ETHICS IN AN ERA OF GLOBALIZATION

Ethics and Global Politics

Series Editors: Tom Lansford and Patrick Hayden

Since the end of the Cold War, explorations of ethical considerations within global politics and on the development of foreign policy have assumed a growing importance in the fields of politics and international studies. New theories, policies, institutions, and actors are called for to address difficult normative questions arising from the conduct of international affairs in a rapidly changing world. This series provides an exciting new forum for creative research that engages both the theory and practice of contemporary world politics, in light of the challenges and dilemmas of the evolving international order.

Also in the series

From Terrorism to Politics
Anisseh van Engeland and Rachael M. Rudolph
ISBN 978-0-7546-4990-8

Emerging Conflicts of Principle
International Relations and the Clash between Cosmopolitanism
and Republicanism
Thomas Kane
ISBN 978-0-7546-4837-6

The Ethics of Foreign Policy
Edited by David B. MacDonald, Robert G. Patman
and Betty Mason-Parker
ISBN 978-0-7546-4377-7

Who's Afraid of Children?
Children, Conflict and International Relations
Helen Brocklehurst
ISBN 978-0-7546-4171-1

Old Europe, New Security
Evolution for a Complex World
Edited by Janet Adamski, Mary Troy Johnson and Christina M. Schweiss
ISBN 978-0-7546-4644-0

Ethics in an Era of Globalization

Edited by

M.S. RONALD COMMERS
Ghent University, Belgium

WIM VANDEKERCKHOVE
Ghent University, Belgium

AN VERLINDEN
Ghent University, Belgium

ASHGATE

Published by
Ashgate Publishing Limited
Gower House
Croft Road
Aldershot
Hampshire GU11 3HR
England

Ashgate Publishing Company
Suite 420
101 Cherry Street
Burlington, VT 05401-4405
USA

Ashgate website: http://www.ashgate.com

British Library Cataloguing in Publication Data
Ethics in an era of globalization. - (Ethics and global
  politics)
  1. Globalization - Moral and ethical aspects
  I. Commers, Ronald II. Vandekerckhove, Wim III. Verlinden,
  An
  172

Library of Congress Cataloging-in-Publication Data
Ethics in an era of globalization / [edited] by M.S. Ronald Commers, Wim
Vandekerckhove and An Verlinden.
     p. cm.
  Includes bibliographical references and index.
  ISBN 978-0-7546-7195-4
  1. Globalization--Moral and ethical aspects. I. Commers, M.S. Ronald. II.
Vandekerckhove, Wim. III. Verlinden, An. IV. Commers, Ronald.

  JZ1318.E8654 2008
  172--dc22

                                                                    2008003957

ISBN 978-0-7546-7195-4

Mixed Sources
Product group from well-managed
forests and other controlled sources
www.fsc.org Cert no. SA-COC-1565
© 1996 Forest Stewardship Council
FSC

Printed and bound in Great Britain by
MPG Books Ltd, Bodmin, Cornwall.

Contents

List of Tables

Notes on Contributors

Gérald Berthoud is Emeritus Professor at the Université de Lausanne, Faculty of Social and Political Sciences. He was visiting professor at a number of European universities, as well as at the University of Niamey in Niger. Prof. Berthoud is one of the founders of the Mouvement Anti-Utilitariste dans les Sciences Sociales (MAUSS).

József Böröcz is Associate Professor of Sociology at Rutgers University, member of the Scholarly Board of the Institute for Political Studies at the Hungarian Academy of Sciences, and a member of the Executive Committee of the Center for Migration and Development at Princeton University.

Peter Caws is University Professor of Philosophy and Professor of Human Sciences at the George Washington University in Washington, DC.

M.S. Ronald Commers is Professor of Philosophy and Ethics at Ghent University. He is the director of the Center for Ethics and Value Inquiry as well as Head of the Philosophy and Moral Science Department at Ghent University.

Nigel Dower is Honorary Senior Lecturer in Philosophy at the University of Aberdeen and academic consultant on "Cosmopolitan Agendas: exploring ethics in a globalized world." He was President of the International Development Ethics Association 2002–2006 (IDEA), and is editor of the Edinburgh Studies in World Ethics, Edinburgh University Press.

Carol C. Gould is Professor of Philosophy and Political Science and director of the Center for Global Ethics and Politics at Temple University. She is editor of the *Journal of Social Philosophy*.

Thomas Mertens is Professor of Legal Philosophy of Law at the Faculty of Law, Radboud University Nijmegen and Professor of Human Rights and Human Responsibilities at the Faculty of Philosophy, Leiden University. In 2003–2004 he was a Jean Monnet Fellow at the Department of Law, European University Institute, Florence.

Rebecca Todd Peters is Associate Professor of Religious Studies at Elon University (Elon, NC). She is also a member of the Environmental Studies faculty and offers courses in the Honors program and the Women and Gender Studies programs.

Asunción Lera St Clair is Associate Professor at the Department of Sociology and Scientific Director of the Bergen Summer Research School on Global

Development Challenges, University of Bergen in Norway. She is also a Senior Research Fellow at the Centre for Development and the Environment (SUM), University of Oslo, and Vice President of the International Development Ethics Association (IDEA).

Wim Vandekerckhove is Assistant Professor of Practical Ethics at Ghent University and a member of the Center for Ethics and Value Inquiry. He is also the coordinator of the European Business Ethics Network Interest Group on Socially Responsible Investment.

Christien van den Anker is Reader in Politics at the University of the West of England, Bristol, England. She is editor of the *Journal of Global Ethics*, editor of a book series on global ethics for Palgrave, and convenor of the British International Studies Association Working Group on Global Ethics.

An Verlinden holds Masters degrees in moral science and in criminology. She is a doctoral candidate at the Center for Ethics and Value Inquiry, Ghent University.

Heather Widdows is Acting Director and Senior Lecturer at the Centre for the Study of Global Ethics, University of Birmingham. She is also president of the Global Studies Association.

Acknowledgments

Chapter 7 is taken from Chapter 5 of the second edition of *World Ethics—the New Agenda* (2007), with new introductory paragraphs and minor changes elsewhere. Reprinted by permission of the Edinburgh University Press.

Chapter 9 is a reprint from "Global Poverty: Development Ethics Meets Global Justice" by Asunción St Clair in *Globalizations* 3 (2006), 139–58. Reprinted by permission of the publisher (Taylor and Francis Ltd).

Introduction

M.S. Ronald Commers, Wim Vandekerckhove and An Verlinden

From the early 1990s on, terms similar to "global ethics" have been used to denominate renewed attempts to discover or construct what binds humans together across cultural and religious differences (Küng's Declaration toward a Global Ethic, Unesco's Universal Ethics and the Global Ethics Project). These attempts, representing global ethics as the search to move beyond relativism towards a renewed conception of ethics for late-modern society, have developed within a wide range of academic (e.g. interreligious and intercultural studies) and non-academic (e.g. within the UN) disciplines. Besides these general proposals, new, concrete issues with global scope have become prominent and have been analysed from a multi-disciplinary perspective, ending up in new academic disciplines, such as development ethics and global justice studies.

The first milestone in the new developing field of global ethics was Nigel Dower's "World Ethics" from 1998, in which he emphasized the importance of global "cosmopolitan" responsibilities to be realized through global institutions. In the same year, Christien van den Anker suggested "global ethics" as the name for a British International Studies Association Working Group in an attempt to capture the developing field of research on ethical aspects of globalization.

Today, what is really new for global ethics is that the search to move beyond relativism and the ethical study of concrete issues of globalization are starting to merge. Already in 1996, the Center for Ethics and Value Inquiry (CEVI), based at Ghent University (Belgium), was launched in order to study the "moral perplexity of our period" in an all-encompassing way, combining both theoretical and practical outlooks and working within a dynamic, multi-disciplinary environment. This moral perplexity concerns what Anthony Giddens has called a "runaway world" meaning a world of transformations, affecting almost every aspect of what we do. We stand perplexed with regard to these transformations simply because humans have never experienced them before. In other words, the problems are new ones. Of course, human interdependence at a global level sustaining human practice within local communities is hardly a recent phenomenon. International trade and migration is at least as old as written history and the capitalistic world-system has since the sixteenth century produced a global reality of world-making. But, starting at the end of the 1960s and rapidly accelerating into the twenty-first century, technological, economical, political and other forces have crafted a world in which this interdependence has reached an unprecedented level and has raised new and pressing moral and ethical issues, such as: the one-sidedness of "economic globalization," the generalized environmental crisis, worldwide social and cultural disintegration, the rise of racism and xenophobia, the sclerosis of lifestyles and life forms, the disruption of social protection, the increase of migration, the violation of public spaces, the growth of media dictated mass consumption couples with earth-devastating waste patterns, ... global ethics, as a specific discipline, addresses these global worries and hence can be called ethics *of* globalization.

But the moral perplexity we experience is not just resulting from new issues or new dilemmatic cases. The perplexity is more profound. It is not just that we do not know the answer yet. It is also that we do not seem to know *how* to answer. The "moral perplexity of our period"—as we coined it at CEVI—cannot be resolved by merely developing new answers. It also requires a new way of answering, so it seems. Moral perplexity is sometimes called "bewilderment" (Morris Ginzburg), "indeterminacy" (Abraham Edel) or even "crisis" (Emmanuel Levinas). The specificity of the "moral perplexity of our period" lies with the growing sense of discontent and unease with post-industrial society, a scientistic ideology and a strict utilitarian obsession of narrow material progress, all of these unaccompanied by a spiritual evolution and a moral development of humankind. The social and political evolutions during the current era of globalization are giving rise to a moral disarray and cynicism, as can be heard in phrases and laments like "the end of modernity," "against ethics," "the closing down of humanism," "expertise-oriented administration of human existence," "moral aestheticism and relativism" and so on. At Ghent University, CEVI aims at establishing a thoughtful defence against this widespread "unhappy moral conscience." CEVI contributes to ethical reasoning that is able to tackle the moral perplexity of our period, through investigations into the value formulation of alternative visions of a citizen-based and nature-respecting consciousness. Global ethics therefore must also involve the critical study of ethics and morality under the conditions of globalization. Ethical reasoning about issues of globalization has now become an issue of globalization itself. Global ethics is not only ethics *of* globalization, but also ethics *under* globalization, or as Nigel Dower calls it: globalization *of* ethics. What is new to global ethics is not just the global worries, but also the fact that we are worrying globally.

It should be clear that at CEVI, we favor an idea of ethical inquiry based on the consciousness of the limits of any general foundationalist philosophy, refusing however the delusions of a fatalist and more than often self-defeating relativistic moral philosophy. In this, we champion the relative autonomy of moral thinking along the lines of what Marcus Singer, who once said that the great difficulty in morals is not really a matter of theory but lies in the resolution of concrete cases. The problems are often so complex and difficult, and no one is omniscient. Yet this is no reason for despair or for scepticism. In the reasonable disagreements of reasonable people we may find, so far as we are reasonable, both hope and enlightenment.

It was with this outlook that CEVI staged a number of events in 2006. We organized a number of seminars and public lectures on world-systems, global justice and global ethics. But we also organized the first international global ethics conference in April 2006. The conference was set up in a conventional way: a number of keynote lectures and a bunch of parallel paper sessions. A selection of papers from these sessions has been published as a special issue of the *Journal of Global Ethics* (Vol. 3, No. 2). This book brings the keynotes and contributions to other CEVI seminars and organizes them to show what that first international global ethics conference was all about. Surely, the issues of cosmopolitanism, global justice, development ethics and the various fields of practical ethics in relation to globalization had already established a tradition as conference themes and research networks. But the conference in Ghent was the first attempt to bundle academic reflection on the ethics *of* globalization. The "bundling" itself, was an exercise in that other dimension of global ethics, namely ethics *under* globalization. Participants in the conference, at which papers on many topics and a variety of approaches were presented, were enthusiastic about the "bundling" of these several approaches. The pressing ethical issues of globalization had not only led to a growth of academic work on these issues but also to an increasing isolation of the various approaches from one another. But globalization and its ethical issues are multilayered and comprise many facets of human life and sense-making. Hence, it was felt very strongly at the conference that a commitment to resolve these ethical issues must go together with the care not to overspecialize in just one approach.

We decided to act upon that strong feeling and create a platform where the two research dimensions of global ethics could intersect: ethics *of* and *under* globalization. And so, at that conference in Ghent and reflected here in this volume, IGEA started—the International Global Ethics Association. IGEA connects today a number of researchers and academic centres spread across the globe (www.igea.ugent.be) and aims at biannual conferences (the second one—2008—being held in Melbourne, hosted by the Faculty of Arts of the Deakin University), joint research projects and other academic exchanges.

This book documents the start of IGEA. The contributing authors in this book have started IGEA simply by linking their approaches, there, in Ghent. These approaches stem from various backgrounds: political economy, social sciences, anthropology, moral philosophy and political philosophy (both analytical and continental). It is also in Ghent that the three questions dividing this book into three parts popped up:

1) What is the task of global ethics?
2) Is global ethics possible?
3) How can we "do" global ethics?

The first part, "The Task of Global Ethics" comprises four agendas for the field of global ethics. In the opening chapter of this book, **Carol C. Gould** puts aside a number of misconceptions with regard to global ethics and then continues with presenting three faces of global ethics. The first face is the analysis of the ethical issues that arise with globalization and of the transformations in applied ethics necessitated by globalization. The two most paramount ethical issues in our era of globalization concern the social responsibilities of transnational corporations and the issue of defining global ecological responsibilities. But the current context in which these issues arise also has implications for the principles of applied ethics themselves. One crucial implication, Gould argues, is that the traditional view that the more remote consequences of action can be given less weight in our considerations, no longer makes sense in regard to globalization and its consequences. The second face of global ethics relates to cross-cultural approaches to key ethical issues. This face concerns universalism and culture, as well as historicity in our conceptions of human rights. Gould argues for a non-relativist point of view based on a conception of human freedom as self-transformation that we can phrase both in individual terms as well as in more collective contexts. In what Gould describes as the third face of global ethics, the notion of "cosmopolitical democracy" is put forward connecting ethics and politics. Gould does not envision a world government. Rather, she emphasizes democratic decision-making in cross-border and transnational communities and associations, such as the EU. The unifying themes of these three faces of global ethics, of what that is and must be, are the recognition of human rights and the norm of solidarity.

In his contribution, **Gérald Berthoud** recalls what in *United Nations* declarations and reports the globalization discourse stands for: a new information society built on shared knowledge, global solidarity, and a better mutual understanding. But he raises the question whether globalization and its resulting worldwide society is something new. He reminds us that globalization started in the fifteenth century when due to Western-European hegemony the world was radically divided in two institutionalized parts: world market and the so-called global community. Heterogeneity and inequality were the mark of this radical division. From then onwards another division captured the minds of the people who were reflecting on it. From the early days of globalization we find side-by-side an economist oriented and a moralist devised discourse on the phenomenon. Berthoud, with the interventions of UN and "civil society" organizations in mind, cautions for the absolute valorization of the market and "its supposedly liberating impact." He refers to the social scientist Marcel Mauss, the linguist Emile Benveniste, and the moral philosopher Paul Ricoeur for proper arguments in favor of the embedded character of intersubjective relationships in a broader framework of societal and cultural institutions. Human relationships, contrary to the market discourse, cannot be "envisaged without an element of gratuity and a certain amount of generosity," he writes. Only in this way we can do justice to the significance of men's practices which are marked by the pronouns: "I," "you," and "she/he," acknowledging that within institutional settings the self and the others are interdependent.

The chapter by **Christien van den Anker** focuses on approaches to ethics in an era of globalization and how these interrelate. This effort is an attempt to move global ethics as a field beyond distinctive and apparently incompatible approaches. Her attempt to bridge the gaps in global ethics starts with the perceived stand-off between universal and contextual theories on global justice and global citizenship. While universalists argue that these subjects are best seen from the perspective of common humanity, contextualists argue that it is the (cultural) difference between people(s) that matters at least as much as what they have in common. The second "gap" is between theory and practice. Christien van den Anker suggests that global ethics consists of adopting a methodology that takes us beyond the rigorous division between these respective areas of work and points to a possible balance between their core concerns.

"Has our world gone mad?," asks **Rebecca Todd Peters** in her contribution on justice and the ethical landscape of globalization. She does so after recalling how private spending on personal consumption in the Western part of the world reveals a shocking picture of the priorities and values. This she confronts with the lacking though necessary expenditures for water, basic education and sanitation of the world population. Conversations about global ethics "must pay attention to the lived behaviors and material realities of real people." It is not by neglecting or ignoring the basic facts concerning the differences in consumption patterns throughout the world that the morality of globalization will get substance. The author agrees with Berthoud in stating that globalization is "not the proper name of a new global era we are entering." It refers to an acceleration of what was already an economic and social reality long before. Today one cannot avoid reflecting on the "epochal transformation necessary to facilitate human and planetary flourishing for the whole world." Recalling her analysis, *In Search of the Good Life: The Ethics of Globalization* (2004), Rebecca Todd Peters discovers four distinct globalization theories, each of which having a proper moral vision: neoliberalism, developmentalism, earthism, and post-colonialism. Using the word "ideology" for "a set of beliefs and assumptions about how the world works," she examines each of the theories briefly in order to consider their moral visions on individual existence, justice, and global solidarity. Acknowledging that the present stage of globalization has the potential to transform our world for the better, it is required to interrogate these moral visions closely and critically. Different theories of globalization are to be compared and evaluated from a moral point of view, for which it is obligatory to establish a set of reasonable standards making the adjudication between the competing theories, visions, claims, and values possible. Rebecca Todd Peters puts her hope on the resources of many faith traditions to serve a prophetic role in world society "by challenging the status quo" and "by working toward social justice."

The second part of this book features four chapters arguing that global ethics is indeed possible. Each of the chapters argues this by doing particular mine-sweeping. **M.S. Ronald Commers** presents global ethics as a "synversalist" approach to ethics. In our era of globalization it becomes possible and desirable to debunk notions of "the end of ethics" and the unbridgeable distinction between "is" (fact) and "ought" (norm). Commers' "synversalist" approach regards a normative-factual continuum as the basis for global ethics. Globalization emphasizes cultural differences and situated knowledge but it also points out that we are not in the first place family members, cultural workers, citizens of the state and only secondly and therefore subordinately human beings. With Höffding, Commers argues that the possibility of global ethics lies herein that it stresses out that within the bonds of specific communities and identities, we should live our lives as human beings and treat each other as human beings. That insight is the basis of the "synversalist" approach and constitutes the possibility of global ethics. Commers articulates that approach by drawing on authors such as Chaïm Perelman, Mikhail Bakhtin, Martin Buber, Vladimir Jankélévitch, John Dewey, and Abraham Edel—authors that wrote on ethics also in a time of an expanding world capitalist system but before the subjective and relativistic turn in ethics. Their works are attempts to tie facts and norms, concrete existence and general values. They conceived ethics as a practically oriented "science" related to the problems of a globalizing world society as it was when they wrote. The researcher in global ethics then is the go-between, always moving back and forth on the normative-factual continuum. The "synversalist" global ethics urges the ethicist today to examine existential assumptions of the signifying concepts used in the post-cold war stage of the world capitalist system. In his chapter, Ronald Commers makes the exercise for "Development" signifiers. Clarifying these existential assumptions allows global ethics to prescribe reforms and action. Its explanation and prescription is based on veracity—stronger than exactness but weaker than truth. The existential assumptions underlie concrete action related valuations and prescriptions. Commers argues that we can regard all world citizen theories and agendas as a normative-factual continuum, because they are related both to ideal conceptions of citizenship and factual or realized citizenship organization and institutions. For example, the UN undoubtedly exists yet at the same time we all are deeply disappointed because the UN has not yet fully realized human aspirations. Hence, for Commers, global ethics is possible as a "Deweyian" pragmatically oriented discipline.

Heather Widdows considers at length the criticisms of both "Asian values" adepts and feminist ethicists concerning the supposedly imperialism of Western discourses in global ethics. In both the "Asian Values" and feminist discourse the argument runs as follows: human rights and concepts of justice do not express universal values for they promote but a Western view on valuation. To contradict the most extreme standpoints and to defend her own stand that the gap between the "ethics of the "west and the rest" has been greatly exaggerated," Widdows endeavors to answer the related questions: "what global ethics?" and "why global ethics?" When ethicists recognize the relationality character of their ethical arguments one may avoid the pitfall of the extreme positions. Referring to the contributions of Carol C. Gould and Virginia Held, she argues that from an ethics of care and an ethics of virtue point of view the exaggerations can be left behind. Acknowledging the value of the criticisms on the "individualistic turn in liberal ethics"—linked with Enlightenment moral philosophy—she pleads for "a globally representative and applicable ethics which recognizes diversity." To a global ethics so conceived of the "relatedness and the richness of lived experience" is of the utmost importance in order to bridge the gap between Western and non-Western insights in the good life, in justice, and rights of the people.

Nigel Dower defends his solidarist-pluralist form of cosmopolitanism against various objections and distinguishes it from moral relativism. The objections to the idea of universal values and global responsibilities—two aspects characteristic to cosmopolitan theories—are consequentialist. One critique is that cosmopolitan theory leads to a world government concentrating power in the hands of powerful nations. A second is that the projection of universal values entails a homogenization of cultures. A third critique fears that introducing ideals into decision-making will lead politicians to do things that are inappropriate in the real world or that this will even lead to the prosecution of Holy War. Lastly, cosmopolitan theory is also accused of undermining the loyalty of the citizen to the state. Nigel Dower accepts that these objections pick out some real dangers, but argues for a version of cosmopolitanism that avoids these dangers. Dower's solidarist-pluralist approach becomes clear as he contrasts it to two other approaches, the idealist-dogmatic and the libertarian-minimalist. His position is a middle one affirming the basic values of peace, access to elements of well-being, a healthy and resource-full environment to live in, stable community and relationships and autonomy. The solidarist-pluralist cosmopolitan denies the importance of promoting other values and beliefs but asserts the importance of obligations at the global level to bring these values into existence. Dower also investigates in his chapter how his approach might combine the strengths and insights of communitarian's thinking with cosmopolitan theory.

In his chapter, **Peter Caws** discusses whether personal moral commitments are compatible with global ethical responsibilities. The question entails a test for global ethics because globalization means that as a moral agent, I am now obliged to think beyond the familial or ethnic or national or regional to remote others whose welfare is inextricably connected with my own. Caws touches upon Kant and Jefferson to point out that what reason prescribes has not been what people have done. And it is precisely the difficulty we seem to have to extend our moral commitments beyond our community. Caws clarifies this gap by referring to Ferdinand Tönnies well-known distinction between *Gemeinschaft* and *Gesellschaft* (community and society). But whereas Tönnies seems to have thought these two to be diachronically related—and where the emergence of modernity accompanies the transition of one into the other—Peter Caws sees them as synchronically coexistent. Community and society represent different ways in which the same subject and agent can and does relate to his or her contemporaries. The question of the possibility of global ethics then is how people can be members at the same time of local communities and of a global society. Caws links the distinctions community/society, local/global and moral/ethic to show that this requires two levels of understanding. Having commenced his chapter by giving reasons as to why ethical interests map awkwardly on to economic ones, Caws concludes that as economic relations have gone before in the process of globalization, they may help to pave the way for the penetration of ethical concerns. Not with the goal of embracing those who suffer as members of a moral community to which we all belong. Rather, those same channels are potential conduits for ethical remedies.

The third part of this book, "Global Ethics—How?" consists of four illustrations of how answering in "the moral perplexity of our period" can take place. These chapters show that reflection on how ethical reasoning can take place in an era of globalization is intricately linked with the ethical issues of globalization. For **Asunción Lera St Clair**, any conception of what may constitute fair globalization needs to address the processes that produce and reproduce global poverty. In her chapter, St Clair argues that the ethical aspects of global poverty lead to a redefinition of both development and globalization. As the "global" impinges on every field of knowledge, so too development, philosophy, and ethics and the relations among these fields must redefine their scope and subject matter. The consequence for the ways in which globalization is treated, and more specifically for global ethics, is that the ethical aspects of globalization are interrelated with an ethical perspective of knowledge and policy for poverty reduction. Asunción St. Clair suggests that poverty needs to be treated globally and not as a social fact that occurs only in developing countries. What is needed is a re-engagement with literature and theories within the field of development studies and with poverty research. Global ethics for Asunción St Clair includes critical engagement with the knowledge production going on inside global institutions, and doing so may lead to stronger formulations for alternative globalizations and for a better understanding of the paths towards fairer development aid policies.

Thomas Mertens reflects on the contributions of Peter Singer and Thomas Pogge to the global justice debate in an effort to evaluate them critically against the background of John Rawls's "duty to assist." Peter Singer in his approach on the ethics of globalization argues in favor of the redistribution between rich and poor communities. He holds that we should shift from the concept of negative to positive duties, implying a transfer from what is superfluous in the rich countries to the poor countries and communities of the global system. His argument is congruent to classic utilitarianism for it is the rich men's duty to contribute to the happiness of all people. John Rawls's arguments on the subject are far less general and radical. In his *A Theory of Justice* he explains that distributive justice applies to rather closed communities only and he pays no attention to the question of worldwide justice. It is not humanity as a whole, such as it is the implication of Singer's arguments, but the relatively closed political communities that we should pay attention to. Moreover Rawls rejected the utilitarian stand. Mertens follows Rawls in his critique on Singer's approach, which is not convincing on the issue where the right motivation for the whole of mankind must be coming from. On this point of the argument in favor of global justice, Thomas Pogge might help to correct the strong utilitarian tenets found in Singer's work. That the rich must help the poor irrespective of relationships of proximity or causality is to remain an utopian creed. Only if we can prove, such as Pogge thinks we can, that on the subject of wealth and fair opportunities the rich stand in a causal relationship with the misery and suffering of the world poor, the moral urgency of "our" duty—as the rich ones—can be made convincing. The rules and institutions of financial, economic and legal relations have a devastating effect on the global poor, Pogge has argued. World poverty cannot be explained in terms of national and local factors only. It is the global institutional order, which is at the origin of misery, slavery and suffering in the world system. In doing so, Pogge tries to correct Rawls emphasis on the closed political communities and strongly argues in favor of a cosmopolitan solution. In contradistinction with Rawls's conception of international justice (*The Law of Peoples*), Pogge opts for cosmopolitan justice. Mertens remains in doubt concerning the correctness and the relevance of this position. Again it seems to him that so little can be done on an institutionalized level, the proper institutional reforms lacking impetus, support, and force.

Following the arguments of Rawls about an all-inclusive League of Peoples, all the while respecting a "global difference principle" and the particular "bounds of affinity between peoples," Mertens believes that the problem of global poverty should be approached through the emphasis on the "legal duty of assistance." The duty of assistance can be made a real moral force by building up decent basic institutions that establish peaceful relations between the existing political communities. Moreover, Mertens argues, this would be more in harmony with the nature of morality in which the *amour propre* of the political communities—such as it is in the case where individuals are the "moral" persons—is not ignored.

An Verlinden starts her chapter by arguing that the current normative approaches to international relations are inapt to address salient normative questions in today's international society, such as questions relating to poverty, the use of arms, the environment, armed interventions by states of other states, or the reception of refugees and migrants. Verlinden reviews ways in which these normative approaches can be classified and develops from that a position for global ethics that moves beyond a dichotomized thinking between ethics and justice. For Verlinden, global ethics is directed both at the level of individuals and collectives as well as at the institutional level of inter- and supra-state relations. She argues this is possible by adopting a contextualized and relational approach that sees ethics as arising from the particular forms of life shared by people within a given culture at a particular moment in history. The contribution of An Verlinden lies herein that she points at the moral philosophy of Martin Buber that allows us to sketch out such a contextualized dialogical or relational approach. Globalization as the increase of global interaction emphasizes the communicative dimension of constructivism and hence brings us to an ethical rationality as a relational affair, which moves beyond merely understanding or "respecting" cultural differences to a kind of "third space." With Buber, she conceptualizes this "third space" as the Interhuman, characterized by the alternation of I-It (abstract principles) and I-Thou (concrete other) emphasis. Contextualized global ethics as the space of the Interhuman is no longer ethics of ultimate ends. Abstract values and principles can be useful and suggestive but is not the starting point of our ethical deliberation. Global ethics is the continuous go-between of universalism and particularism, objectivism and subjectivism. An Verlinden suggest global ethics to be the research into current conditions of, possibilities for and obstacles to the Interhuman–*Zwischenmenschliche* or interaction between complete and thoroughly responsive persons.

Redistributing global inequality is the aim that **József Böröcz** sets himself in his daring thought experiment. From a critical reading of the 1995 UN Resolution on the eradication of poverty, indicating the ahistorical character of the UN global inequality analysis, he focuses on the fiscal feasibility of his global inequality proposals. He puts forward that these proposals can "be defined as a large-scale, historic social process of social change." The outcome of this social change process would be the diminishment of what Giovanni Arrighi called "oligarchic wealth." This would be in favor of "democratic wealth," resulting from a far less extremely "unbalanced structure of distribution." The project of global action is inexistent, but the author endeavors to provide an empirical assessment of the volume of resources needed to redistribute in order to reach a more fair state of global inequality. This global redistributive scheme of possible action is the counterpart of an "already existing global market system of capital accumulation." Böröcz develops some striking numerical examples in an exercise that he qualifies himself as utopian. Nevertheless he considers a "controlled utopianism" both urgent and indispensable to think beyond the actual institutional system worldwide. His exercise addresses the question what it would take if a "global redistributive mechanism were to bring the world's states closer to the world mean." He leaves no doubt on the subject of the economic, social, and political chances to execute the proposed global redistributive scheme. But even so, the exercise enables us to question the tenets of global economic liberalism and the inevitability to consider world poverty and its eradication in monetary terms. He puts forward the question what would happen if global economic liberalism protagonists could support "a more reasonable and acceptable form of social organization," providing a less unequal global distribution of income. Given the amount of today's worldwide inequality humanity is left with two alternatives: either the creation of an organizational framework suitable for global redistribution, or continuing and perhaps even augmenting the present state of inhumane inequality. For "the moral unity of humankind" it would be beneficial to refuse choosing the latter. The global structure of inequality that splits humankind in two separate groups "opens an abyss of unforeseeable consequences concerning the survival of humankind."

The chapters in this volume represent what IGEA—International Global Ethics Association—is as a platform: examples of ethics in an era of globalization. At the Center for Ethics and Value Inquiry (Ghent University), we are convinced this is possible and the authors in this volume have gladly accepted our invitation to show just how this might be done. They show global ethics as a domain that thinks not in opposites or distinctions but in continua and in bridges between objectivism and subjectivism, facts and values, universalism and particularism, institutions and persons. They show global ethics as not just discussing authors but also and mainly as finding solutions for our sense-making of and in the world today. Therefore, this volume has strived for a sophisticated equilibrium between academic depth and rigorous ethical argumentation on the one hand and the more lived activism and engagement of practically oriented researchers on the other. In this way, the editors hope that this volume will find its way to academics as well as to practitioners who are interested in both the philosophical underpinnings and the practical, applied aspects of the manifold questions of global ethics.

PART I
What is the Task of
Global Ethics?

Chapter 1

The New Global Ethics
and its Three Faces

Carol C. Gould

In this chapter, I attempt to explicate the project of a global ethics, in some of its core aspects. I will begin with a consideration of what global ethics is *not*, that is, some common misinterpretations of what a global ethics is supposed to do. Then I will analyze the three aspects or faces referred to in the title. This reflection is intended to serve as what philosophers have called a propadeutic, in that it is explicitly preparatory and oriented to helping guide future research in this field. I will then turn in the final section to two core concepts within global ethics, namely human rights and solidarity, which in many ways run through the three faces and which I regard as crucial for the further development of the field. I will also consider the relation of these two concepts to each other. Throughout this chapter my concern is to highlight some of the difficult philosophical questions that arise in global ethics and to begin addressing some of them.

What Global Ethics is Not—Some Common Misinterpretations

The notion of a global ethics can easily be misunderstood, in the first place as implying that what we are seeking is a single ethics for everyone in the entire world. Philosophers have made us keenly aware that normative ethics and the various areas of applied ethics admit of many variants and a diversity of approaches, and so too, I suggest, does global ethics. Thus, global ethics should not be interpreted as requiring worldwide agreement on a single set of norms or moral principles.

Secondly, global ethics is not a global religion. Although many of the moral issues have also been addressed by religious thinkers, I think we need to distinguish global ethics from religion. Rather, as a part of ethics, it is properly a branch of philosophy, although it engages many other disciplines and approaches including political theory, political economy, public affairs, and international relations theory. Thus, the ethical, and more generally, the normative approaches incorporated in the concept of global ethics should be susceptible to some degree of rational justification and be supported by arguments. Even where there is appeal to feeling, this cannot involve appeals to higher authority but rather involves intersubjectively shared and well-evidenced claims about human experience.

Third, global ethics is not simply the same as international ethics, but involves normative principles that emerge from and are applied in the newer transnational or global contexts that increasingly characterize our interconnected world. Thus, the interesting area for philosophical research concerns norms for relations that are distinctively transnational, if not fully global, rather than for more traditional relations among nation-states.

Fourth, global ethics cannot be limited to principles or other sorts of ethical guidelines that apply only to individuals in their specific interactions with other individuals. Thus, global ethics includes also social ethics, which implicates the relations among associations or groups as well as individuals. In addition to the transformations in moral principles or moral reasoning for individuals that may be required then, global ethics centrally deals with global justice, cosmopolitan democracy, and other more social, political or economic normative concepts.

But fifth, and conversely, global ethics is not simply a part of political philosophy, nor can it be reduced to social and political norms. It also marks out a place for reflecting on the type of informal, interpersonal social relations that are required by globalization. One question will be whether any specifically new modes of interaction are needed or instead whether it is just a matter of a greater extension of traditional values, i.e., of the domain over which they range.

The First Face—Ethics and Globalization

The first dimension of global ethics concerns the analysis of the ethical issues that arise with globalization, as well as the transformations in traditional applied ethics that globalization may necessitate. The first of these tasks has been rather intensively investigated already in philosophy, especially within the field of international ethics or as part of business ethics or environmental ethics, though the specifically global, rather than purely international, aspects are only emerging clearly of late.

Although the ethical issues raised by globalization are quite vast, perhaps the paramount ones concern the social responsibilities of transnational corporations and more broadly questions of global justice, as well as the issue of defining global ecological responsibilities. In regard to the first of these, global corporate responsibility, it can be observed that the question of the obligations of corporations to respect human rights has been thematized, but the scope of this responsibility remains unclear. Thus Thomas Donaldson, in his classic account of moral minimums for corporations, refrains from suggesting anything more than that corporations should avoid depriving workers and others in the host countries of their rights, though in some cases they should go beyond this to prevent the deprivation of rights, e.g., by providing workers with protective goggles where necessary (Donaldson 1999). But he holds that there is no specific obligation for corporations to assist people in gaining their human rights. Yet, we may raise the question of whether the division is as neat as Donaldson proposes and whether his account is sufficiently demanding. He also addresses the difficult question of whether corporations should use the standards of the home or host country, but like most business ethicists, he leaves this unanswered beyond an appeal for practical reasoning to determine it.

In addition to these corporate social responsibility issues, economic globalization poses more sharply than previously the question of articulating the requirements of global justice in dealing with the unjust distribution of resources among nation-states, as well as the exploitative aspects of the more global forms of capitalism that have emerged. Since this topic is addressed in other chapters of this book, I will not address it here, although it is a central issue for global ethics.

The second crucial set of applied ethics issues concerns global ecological responsibilities. We can call attention here to the important work of theorists like Tim Hayward who approach global ecology in terms of the idea of human rights. While such an approach may seem surprising in view of the prevalent tendency to emphasize ecological values for their own sake or in regard to animal rights, it is apparent from accounts like Hayward's that human rights can also provide a helpful perspective in this connection.

Reflections on Globalization and the Transformation of Applied Ethics

We can go on to ask whether traditional applied ethics need to be changed in view of the development of increasingly global interconnections among people in economic, technological, and political contexts. While ethicists have begun to address some of the specific issues that in this new situation—e.g., the previously mentioned issue of the contrast in business expectations in a host vs a home country or the difficulty in imposing any regulations on the internet with its global reach, or the new groups of stakeholders that need to be taken into account, or the role of collective responsibility where the agents are now transnational—to my knowledge there have been few reflections on the basic principles and categories of applied ethics in this new context and specifically whether the traditionally-recognized ones require serious transformation. Yet it is becoming increasingly apparent that leading ethical approaches—rights-based, consequentialist, and communitarian views, along with the lower-level guidelines to which they give rise, confront unexpected difficulties when put into this increasingly global perspective, with new networks across borders that may render problematic the frameworks, rules, and practices that were developed primarily for relations among individuals within nation-states. I will suggest that, in an interesting way, human rights perspectives may fare better than consequentialist or communitarian ones in this new situation.

In one sense, the need for a reformulation of global ethics is trivially true—namely, inasmuch as there are new issues within this domain, for example, outsourcing, or again, divergent cultural expectations, e.g., regarding the acceptability of bribery in business. Yet, I would suggest that beyond this the impact of globalization may engage the principles used in applied ethics themselves. In one reading, this may also not engender much interest, if one has in mind lower-level guidelines derived from fundamental ethical principles, e.g., the idea of informed consent in medical ethics as a specification of the respect for persons characteristic of Kantian deontological views. However, I want to propose—or at least consider—something a little more radical here: namely, that the basic approaches that have governed applied ethics may themselves require reformulation.

In order to see this, it is necessary to back up for a moment in order to consider the status of theoretical approaches as they function in applied ethics. In the standard view, as presented by Richard DeGeorge among others, basic ethical principles are regarded as unaffected by practice. Thus DeGeorge writes,

> If general ethical theories of the standard kinds are correct, they are not dependent on particular circumstances, even though one must consider particular circumstances in applying them. But utilitarianism and Kantianism do not depend on particular circumstances for their defense. (DeGeorge 2002: 458)

I would not follow DeGeorge in regarding these fundamental ethical approaches as being wholly independent of practice, implying that they exist *sub specie aeternitatis*. Rather, my own view is that while these approaches do have some universalistic dimensions, they nonetheless emerge historically and are partly dependent on social practices.

In terms of the foundational approach to applied ethics developed by Beauchamp and Childress in their classic work *Principles of Biomedical Ethics*, we might say that DeGeorge tacitly appeals in the passage above to the model of ethical reasoning that they call deductivist or the covering precept model, where moral judgments are held to be deduced from precepts or rules that cover it (Beauchamp and Childress 1994: 14). Beauchamp and Childress argue instead that moral reasoning proceeds inductively as well as deductively (Beauchamp and Childress 1994: 17), and they too argue for a dialectical relation between theory and practice, or what they come to see in later editions of their book as an application of Rawls's idea of reflective equilibrium in this context. In such a coherentist approach, as they call it, one begins with considered judgments and goes back and forth with the theoretical principles that can guide and refine them (Beauchamp and Childress 1994: 23–6). These authors also follow Henry Richardson in emphasizing the importance of specifying norms for concrete situations, along with balancing the various norms involved (Beauchamp and Childress 1994: 28–37). DeGeorge does in fact recognize a role for such specification of norms when he turns to business ethics itself. Thus he observes that it "necessarily depends heavily for its content on the structures that define business and in which business operates" (DeGeorge 2002: 458). But the question I am raising takes this specificity further and asks whether globalization as a powerful contemporary phenomenon has implications for these principles of applied ethics themselves.

The consideration of the impact of globalization suggests some new foci and interpretations for existing normative frameworks. For one thing, it is apparent that considering the consequences of decisions and policies on those affected by them at a distance requires considering the effects of these policies on people from diverse cultural backgrounds. And most basically, it suggests that it is no longer possible to disregard these remote consequences of actions or policies as the philosopher J.J.C. Smart believed, whether these consequences are interpreted temporally or spatially. In a famous passage in his essay in *Utilitarianism For and Against*, Smart proposed that the situation is analogous to casting a stone in the waters of the pond, where the waves even out at a distance. He wrote,

> We do not normally in practice need to consider very remote consequences, as these in the end approximate rapidly to zero like the furthermost ripples on a pond after a stone has been dropped into it. (Smart and Williams 1973: 33)

But does it in fact make sense to suggest that we can often leave out of account the remote consequences of an action or decision, especially in regard to globalization and its consequences? For here, economic decisions and actions, especially of global corporations with regard to e.g., outsourcing or foreign direct investment, along with the political actions and social policies of nation-states, have crucial impacts on those at a distance and on their life chances. And of course, there are the environmental impacts, not only on presently existing individuals (where even these impacts can often not be fully anticipated), but even more crucially, the effects on future generations. Accordingly, although not a utilitarian theory per se, stakeholder theory likewise comes up against the problem of the assessment of consequences and the impacts of decisions, actions, and policies on people who live at a distance, where these effects can clearly not be disregarded as Smart had (seemingly naively) hoped. Interestingly, we may add that Smart himself recognized that the unknowability of the course of future technological advancement makes utilitarianism very difficult to apply (Smart and Williams 1973: 64).

I have suggested elsewhere (Gould 2004: ch. 10) that if the needs and interests of stakeholders at a distance are to be considered, it is necessary for concerned managers and others to find ways to actively solicit their input rather than simply considering these interests on their own without hearing from them in some way. Further, to the degree that managers and others give thought to the needs and interests of remotely situated people, I have argued that they need to attend to the basic human rights that are at stake and not only to rights as traditionally construed within a given nation-state context. These human rights include not only certain fundamental civil and political rights but also basic economic and social rights as well.

Beyond this, where genuinely cross-border issues are at stake, it may be necessary to devise modes of democratic participation in decisions that extend across traditional nation-state boundaries. The Internet is often pointed to as providing crucial help in this enterprise and it is promising in this respect. But there are well-known problems with just distribution of access to the Internet (the so-called "digital divide"), along with the potential for manipulation. as well as increased threats to privacy of these new uses of networking. Clearly, too, the Internet and the social and political networks that make use of it, cut across the bounded communities with which most communitarian approaches have operated.

New communities are created in this process, where these are potentially more intercultural and transnational than earlier ones (Gould 2004, 2007a).

The discussion of international ethics poses the sharp requirement of respect for cosmopolitan human rights. But phenomena such as global terrorism suggest the normative relevance not only of human rights but also of empathy and solidarity, both in understanding what is ethically wrong about terrorist acts and in attempting to eliminate the conditions that may give rise to them (Gould 2004). More generally, in international contexts, care cannot be restricted to those near to us. New theories of the extension of care and empathy to those at a distance need to be devised, with the understanding that it will not be possible to restrict this to traditional models of mothering or nurturance, which are suitable for particular others standing to us in close personal relationships (Gould 2006, 2007b). In addition, of course, the role of democracy is increasingly relevant in this area of international ethics, and not only in the form of liberal democracy but in more substantive and empowering interpretations.

We can summarize these and related new directions for applied ethics. Of necessity, these are posed here schematically as topics for further discussion and debate. It can be suggested that when the impact of globalization is considered:

1) it may be necessary to move from a consideration of the consequences of a given policy to the solicitation of active input by those remotely affected (leaving aside the difficult issue of future generations), whether this input is provided directly or through representatives;
2) it may be necessary to move from a focus on the rights of citizens within nation-states that are implicated in a given situation to the human rights involved;
3) traditional considerations of just distribution (previously thought to pertain to a given political society) need to take account of global justice issues;
4) communities as sources of identity or value need to be interpreted as going both beyond and beneath national ones. Whereas communitarians have often focused on local communities, the new model of networks of relations, often cross-border, requires further articulation;
5) the idea of care for particular individuals who are close to one needs to be extended in new ways to modes of empathy and solidarity with those at a distance.

The Second Face: Cross-cultural Approaches to Key Ethical Issues

Globalization in its universalizing dimension brings diverse cultures increasingly into contact with each other. And much as we have come over time to value the possibility of belonging to more than one culture, or of bridging diverse cultures, or even of cultural fusion, it remains the case that there are substantial differences in the approaches that various cultures take regarding key ethical concerns—not only human rights and justice, but duties and obligations, along with virtues, whether of individuals, citizens, and societies more broadly. Positively, these differences can remain the source of moral invention when cultures come into contact with each other. Nonetheless, there are also regressive features to various cultural perspectives, including our own, and these need to be understood and criticized.

Cross-cultural ethics raise several questions for us: How can we incorporate openness to diverse perspectives while still retaining certain elements of a liberal or individualist ethics? What sort of approach will allow us to give an important role to freedom and its conditions, while still recommending a dialogue among various perspectives and learning from other cultural points of view? To what degree should we follow Rawls in a (political but not metaphysical) direction of overlapping consensus, or should we just content ourselves with a *modus vivendi*? What, moreover, should we say when people fundamentally disagree on norms, or more difficult, when they act in ways that we judge to be oppressive? Is it sufficient to call for education, persuasion, dialogue, or is something stronger required?

A related set of questions concerns the role that is to be given to history and the process of emergence of universal norms (like human rights) within the philosophical account of the principles of global ethics This question is related to the preceding ones concerning culture inasmuch as it directs our attention to the relative youth of explicit human rights norms and to the fact that they have not been much respected over the course of human history. They appear as contingent and limited (i.e., supposedly Western) constructions, rather than universal as they claim to be.

These issues of universalism and culture, as well as of historicity in our conceptions of human rights, have been much discussed by philosophers of late, and I myself have advanced a nonrelativist point of view in my book *Globalizing Democracy and Human Rights* and in recent articles. I propose a social ontological approach but one based on an open conception of human freedom as self-transformation, taken in both individual terms as well as in the collective contexts of social and cultural activity (Gould 2004: chs 1 and 2, 1988: chs 1 and 3). Whereas Richard Rorty observes this feature of change and transformation and sees it as entailing a thoroughgoing relativistic constructivism in ethics, I see this same agential mutability and the human capacity for self-transformation as providing the social ontological basis for human rights. I have argued further that human rights specify the conditions for freedom and dignity of individuals as social beings, that is, the conditions necessary for their self-transformative activity. Among these human rights, I have distinguished between basic and nonbasic ones, where the basic ones are conditions for any human activity at all, and include meeting fundamental needs, while the nonbasic ones specify conditions for people's further flourishing beyond this minimum (Gould 1988: chs 1 and 7, 2004: chs 1, 8 and 9).

As I have suggested in *Globalizing Democracy and Human Rights* (Gould 2004: ch. 2), human rights have themselves come to be recognized through a dialogue among perspectives that represent divergent cultural emphases and have furthermore been interpreted from within diverse cultures, including Confucian, Buddhist, and Muslim, among other perspectives. Especially to the degree that human rights emphasize the requirements for human *dignity*, they are thus susceptible to more than Western interpretations. Further, there is no question that human rights require local and specific cultural appropriations and interpretations in order to determine the particular requirements to which they give rise. However, we should add that human rights are not infinitely malleable, and require some basic forms of equality for women, which is a particularly controversial feature of them at present (Gould 2003, 2004: ch. 6).

When people disagree that human rights are important, we can subject their views to overt criticism and attempt to persuade them otherwise. Further, it is entirely legitimate to support local groups who are attempting to protect or expand human rights in a given country. But this does not justify military intervention by one country into other to realize human rights. This is not to say that intervention is never justified in defense of socially basic human rights, to use David Luban's phrase in his early article on this subject (Luban 1980). But the principle of legitimate authority comes into play here too. Legitimate interventions should be undertaken under UN auspices, and eventually under an expanded and more legitimate security council or a global people's assembly, as advocated by Richard Falk and Andrew Strauss, as well as by David Held (1995: 273–4; Falk and Strauss 2001).

In regard to the historicity of the concept and practice of human rights, we can grant a considerable role to social construction and to historical emergence. Nonetheless, to the degree that people as agents constitute the basis of human rights, that feature has been present all along though it has only rather recently come to be recognized as a universal attribute, in part as a result of social struggles and political and social movements to overcome oppression and restrictive applications of human rights in regard to particular social classes or groups. Nonetheless, the full articulation of the idea of human rights is a project for future generations, and it does not lose its power on that account. When it is recognized that these sorts of universal concepts partly emerge through their social and historical construction, as well as through the growing universalization of relations of people in practical social life, we can see that what is needed is what I have called a conception of *concrete universality* to supplement the abstract universality of traditional liberal norms (Gould 2004: ch. 2).[1] Moreover, these norms not only emerge in part through such interactions but also need to be embodied in institutional contexts that can alone permit their fuller expression.

A final consideration here is that the critical interchange among cultural perspectives crucially needs to proceed on the basis of self-criticism if it is to be successful in justifying reasonable norms on which people can converge. The role of self-criticism, as well as the critique of ideological or one-sided perspectives, has not received sufficient attention in social and political philosophy in recent years.[2] One can say that self-criticism is an essential preliminary to the criticism of others if dialogue is to be productive of genuine and legitimate agreements on fundamental norms and their implementation. Further, this sort of normative critique needs to be grounded in social critique, in which the functioning of

---

1   See also the discussion of the concept of concrete universality in Gould 1976.
2   A recent exception is Mills 2005.

institutions to preserve the status quo is subject to empirical analysis and critical scrutiny in the interest of advancing global justice.

The Third Face: Cosmopolitanism in Ethics and Politics

The third aspect of global ethics is the crucial one of developing a more cosmopolitan normative approach in both ethics and politics. I cannot attempt to lay out the details of a philosophical theory of this sort here, but will only point to certain features (again drawing on some of the points in my book *Globalizing Democracy and Human Rights*).

Cosmopolitan democracy, or what I called in *Rethinking Democracy* *"cosmopolitical democracy"* (Gould 2004: ch. 12), is not a model of world government. Rather, in the form of *transnational democracy*—a vision closer to what can be envisioned in contemporary societies—it places emphasis on the development of democratic decision-making in emerging cross-border and transnational communities and associations. These include local, as well as broader, communities organized around economic or environmental concerns, Internet forums, and larger regional associations, like the EU. I also propose the need for the extension of democratic forms of decision-making to firms and social associations. Of course, by democracy we do not necessarily mean only majority rule and free and fair elections. There is a fairly wide range of procedures—formal and informal, representative, and direct—that can apply, and these have to be construed as extending beyond our favored US and European modes of electoral democracy. Moreover, it is important to recall that procedural democracy is insufficient without more substantive modes of recognizing people as co-participants and co-determiners in these contexts of what I have called "common activity."

Yet another aspect of transnational democracy involves making room for input from those at a distance who are importantly affected by the decisions of global corporations and nation-states, as well as by the institutions of global governance like the WTO and the IMF. This requirement goes considerably beyond the notions of the required consideration of stakeholder interests, and entails stronger notions of democratic participation or transnational representation in these decisions. Given the impact of decisions at a distance on the lives and well-being of people, mere consideration of their interests on the part of elites is not sufficient, and there is a need to devise ways of hearing from them directly, giving them voice in the process. The mechanisms for such participation and representation largely remain to be invented.

Besides transnational democracy, a second key idea of a cosmopolitan ethics and politics is that of human rights, which in my view apply to both individuals and groups, as well as to the more traditional structured political forms of activity. In this conception, human rights have a scope beyond their original function as limitations on the actions of nation-states, where they have been taken centrally and importantly to be concerned with the prohibition on torture and the protection of life and liberty. Feminist theorists have argued that human rights need also to be "brought home," as it were, to protect against domestic violence. Additionally, in my perspective, human rights can legitimately serve to constrain decisions, even democratic ones, within transnational associations at regional as well as local levels. The jurisprudence regarding these uses of human rights is only in the process of being constructed.

Positively, too, human rights have a central role to play in cosmopolitan politics, by providing relatively well-agreed standards that both states and transnational actors and associations ought to strive to fulfill. Human rights here include not only basic civil and political rights but economic and social rights as well. Beyond this, I have argued in *Globalizing Democracy and Human Rights* that we can find guidance for delimiting the democratic principle that all affected have a right to participate in decisions that affect them by appealing to impact on basic human rights. To explain briefly, the problem with the "all affected" principle in transnational democracy is that nearly everyone is potentially affected by many decisions, down to future generations. My recommendation in this connection is that we look to those who are importantly affected in their possibilities of realizing basic human rights. Where people at a distance are affected in this way, I propose that they have rights of input into the decisions in question, either directly in some way or more likely through new forms of transnational representation.

Beyond this, human rights have an ethical side and need to be recognized in forms of individual and social interaction. As I will explain in the final section below, the sort of *recognition* entailed here involves a cognitive and rational recognition of people's equality, but is importantly aided by two more emotional modes of interrelation—namely, *empathy* and *solidarity*.

Before turning to these dispositions, I would like to mention a third key aspect of cosmopolitan norms, global justice. Since human rights on the approach taken here include economic rights to means of subsistence, as well as rights to health, global justice is implicated already in an adequate notion of human rights. Moreover, the achievement of an effective system of global justice requires the development of a framework of transnational democracy that will give people involved in the distribution and redistribution more say in determining the means for achieving this end. In addition, we can say that the requirement for economic human rights demands a reconsideration of the functioning of the economic system to make it more conducive to people's fulfilling their basic needs worldwide. But that topic would have to be developed in future research.

Unifying Themes for a Global Ethics—Recognition of Human Rights and the Norm of Solidarity

In this concluding section, I would like to briefly consider human rights and transnational solidarity as key norms for global ethics and also make a few remarks concerning their relation to each other. Of particular interest here is understanding how the classic notion of the reciprocal recognition of the equal rights—in this case, human rights—is related to the more emotive conceptions of empathy and solidarity, and indeed whether universal human rights can be advanced through these more particularistic notions.

The motivation for such an analysis arises from the limited potency of rights taken alone, even as embodied within formal legal systems. Thus rights, including human rights, have tended to remain formal and have often been disregarded in practice. This has led some theorists to claim that they are irrelevant and need to be replaced with a reliance on feelings of empathy for particular others. My own view is different: I suggest that the recognition of rights needs to be supplemented with, though not replaced by, feelings of empathic understanding and solidarity (Gould 2004, 2006, 2007b). Yet, the question remains how these two sorts of notions can be seen as mutually supportive. We would presumably need to show how this is possible without supposing that the particular feelings involved in empathy and solidarity are directly universal in scope, because that would seem overly demanding and not realizable. Positively, we would need to explicate how feelings of empathy and actions in solidarity with distant others can help to bring about the recognition of the equal status or persons and of human rights. Since I have addressed these questions in some detail elsewhere (Gould 2006: 255–6, 2007b: 160-1), I will only make a few observations about this in conclusion here.

The idea of recognition of equal rights is already well understood, despite the many philosophical questions that can still be posed about it. Such recognition has its proper home in the *cognitive* and *rational* acknowledgment of others, as individuals or groups, and of their (equal) rights. Yet, in Hegelian terms, such an acknowledgment of others is not understood as a simple mental act, but rather as emerging from a struggle for power or domination, where the drive is for the recognition by another of the self as free or self-determining. Empathy, in contrast, signifies a feeling-based or imaginative identification with another and the other's perspective and situation (Gould 2004: 251–7). While often felt for those who are in a situation of suffering of some sort, who may thus be less well-off, empathy avoids any idea of a struggle for power or even a power differential between the relevant individuals. Yet, empathy has a cognitive aspect too, since it involves attempting to understand the perspective of the other; but it highlights the emotional grasping of the feelings and situation of the other. Ethically, it is directed to the needs and vulnerabilities of others.

It is evidently of contemporary relevance to develop wider empathy and solidarity with those situated at a distance, in the present global situation characterized by serious inequalities and tendencies to domination by one nation-state over others. I have suggested the need to cultivate a *disposition to empathy*, as a tendency to take seriously the concrete needs of others in their specific situations, including of people remote from us, and a *disposition to solidarity*, as a tendency beyond this to act in support of these others when necessary (Gould 2007b).

With regard to the charge of implausibility in expecting a wide diffusion of these dispositions, we can remark that such diffusion is not impossible inasmuch as empathy does not require actually knowing what goes on in the mind of all others (which would be impossible) or accepting their viewpoint. Rather, it entails listening to others and reconstructing their views for oneself with fellow feeling

(Gould 2004, 2007b). There is also no expectation of empathy and solidarity directed at all others, but only of networks of overlapping mutual empathy and solidarities. So, when interpreted in this alternative and more limited way, it can be suggested that empathy contributes to an enlarged perspective by imaginatively taking other individuals or groups into account, thinking about them, and presenting their situation—seriously though sometimes critically—to oneself. In this view, this enlarged perspective is in fact one of equality but in a sense that recognizes differences. It thus instantiates what I elsewhere have called a *generous* rather than a *rigorous* form of recognition, where the latter limits equality to sameness while the generous form recognizes equality through differences (Gould 2006: 255).

It should be emphasized, however, that at the level of human interaction and global ethics, empathy and recognition have to be supplemented by solidarity, in order to account for normatively desirable relations to others, within one's own polity or at a distance. Solidarity as a sort of social empathy can hold not only between individuals but between groups or associations and a new and growing literature has emerged about it (see Bayertz 1999; Mohanty 2003; Dean 1996). People are understood as potentially feeling solidarity with the suffering of others or as standing with them in their struggles. And some theorists are beginning to apply this concept beyond its original home in the ties that bind the members of a given and delimited social group to those that characterize our relationships to distant people, particularly to those who are oppressed or needy.[3]

Given the more transnational interrelations engendered by globalization in its economic, technological, and communicative modes, we can even use Emile Durkheim's original notion of solidarity established through a division of labor (Durkheim 1964) to show its contemporary relevance and increased scope. We can further suggest that the overlapping interrelations among people at a distance generate a new form that we can call *network solidarities*. When people or associations stand in solidarity with others at a distance within networks of interrelations and affiliations, they can come to identify with these others in their efforts to overcome oppression or to eliminate suffering, and they may take action to aid these others, or stand ready to do so if called upon. A shared commitment to justice characterizes these solidarity groups, or perhaps, in more consequentialist terms, a commitment to the elimination of suffering. Yet, solidarity is a disposition to act toward others who are recognized as different from oneself, in the sense of being differently situated, and in this way, it is not limited to a Rortyan recognition of others who are "one of us" (Rorty 1989: 189–98).

However, solidarity cannot be limited to either cognitive understanding or empathy, but moves beyond these to the readiness to take action in support of others.[4] I have argued that *deference* is a crucial notion here, designating the requirement to allow the others to determine the forms of aid most beneficial to them. This interpretation attempts to avoid imposing on others the customary

---

3   For my own approach to this, see Gould (2007b). See also the essays by Joseph Schwartz, Max Pensky, and Larry May in Gould and Scholz (2007).

4   See also the discussion in Stjerno (2004: 326).

expectations and practices of those offering aid, and instead recognizes that it is the people in the oppressive or needy situation who are usually best able to say what support they wish and from which they would benefit. Further, the connection of solidarity to action, in constructing ties among multiple individuals or associations, reveals its relation to the older notion of *mutual aid*. And solidarities of this sort can exist among civil society associations and social movements, as well as individuals.

Although it is unreasonable to suppose that people will feel solidarity with all other individuals or groups, particularly because of the fact of conflicting interests, nonetheless I have suggested that some sort of human solidarity is possible as a *disposition* toward empathic understanding of the common needs and interests of others and a disposition to stand with them where necessary in view of these. This sort of solidarity can exist through differences, where the distinctive social situation of the others is empathically understood, including their specific challenges and even conflicts, or again where the interdependence with these different others comes to be recognized.

Finally, unlike care or empathy, which apply to a very limited subset of individuals, solidarity networks permit broader interrelations with a range of other individuals and associations who share in a situation of being oppressed or who, more generally, are suffering through no fault of their own. Since such solidarities are constructed through the interactions and understandings of groups or individuals over time, the sort of universality that is possible here is what I have previously called a *concrete* one, in contrast to the abstract universality of traditional moral principles (Gould 1976, 2004: ch. 2).

A notion of solidarity of this type, then, which sees it as requiring openness and receptivity to the situation of other individuals and groups, is an ethical disposition that supplements a theory giving a central role to democracy and human rights. Indeed, solidarity suggests the importance of supporting others in their own efforts at democratization, and I have therefore called it a conception of *democratic solidarity*. To the degree that others are both empathically and cognitively respected in their equality (and in their differences), the norms of solidarity and the recognition of human rights can be seen as mutually sustaining. I propose that the further elaboration of each of these norms and of their relations to each other would be important future tasks for global ethics.

References

Bayertz, K. (ed.) (1999), *Solidarity*. Dordrecht: Kluwer.
Beauchamp, T.L. and Childress, J.R. (1994), *Principles of Biomedical Ethics*. New York: Oxford University Press.
Dean, J. (1996), *Solidarity of Strangers*. Berkeley: University of California Press.
DeGeorge, R.T. (2002), "International Business Ethics and Incipient Capitalism: A Double Standard?," in Donaldson, T. and Werhane, P. (eds) *Ethical Issues in Business*. Upper Saddle River, NJ: Prentice-Hall.

Donaldson, T. (1999), "Moral Minimums for Corporations," in Rosenthal, J.H. (ed.) *Ethics and International Affairs*. Washington, DC: Georgetown University Press, 455–80.

Durkheim, E. (1964), *The Division of Labor in Society*. New York: The Free Press.

Falk, R. and Strauss, A. (2001), "Toward Global Parliament," *Foreign Affairs* (January/February).

Gould, C.C. (1976), "The Woman Question: Philosophy of Liberation and the Liberation of Philosophy," in Gould, C.C. and Wartofsky, M.W. (eds) *Women and Philosophy*. New York: Putnam's, 5–44.

Gould, C.C. (1988), *Rethinking Democracy*. Cambridge: Cambridge University Press.

Gould, C.C. (2003), "Women's Human Rights and the US Constitution: Initiating a Dialogue," in Schwarzenbach, S. and Smith, P. (eds) *Women and the US Constitution: History, Interpretation, Practice*. New York: Columbia University Press, 197–219.

Gould, C.C. (2004), *Globalizing Democracy and Human Rights*. Cambridge: Cambridge University Press.

Gould, C.C. (2006), "Recognition, Care, and Solidarity," in Bertram, G., Celikates, R., Ladou, C. and Lauer, D. (eds) *Socialité et reconnaissance. Grammaires de l'humain*. Paris: Editions L'Harmattan, 243–56.

Gould, C.C. (2007a), "Global Democratic Transformation and the Internet," in Rowa, J.R. (ed.) *Technology, Science and Social Justice, Social Philosophy Today* 22. Charlottesville, VA: Philosophy Documentation Center.

Gould, C.C. (2007b), "Transnational Solidarities," *Journal of Social Philosophy* 38(1), 146–62.

Gould, C.C. and Scholz, S.R. (eds) (2007), *The Journal of Social Philosophy, Special Issue on Solidarity* 38(1).

Held, D. (1995), *Democracy and the Global Order*. Stanford: Stanford University Press.

Luban, D. (1980), "Just War and Human Rights," *Philosophy and Public Affairs* 9(2), 160–81.

Mills, C.W. (2005), "'Ideal Theory' as Ideology," *Hypatia* 20(3), 165–84.

Mohanty, C.T. (2003), *Feminism without Borders: Decolonizing Theory, Practicing Solidarity*. Durham: Duke University Press.

Rorty, R. (1989), *Contingency, Irony, and Solidarity*. Cambridge: Cambridge University Press.

Smart, J.J.C. and Williams, B. (1973), *Utilitarianism For and Against*. Cambridge: Cambridge University Press.

Stjerno, S. (2004), *Solidarity in Europe: The History of an Idea*. Cambridge: Cambridge University Press.

Chapter 2

Globalization Between Economism and Moralism

Gérald Berthoud

The world has not only been the subject of endless discussion and passionate debates for more than a decade, but also of unfounded hope and illusory beliefs. In economic and academic environments and with "alter-globalist" (*altermondialistes*) militants, many are those who think that borders no longer have a *raison d'être*, particularly any political frontiers. Their thinking has come to a point where they defend the idea of a new era, termed "global." This worldview has spread very quickly throughout the media so that it has become a commonly held public opinion.

This chapter tries to argue that the hegemony of the borderless market makes the idea of a common humanity inconceivable. The chapter is structured as follows. The first section points out that the notion of globalization as the unification of humanity is not new, but regains momentum connected to technological innovations. However the current beliefs about globalization mask the fact that the world is characterized by a radical division between two institutionalized parts: the market and the international community. The second section argues that since the seventeenth century at least the market tends to be viewed as the only way of creating a peaceful world. In the following section, I point out that globalization cannot be taken seriously without considering the role of the international community. But, within the hegemonic economic ideology, the planetary solidarity is simply complementary to economic development. Aid and poverty reduction are means to allow the poor to participate in the world market. As I show in the section after that, market globalization seems to be an inevitable force, as it is based on the widespread belief that human being is strictly motivated by self-interest. Market is thus presented as the single system for poor and rich to improve without any limits their material conditions of life. Such is, for a utilitarian ethic, the ultimate aim of human existence. In the subsequent section, I outline another view of ethics with Aristotle and Ricoeur. Against the apparent evidence of a naturally egoistic human being what is defended is the fact that the human being is always a social being. He or she is therefore always included into a specific context. In this sense, ethic must favor living together. In the concluding section I discuss what would be the conditions of a possible global society against the absolute valorization of market.

Only One World?

This belief in a globalized future for the whole of humanity is found, for example, in the incantatory expression of an "information society," itself closely linked to the subject of globalization. Promises of humanity finally living in peace and prospering are so widespread that they are now being presented as evidence. This is the message from the World Summit on the Information Society (WSIS 2003) approved by all Member States of the United Nations:

> We are firmly convinced that we are collectively entering a new era of enormous potential, that of the Information Society and expanded human communication. In this emerging society, information and knowledge can be produced, exchanged, shared and communicated through all the networks of the world. All individuals can soon, if we take the necessary actions, together build a new Information Society based on shared knowledge and founded on global solidarity and a better mutual understanding between peoples and nations. We trust that these measures will open the way to the future development of a true knowledge society.

This illusory view of globalization is not new. This becomes clear when we cast the current phenomenon of globalization as part of a movement that historically originated at the beginning of the fifteenth century with the "discovery of the New World." But in more concrete terms, an initial stage can be effectively identified in the major technological innovations in communications (transport and transmission) during the nineteenth century. For example, the railway and the telegraph revived the hope of uniting the "great human family." At the start of the twentieth century the "fairy" of electricity was going to enable the renewal of the, up till then, unfulfilled promises (Berthoud 2000: 173). However, revival of the utopian technological promises had to wait until the middle of the twentieth century and the "information revolution."

The fact remains that globalization in its current form is not only a disparate collection of beliefs but also refers to previous innovations such as the general circulation of money, of goods, information, and to a lesser extent, people. It still corresponds to economic policies that have and have had a considerable impact on institutions as well as on individual and collective practices. At this level of policies and practices, the question is no longer one of knowing what globalization effectively is because this has been measured. Various institutions think that they can establish an index of globalization so that countries can be classified. This "truth about figures" at least highlights the enormous gap between winners and losers, as much between countries as inside each one of them. But the method of comparing figures, of encapsulating the complexity of the phenomena known as globalization, is to say the least unsatisfactory. Above all, the world is characterized by a radical division between two institutionalized parts: the world market and the so-called international or global community. A system basically marked by various forms of heterogeneity. On the geopolitical map the West is ever more confronted by growing powers such as China and India. In a wider sense the heterogeneity is also cultural. At the moment there seems to be a variety of largely incompatible truths throughout the world, even if the Member States of the United Nations recognize all the universal values put forward in numerous documents.

The World Market

Market dynamics—as both rich and poor parts of the globe are aiming at or trying to aim for the same things—is one of several processes uniting the planet. All of these are to some degree subject to the power struggle characterizing the international division of labor. Generalized commodification has certainly not been fully realized yet. But it would be naïve not to consider the hegemonic worldwide reach of such a movement. In following the same rule the market tends not to make any distinction between those who are near and those who are far away. Or yet again, it boils down to considering the familiar and the unfamiliar or foreign in one functional and impersonal register. This way of viewing the liberating reach and range of economic relationships is not new. In the second half of the seventeenth century an English writer Dudley North observed:

> the whole World as to Trade, is but as one Nation or People. (See Appleby 1978: 277)

Taking the same point of view during the same epoch, the Italian Montanari noted:

> Intercourse between nations spans the whole globe to such an extent that one may say all the world is but a single city in which a permanent fair comprising all commodities is held so that by means of money all the things produced by the land, the animals and human industry can be acquired and enjoyed by any person in his own home. (See Marx 1970: 153)

Nearly a century later, Montesquieu could only confirm the same globalist position. For him:

> [...] household effects, like money, banknotes, bills of exchange, the effects of the companies, ships, all merchandise, belong to the whole world that in this respect simply forms one unique State, of which all societies are members. (Montesquieu 1979: 24)

Lastly, for Adam Smith the market is a space where expansion is not subject to any pre-established limits. For example:

> a merchant [...] is not necessarily the citizen of any particular country. It is in a great measure indifferent to him from what place he carries on his trade; and a very trifling disgust will make him remove his capital, and together with it all the industry which it supports, from one country to another. (Smith 1976: 426)

Of course, these were prophetic views. At that time capitalism was largely contained within social, cultural, and political limits. Contrary to that, the economic system today tends to be autonomous and to be free from any obstacle to its expansion. In fact, joint radical transformations of a technical and economic nature impose a logic of organization, which completely breaks with all ideas of limits and clearly defined places.

Already for Montesquieu, the idea of a world market could be viewed as the perfect expression of "doux commerce" or gentle commerce. In the same way today, commerce is considered to be the only way of progressively building and creating peace and prosperity in the world. The growing interdependence produced by international commerce is perceived as the best way of, little by little, removing all legitimacy from national borders between sovereign states. There is the belief that one market can create one world and unite all humanity conquered by the idea that the individual and collective interest of the others is also my own interest. However, the pacifist inclination of the market must be forcefully put into perspective. With great clarity, Montesquieu shows the dark side of "doux commerce." Indeed, for him:

> in countries affected by a commercial spirit, one traffics in all human actions, and all moral virtues: the smallest things […] are made or given for money. (1979: 10)

The International Community

Nevertheless, it would be simplistic to reduce globalization to the single domain of the economic. The existence of a developing world market cannot be envisaged without taking the international community into consideration, in agreement with an established vocabulary. Though in the current world context, does such a formula need to be taken seriously? Did it not become a simple custom of language with the passage of time? From a swift evaluation of the effective situation in the world, it seems the answer to these questions is positive. In fact, this international community is racked by harsh imbalances, economic and technoscientific certainly, but also strategic and military. And above all, it is perverted by a divide between the global wealth of the North and the widespread poverty of many countries in the South. A kind of wide separation irresistibly evoking the existence of two worlds lacking common positions, although the question of poverty should not be focused on the so-called "developing countries" only.

However, without denying the pertinence of these and other assessments too, there are serious reasons for taking the mobilizing idea of international community into consideration. Starting with the existence of international organizations, which proves the inevitability of interdependence between states, including those countries most hostile to any encroachment on their sovereignty. A manifest tendency has developed in which an increasing legitimacy is being conferred on a separation of responsibilities between states and various global institutions. Certainly, even the United Nations as it is now, is not suitably constituted for an inclusive political community in which the responsibilities would be to ensure that the whole of humanity were "living well together." Nevertheless, the hypothesis of a developing international community can be supported. Among other things, its existence becomes apparent in partial and selective localized actions marked by the moral demands of a planetary solidarity.

Some kind of division of tasks is established on a planetary level between the economic world and the international community. The former must promote a market that is as free as possible, while one of the aims of the latter is to resolve the problem of world poverty. For the advocates of "unbridled markets," the slogan "trade not aid" has all the appearance of an indisputable truth. It also frequently serves to justify economic policies liable to destabilize social cohesion because they promise to improve the well-being of the many.

Nevertheless, the enthusiasm for the globalized free market is far from eclipsing various forms of benevolence and generosity, which can all be included in the general category of aid. Both, the moral duty and the "truth of trade," have to be considered within a widespread way of thinking, based on a double representation of individual and collective actions, and institutions. On one side, the figure of *homo oeconomicus* driven by a rational self-interest, and a clearly marked indifference to others; on the other, the ideal of a human being showing empathy through altruistic actions. Such a radical contrast is a perfect illustration of the traditional dualist views of economism and moralism. But within the very powerful economic ideology, aid must be viewed simply as a type of moral complement to economic development. So the slogan could be "aid for trade." Aid is viewed as the means for a large part of humanity to escape from the "poverty trap" by participating in the world market. In particular, public aid for development must transform the excluded into actors in increased economic competition. This "fight against poverty" tends to divide humanity into those who have the duty of helping and those who have the right to receive. But the moral obligation of the former does not lack a rather marked economic interest. The latter cannot receive but have to give back in one way or another. Too often though this right to receive is the same as reducing the beneficiaries to being a veritable object of charity. This possible perversion of aid illustrates the strong tendency of the world system to base human relationships on technical and economic efficacy. In agreement with this logic, not being able to participate in such a system, can it not be considered useless?

A Utilitarian Ethics

Those who are included in the globalized market, certainly very unequally, and those who are excluded from it are all simultaneously subject to and fascinated by globalization. Globalization has all the appearance of an inevitable force against which resistance would be futile. But opposing this dark side of globalization is the bright face of a process in a position to produce limitless goods and services. The route that should lead to such happiness is of course that of the unrestrained market. This is a route presented as being universally applicable because it rests on the belief of a human person being naturally inclined to care first and foremost for him or herself. From this point of view, the main condition to free the individual would be the instrumentalization of the world. Economic growth is therefore the condition sine qua non tending towards this objective. In particular, since the fall of the Berlin Wall in 1989, the ideal of material well-being has become fully established throughout the world. A truly economic race between countries is taking place. The world is not only divided between rich and poor countries of course, but also into emerging and newly industrialized countries, to cite only the most up-to-date labels. In other words, in willingly following market wealth or having this imposed on it, the world is fragmented well beyond the simple dichotomy between included and excluded.

This unrelenting search for an improvement in the material conditions of life, even for the most rich, very immediately appears to be the ultimate aim of human existence. This quest possesses the main characteristic of not placing any limits on the search for well-being. This generalized view of *homo economicus* must correspond to ethics that are utilitarian. In other words, all that would permit well-being or the happiness of the individual to increase, to use vague but commonly used terms again, would be the criterion par excellence for saying simultaneously that this is true, good, and just.

Following these utilitarian principles, fighting poverty and promoting growth is therefore to act for the good of everyone. Every person could also increase their participation and ability to act in the economic world of production and consumption. But in hoping to reach such a level of freedom and prosperity, what means are to be used? For several experts aid will only be the manifestation of "good intentions" producing debatable results, or even clearly negative ones. In other words, the market would seem to be the only natural way of organizing the entire world. This comes back to considering all the discussion that the "good life" and the "just society" will have no *raison d'être*. Such an extreme position of course evades the basic question of the aims of human existence and their corresponding values. Therefore, the legitimacy of the market order is often expressed in what could be viewed as ethical language. For a whole tradition of thought, based on the idea of institutions as the consequences of unintended action, or, more precisely, on the view of the spontaneous order of the so-called free market, there is no fundamental antagonism between individual interest and the common good. On the contrary, trying to satisfy first your own needs and desires has a positive effect on society as a whole. The position taken by Mandeville is worth recalling, that is, his belief that "private vices are public benefits" as well as the idea from Adam Smith of the "invisible hand." Similarly, for Friedrich von Hayek, a major representative of the doctrine of the "spontaneous order," such a view assumes a "society of rights" or an "open society," characterized by abstract and universal rules. The situation therefore becomes one of "maintaining that which poor neighborhoods will undoubtedly need and using this to meet the anonymous demands of thousands of strangers" but that is still to say "seeking the maximum benefit leads to good being done for a much greater number of people" (Nemo 1988: 298). Such an ethical principle is no longer based on traditional moral precepts like duty and obligation. On the contrary, it is paradoxically founded on the competition of mutual interests between individuals who are indifferent to each other within an idealized free market.

Another View

Unlike this individualist vision, a different view of the world, of relationships with nature and with the others, near and far, must be considered. However, this view on the possible and the desirable cannot be radically different to the point of breaking completely with the present situation. Nevertheless, let us try to outline a theoretical way of viewing the human and social reality differently from that which imposes the economic vision of the world on us. Therefore, the premise of a naturally egoistic human being, which for the most part seems to be blatantly obvious evidence, must be examined. A being whose apparently altruistic behavior is only an indirect means of satisfying necessarily egoistic tendencies. This viewpoint is expressed in the all powerful language of interest. A language emphasizing that which divides and that which opposes, and that is viewed as the only suitable way of saying that this is truly human. In particular, the use of economic categories such as "interest," "exchange," "capital," and "market," to express all the aspects of individual and social life, is without doubt the best way of blocking all effective comprehension of the human condition solely on the dimensions of a rational calculation between pleasures and work effort, and the costs and benefits. For example, treating a human being as capital means evaluating it only as a source of wealth or profit. Social relationships are also represented as capital amounting to the favoring of a world in which everything is instrumentalized. In a World Bank report published in 2006 entitled *Where is the Wealth of Nations? Measuring Capital for the Twenty-first Century*, wealth takes the form of natural capital, human capital, and institutional or social capital. The human being is thus conceived as an element in a universe of things to be developed. Using such a representation of economics, the danger is that in simply repeating the immediate representations that our society makes of itself, we err about the profound significance of our practices and our ideas. Is it necessary to consider that actions cannot be motivated by pleasure, disinterestedness, or yet again, duty? So what is to be done with the perception of common sense, but also with the observations of empirical reality that, to say the least, show the limits of the premise of psychological egoism?

But for the orthodox view of modern thought, human being is conceived logically and chronologically as a pre-social one. Therefore, within the limits of this prevailing kind of individualism, our own representation of ourselves tends to minimize, or even conceal, the multiple forms of interdependence to which we are necessarily subject. Only viewing the individual without others should not be conceivable. There is no existence of self without coexistence. But this indomitable social dimension seems to be purely a constraint, or on the contrary, a free relationship. This truncated representation of the social is composed of a double conception well attested to in orthodox scholarly thought. Thus, in conceiving what fundamentally holds the members of a society together, the theories inherited from the philosophical tradition divide it into political and economic life. It suffices to evoke the emblematic figure of Thomas Hobbes, as the main symbol of the doctrine of the social contract, and that of Adam Smith, who is most often simplified to the point of symbolizing the logic of the free market. Today, the human being is seen as being liberated from his direct relationships with others. Inclined more to oppose all constraints so that the human being tends to act as an individual who no longer thinks that he or she is also a social being. However, before being defined by his political allegiance and by his economic freedom, the individual is a human being recognized as such in his interpersonal relationships. No human being, as individualized as he may be, can be without a group of appropriate institutions to inscribe his actions and ideas within a more or less well defined prescriptive regulated world. That is to say, the human being is always already a social being and that he is therefore always integrated into a determined context. Again, all intersubjective relationships are not completely free but are set within and affected by a framework of institutions. The idea of institution must be considered by using a broader meaning as public rules for action and thought (Mauss 1968: 25). From this point of view, "language is the great institution—the institution of institutions—which always precedes each of us" (Ricoeur 1985: 400). Human relationships are therefore fundamentally triadic. All sociality is clearly expressed in the set of the three pronouns "I," "you" and "she/he" (see Benveniste 1966). This intrinsic inseparability of self and others through the mediation of third parties assumes a certain tension between asserting his/her subjective identity and being recognized as such by the others and conforming to the demands and requirements imposed by the social order as a "we."

Personal and social recognitions are expressed through the circulation of things and words that become symbols in order to create, maintain, and renew human relationships. This is the foundational requirement of our humanity, expressed according to the context by concepts such as dignity, identity, respect, honor, reputation, and many more besides. In all cases, the individual human being aspires to be recognized and treated as a person. Isn't this desire for recognition that which enables human beings to act? Or at least, isn't such a desire for recognition more fundamental than just having the mere material objective to become rich? Through his multiple actions the human being manifests his own value and merits, comparing himself to the others in one way or another. This implies not having to fight or struggle for survival. But this ability also assumes a person can impose himself at the expense of the others. So that they can survive and exist, people certainly do things with the others, but also, in a paradoxical and ambivalent way, against the others.

This alternative view of the human condition can only be reflected in the way the main questions of ethics are viewed. The prevailing individualism of the self-interested person reflects a representation of self and society that are ultimately destructive. It conceals or even devalues all that favors living together. An ethical requirement makes it necessary to transcend what divides and makes human beings oppose each other. From this point of view, ethics must be assimilated into a wisdom and knowledge of purely human relationships. Relationships that cannot be envisaged without an element of gratuity and a certain amount of generosity. It is in this sense that ethics must be very clearly formulated, following Ricoeur, as an "aim of the good life, with and for the others, in just institutions" (Ricoeur 1991: 257). By using this definition, ethics comes within the realm of the desirable and differentiate itself as such from the moral, which is in line with the world of the prescriptive and normative. Above all, it reflects a conception of the human being unrelated to all economic reductionism. In possessing the ability to act and being able to take the initiative, in a determined institutional context, the self and the others are interdependent. However, confronted to the relentless complexity of the human condition, it would be absolutely illusory to put forward great ethical principles. It would be futile to proclaim ideals that would be humanly unobtainable. The ethics of the "happy medium" should be viewed as a way so as to avoid falling into one extreme or another. Speaking of human actions in *Nichomachean Ethics* (II, 5, 1106^b 27), Aristotle states:

> there can be excess, defect, or mean... the mean is subject to success and praise, a double advantage peculiar to virtue. Virtue is therefore a type of mediety in the sense that it aims at the mean.

This ethics is closely related to practical wisdom. The latter, expressing in a way human fragility, allows arbitration of the inevitable conflicts of values in multitudes of concrete situations and the continuous search for the best equilibrium to take place everywhere. Unlimited economic growth is surely one of the largest obstacle to elaborating an ethics of the happy medium. Admittedly the economic sphere, caught up in a never-ending trend of technoscientific development, is the most demanding manifestation of rationality. But in fact, as much in terms of production as consumption, the economy with its constant innovations eludes and escapes from all limits of sensible moderation. In the endless competition between economic rivals, the distinction between rational calculation and reasonable attitude tends to become confused. With regard to production, the ability of entrepreneurs to act tends to be corrupted into a power to produce the largest profit. The absence of any limit establishing a maximum income, and the widely diffused lists of the richest men and women in the world, clearly legitimize this race for profits. Isn't this the most evident manifestation of a veritable culture of excess? This never ending search for monetary returns has corresponding unlimited consumer demand. Freedom of choice and access to all things are thus viewed as legitimate democratic demands. But isn't everyone under the influence of conformity and conventionality, dictated by a truly overdeveloped economic order and as such an illusory promoter of happiness for all?

A Viable Global Society?

In the same way as the economic order has all the appearances of an implacable reality, globalization is seen as inevitable. It tends to impose itself on everyone as being the result of a law of necessity. Pushed to its extreme limit, this point of view may be defined as economic globalism. The planet is strictly viewed as a whole in which everything, things and beings alike, circulates freely and are necessarily interconnected. This drift into globalization could be imagined as liberating individuals from all social obligations and all political constraints. The ideal is a homogeneous economic space on a planetary scale. The human being is therefore no longer viewed as a concrete being, defined among other things as being peculiar to a specific context. It is therefore logical that this globalist representation of the world involves a systematic devaluation of organization at the local, regional, and national level. All claims on identity at one or another of these levels have to be condemned as obstacles to peace and prosperity for the whole of humanity. In the name of those two key values in modernity, reason and progress, such a claim is only the irrational manifestation of a localism, a regionalism, or then again, nationalism, all three supposedly trapped inside the chains of tradition.

Undoubtedly, unification of the planet is possible and desirable. In addition, owing to threats, risks, and uncertainties experienced by the whole of humanity, this unification has become a necessity. Thus the entire planet must also be seen as a regulated space, viewed simultaneously from the moral and the legal angle. But above all it must be thought of in its political dimension as a set of institutional mediations ensuring the regulation of a fundamentally heterogeneous world. However, being unable to confront this complexity from the outset, let us tackle only the level of values and their shaping in that they can be defined as a "metanarrative" or "grand narrative," to use the expression of Lyotard (1984).

On this level the issue is relatively clear. Is elevating economic growth to a fundamental value the most assured way of allowing the inhabitants of the planet not only to survive, but also to exist fully, and lastly, to become more human? Is it conceivable that a narrow community of interest, or yet still a "community of means," according to the idea of Hayek (Nemo 1988: 193), might allow the world to globalize? The search for an unlimited power in the related domains of technoscience and economics is translated into the field of consumption by a type of frenzy for "ever more" and the "always new." Several authors have insisted on the fact that market capitalism implies a moral contradiction between a puritan or ascetic side, characterizing the field of production with its imperative of rationalization, and a hedonistic side characterizing consumption which is viewed as a sphere of individual liberation and pleasure (Bell 1976). Already for Marx, such a contradiction was quite obvious:

> As capitalist production, accumulation, and wealth become developed, the capitalist ceases to be the mere incarnation of capital. [...] his education gradually enables him to smile at the rage for asceticism, as a mere prejudice of the old-fashioned miser. While the capitalist of the classical type brands individual consumption as a sin against his function, and as "abstinence" from accumulating, the modernised capitalist is capable of looking upon accumulation as "abstinence" from pleasure. (Marx 1967: 593)

In this race to a well-being never attained for anyone, the development objectives of the United Nations (UN 2000) for the Millennium have hardly any chance of being achieved, unless a real revolution in values and an institutional transformation corresponding to a globalized solidarity occurs. But is it still necessary to ask if unlimited growth, leading to a tendency to excess in many situations in social life, is equivalent to a natural movement? In this case, everyone would have to be evaluated according to his ability to adapt. Though would it no longer be right to see in this absolute valorization of growth—and of all that comes with it—a general orientation of the modernity resulting from a global choice?

In contrast to a humanity subject to adaptive constraints only, an ethical questioning must concern a possible principle of autolimitation, as formulated by Cornelius Castoriadis (see, e.g. Castoriadis 2005: 227 and 250). It is certainly not easy to specify the values in the name of which another type of globalization would be possible. Can a society in the making be spoken of? While the notion of society might become problematic, it still conveys the idea of a will to live together. It cannot therefore be reduced to technoscientific and economic issues. It does not simply bind actors for whom the only mediation would be the prices on the ever more developed and extensive market. However, the perception of this world of things as a space characterized among other things by flexibility, novelty, and opportunity is largely seen as being favorable. But how could such poor sociality keep humanity together?

Postulating a hypothetical world society, ecologically and humanely viable, would assume an internal complexity composed of a threefold level of sociality. To start with the first level, that of "modes of authentic relationships" in which "the individuals have a concrete knowledge of each other" (Lévi-Strauss in Charbonnier 1961: 58). Such sociality, based on principles such as trust, loyalty, and generosity, characterizes all interpersonal relations, especially in the domains of family ties and friendship, or yet again in proximal relationships, in the neighborhood, and in multiple communities. But this fundamental sociality takes place in the context of a defined national unity, composed of individuals linked impersonally by administrative, technical, and market mediations. However, more radically imaginary and symbolic components provide meaning to these functional relationships.

At the very level of globalization, as far as it is not reduced to the universal expansion of the market, humanity is a whole in which principles of reciprocity and solidarity must operate in order to exceed instituted limits of a national, religious, or cultural nature. For example, natural resources like climate, atmosphere, or water, but also cultural heritage like architectural and works of arts are conceived and more and more presented as parts of common goods, or global commons for current and future generations. Their safeguarding and protection should involve a planetary consciousness, and above all, appropriate actions. But to go in this direction human beings must feel imperatively responsible, individually and collectively. Without considering the possibility or not of a transnational State, could global citizenship be spoken of? For instance, the recognition of a common humanity is a feature characteristic of the representatives of the so-called civil society, or NGOs, when they participate in alterglobalist forums, or in the "Summits" organized under the aegis of the

United Nations. These representatives, in spite of their heterogeneity, are often considered to be "citizens of the world" or "universal citizens," who should manifest an ability to transcend national boundaries and to be associated in defence of the global common good. They are, in one way or another, opposed to world capitalism and to the hegemony of market, viewed as a spontaneous social order. Against such an absolute valorization of market and its supposedly liberating impact, they are trying to counterpose ethical values that are not based on a reductionist presupposition of a strictly self-interested human being.

But the possible existence of such a universal citizenship would have to be constituted without denying, or without marginalizing, the complexity of the levels of sociality and their corresponding values. But the problem is not so much isolating the social nature peculiar to each one of these levels than tackling the way they are imbricated in reality. For example, the functional relationships of the market, or the administrative authority, would not be supportable if it did not include, according to certain variable degrees, qualities suitable to the register or style of interpersonal relations. But from "authentic" sociality to "planetary" organization, with the inevitable national and regional levels, the ethical aim should always be the same: to create and maintain values for a truly human life against the violence of economic instrumentalization, political oppression, cultural discrimination, and social exclusion.

References

Appleby, J.O. (1978), *Economic Thought and Ideology in Seventeenth Century England.* Princeton: Princeton University Press.

Bell, D. (1976), *The Cultural Contradiction of Capitalism.* New York: Basic Books (new edition 1996).

Benveniste, E. (1966), "Structure des relations de personne dans le verbe," in *Problèmes de linguistique générale I.* Paris: Gallimard, 225–36.

Berthoud, G. (2000), "La "société de l'information:" l'utopie du XXIe siècle?," *Revue européenne des sciences sociales* 118, 163–80.

Castoriadis, C. (2005), *Une société à la dérive.* Paris: Seuil.

Charbonnier, G. (1961), *Entretiens avec Claude Lévi-Strauss.* Paris: Plon.

Lyotard, J.-F. (1984), *The Postmodern Condition. A Report on Knowledge.* Manchester: Manchester University Press (first publication in French 1979).

Marx, K. (1967), *Capital. A Critique of Political Economy. Vol. 1 The Process of Capitalist Production.* New York: International Publishers.

Marx, K. (1970), *A Contribution to the Critique of Political Economy.* New York: International Publishers.

Mauss, M. (1968), *Œuvres 1. Les fonctions sociales du sacré.* Paris: Minuit.

Montesquieu (1979), *De l'esprit des lois* (vol. 2). Paris: Flammarion (first publication 1748).

Nemo, P. (1988), *La société de droit selon F.A. Hayek.* Paris: Presses Universitaires de France.

Ricoeur, P. (1985), *Temps et récit 3. Le temps raconté.* Paris: Seuil.

Ricoeur, P. (1991), "Ethique et morale," in *Lectures 1. Autour du politique.* Paris: Seuil, 256–69.

Smith, A. (1976), *An Inquiry into the Nature and Causes of the Wealth of Nations* (vol. 1). Oxford: Clarendon Press (first publication 1776).

UN (2000), *United Nations Millennium Declaration*. New York: The United Nations.

World Bank (2006), *Where is the Wealth of Nations? Measuring Capital for the Twenty-first Century*. Washington, DC: The World Bank.

WSIS (2003), *Geneva Declaration of Principles*. Geneva: World Summit on the Information Society.

Chapter 3

Bridging the Gaps in Global Ethics: Grounded Cosmopolitan Praxis

Christien van den Anker

Global ethics as a field of study is a relatively new subject of discussion. When searching for it on the internet, the references to global ethics more often than not refer to a group of people who stand for a particular ethic which they would like to see globalized. Even sites that purport to study global ethics rather than impose them often have a religious motivation. There are, however, increasing numbers of people who engage with global ethics from a secular or a multi-faith perspective. These can either be based in philosophical argument and political thought or in the actions aimed at bringing about social transformation. Running through these two dividing lines 1) of comprehensive versus procedural engagement with Global ethics and 2) theoretical and practical forms of developing a position on global ethics, is a third one, namely 3) the central debate over the right balance between universalism and contextualism within global ethics.

The chapter is divided into several sections. First, I investigate the role of universalist and contextual theories in global ethics and argue for a balance between the two. In the next section, I use the example of the liberal-multicultural debate to show the relevance of looking for a balanced perspective. Finally, I present a method of ethical reflection to illustrate the practical possibilities of this balance between the core concerns of universalism and contextualism. I conclude that the importance of contextualism is in itself a universal value and universal principles always need to be expressed locally and embedded in particular behavior and practices. The dangers of the strong versions of either approach need to be avoided while the core concerns of both need to be preserved.

Universalism and Contextualism in Global Ethics

Universalism is widely regarded as a characteristic of any theory of global ethics, simply because of the focus on the global context in this field. Universalism has its historical roots in the cosmopolitanism of Ancient Greece where it contrasted with the focus on the scope of morality as within one city-state; in Christianity and Judaism there are references to universalism in the Golden Rule of ethics not to do onto others what one doesn't want to have done to oneself and the parable of the good Samaritan; during the period of the Enlightenment universalism found its most famous expression in Kantian cosmopolitanism.

Contextualist or particularist perspectives on global ethics often developed either from a Realist perspective on power or from a critique of liberalism, specifically criticizing the universalizing project of liberalism that is present in cosmopolitanism. A major question raised in the debates on global ethics is to what extent can the global political context be moral? Longstanding disagreements in International Relations have included major contests between Neo-realism and normative International Relations (Booth, Dunne and Cox 2001). Liberal cosmopolitans hold that the global order is a rightful subject to moral argument, whereas (Neo-)realists emphasize the right and even duty of nation-states to first protect "their own" citizens. Contextualist critiques of universalism have usually held that the appropriate local context of culture, politics and morals was overlooked. Moreover, the calls for global justice were interpreted as hierarchically trumping justice at home. Cosmopolitanism has in particular been criticized for demanding forms of solidarity across borders which are simply not feasible in the current global context (Miller 1995).

In the debate on the possibility of global norms including the justification of human rights, universalism is also frequently criticized by relativism or particularism. (Wilson and Mitchell 2003). These objections to universalism can be found in various forms in a range of approaches. Critical theorists object mainly to abstract impartiality for its implicit support for the dominant power in the status quo; instead, it favors a critical stance for social change which includes support for the powerless (Jones D. 1999). Postmodernism centres mainly on the essentialist nature of universalism, which generalizes a minority experience as if it was applicable to all; it argues instead for deconstructing existing discourses and exposing the role of language in perpetuating power differences (Critchley 1992, 1999). Feminism is critical of universalism as it has left out women's concerns in the past by generalizing male experiences. Feminist proposals for contextualizing emphasize particularity and argue for situating women in their specific social contexts rather than focusing on them as genderless individuals (Hutchings in Dower and Williams 2002). In addition some feminists have proposed to add a concept of care to universalist theories of global justice in order to avoid the disconnected trace of impartiality (Robinson 2006). Post-colonial theory contributes to the debate by being critical of liberal cosmopolitan universalism for its bias towards the West, again taking their own experience as most important, while excluding the perspective of non-Western people(s) as a result of its history of colonialism and later forms of imperialism (Grovogui 1996, 2006). Post-development theory rejects the hierarchical theories of development that use the term as if part of a civilizing mission (Rahnema and Bawtree 1997). All these criticisms of universalism have their own specific angle and propose different ways forward. Yet, despite their differences, contextualists have in common that they emphasize the particular, the context, the interrelatedness of people and of people with the non-human environment as well as (in most cases) attention for power relations and structural inequalities. In addition, as will be expanded on in the next section on liberalism and multiculturalism, contextualists aim for inclusion of minorities which requires recognition of difference beyond liberal toleration.

So far, moving in the direction of contextualism looks pretty attractive as it involves addressing the historical inequalities at least ignored and at worst perpetuated by liberal cosmopolitanism. However, this image of particularism leaves out three important contested elements in the debate between universalism and contextualism. Firstly, it does not recognize that the strongest versions of cultural relativism lead to political inaction and therefore run the risk of perpetuating the status quo instead of challenging power relations. Secondly, where particularism leads to political stances, as in Critical Theory, there is always also a universalist value at the heart of the approach: justice, care or autonomy are universalizing projects whether they are labelled liberal or critical. Thirdly, many critics of liberalism end up viewing their approach as complementary as they still adhere to at least part of the liberal project in terms of freedom, human rights, equality or democracy. To some extent the contextualists have accepted this and some therefore make a move towards pragmatism in response (Rorty, in Shute and Hurley 1993) or postmodernism where the contradiction between holding liberal values while criticizing liberalism for its lack of foundations is overcome by no longer claiming any ultimate justification for a liberal stance. Therefore, shifting all the way into a particularist version of contextualism, has connotations that are potentially as bad or worse than blind and unspecific universalism that pretends the views and experiences of one historically dominant group reflect what is relevant to all of humanity. The best way forward would be to find a balance between the concerns with strong universalism while not giving in to the risks of strong contextualism. There is some evidence in the literature that other people, too, are looking for a middle way to try to include the core concerns of both approaches (Erskine 2000; Beitz in Brock and Moellendorf 2005). This is sometimes viewed as a consensus on a minimum of common values or is presented as a strategic choice in order to create the broadest coalition. However, I view the middle way as an acknowledgment of the importance of the core concerns in both perspectives and not necessarily minimizing these concerns. The precise conceptualization of the middle way is important to debate in more detail. Jack Donnelly's work on universal human rights sketches a universalist approach which allows for contextual interpretation (Donnelly 1989). This may function as an example for the kind of balance that is possible between universalism and contextualism more generally. In order to illustrate the need for contextualizing the universal project of liberal cosmopolitanism, and to develop a more precise picture of the middle way between universalism and contextualism, let me now elaborate on the example of the debate between liberalism and multiculturalism on the question of developing the principles of either approach into global norms.

The Example of Liberalism versus Multiculturalism

To sum up, we saw in the previous section that there is a need in global ethics to find a balance between the core concerns of contextualism and universalism.

Neither are satisfactory without taking into account the other. The debate between liberals and multiculturalists reflects this stand-off on universalism and contextualism in more than one way. Within one society they disagree over the relevance of group identities; on a global scale they each defend a universalist or a contextualist approach to global norms protecting minorities.

First of all, the concept of multiculturalism is used in two very different ways. The descriptive use of the term is relevant for all societies that consist of more than one cultural group; liberals and multiculturalists agree that this circumstance is increasing within societies (Kelly 2003). Due to increased migration, most societies consist now (if not before) of several communities with different values due to either differences in ethnicity, religion, nationality or culture. Multiculturalism meaning the circumstances for intercultural dialogue is also used to refer to the perceived need to communicate peacefully with other cultures as represented by nation-states. Especially the opening up of the Chinese market and the Chinese streams of travellers, students, businesspeople and migrants lead to engagement with this type of concern. The second use of the term is in a normative prescription of how to address these differences through public policy and formal human, minority and citizenship rights. These two meanings will both be relevant in this chapter.

In the discussion on how to treat cultural differences liberals advocate toleration of individual differences as a basic human right to live autonomously and free from (unnecessary) state interference whereas the multiculturalist approach would argue on the one hand for more than that: cultural differences require not simply acceptance as legal, but recognition as of equal value to the mainstream cultural practices of the (local) majority. Yet, on the other hand, multiculturalists may be allowing less individual freedom in cases where group identities lead to strong imposition of values by the group on the individual.

A further dispute between the two approaches relates to how differences in identity should be translated into the law. According to Parekh, acceptance of differences requires changes in the legal arrangements of liberal democracies. Respect for differences also requires changes in attitudes and ways of thought. And sometimes it may mean public affirmation of differences by symbolic or other means (Parekh 2000: 2). This would go against the liberal model of dealing with value pluralism which has been to invoke the public private distinction and to be guided by the liberal theory of toleration. The principle of toleration means that one has to tolerate what is not harmful to others even if one strongly disagrees with it or even if one is deeply upset by it. Toleration, according to multiculturalists, gives the impression that the offending behavior is not valued as much as the typical behavior in the mainstream culture. Therefore, in order to move beyond toleration, multiculturalists argue for public recognition in the form of language rights and public holidays on important days for minority festivals and religious celebrations, for example. This is all in order to recognize differences as positive (Kymlicka and Wayne 2000: 25–9).

For most liberals, this goes against one of their core values and the main principle of liberalism: universality. Brian Barry, for example, holds that "universalistic moral ideas alone make sense of efforts to enforce human rights and punish violators of them" (Barry 2000: 5). Susan Mendus, too, argues in favor of a liberal model of toleration emphasizing that there is a need to recognize the similarity between people rather than the difference (Mendus 1999: 9). This further illustrates the gap between contextualist multiculturalists and universalist liberals.

In response to the multiculturalist critique of liberalism, liberals have also formulated several criticisms of multiculturalism. They maintain that it holds on to a static understanding of culture and a conservative and essentialist view of the main representation of a culture (Wilson and Mitchell 2003). Some liberals are principally against group rights, and defend only individual rights. Waldron, for example, argues that the aim of protecting existing cultures is equivalent to creating a new Disneyland (Waldron in Kymlicka 1995). However, several liberals incorporate notions of group rights in their approach. Barry, for example, develops a liberal theory of group rights which includes exemptions and special measures like quotas but justified on the basis of individual rights. He accepts that liberal formal rights have not brought equality in the countries that have adopted the liberal model, and therefore accepts the need for affirmative action programmes "to help groups whose members suffer systematic disadvantage," as long as the "'disadvantage' is defined in universal terms—as the lack of things (resources and opportunities) whose possession would generally be agreed to be advantageous" (Barry 2000: 12). In Barry's view, these group rights for special treatment should only be temporary, for as long as the disadvantage lasts. Caney, too, defends a liberal model of human rights and equality of opportunity. However, he moves on even further and argues for the protection of people's cultural interests (Caney in Kelly 2003).

The central area of disagreement is therefore not over group rights versus individual rights, but over the grounds on which group rights could be justified and the area in which group rights ought to be established. Most liberals would agree to group rights on the basis of unfair disadvantage in socio-economic terms and do not require all voluntary associations to comply with liberal principles (Barry in Kelly 2003: 232–3). Yet others, like Caney, think they could also be justified on the grounds of cultural difference and therefore apply to the area of cultural rights (Caney in Kelly 2003). Donnelly, too, aims to create a model of universal human rights that takes into account the need for local interpretations (Donnelly 1989, 1997). Moreover, recent textbooks on human rights now include entries on faith-based and regional conceptions of human rights (Smith and van den Anker 2005).

Having set out the major disagreement between liberals and multiculturalists, let us now look into a possible synthesis between liberalism and multiculturalism as an example of a balance between contextualism and universalism. Kymlicka has developed a perspective which he calls liberal multiculturalism. He views multiculturalism as "a response to the pressure that Canada exerts on immigrants to integrate into common institutions" (Kymlicka 1998: 40) He clearly puts the pressure to assimilate at the centre of the debate of multiculturalism. The renegotiation of the terms of integration between minorities and the majority in order to make them fairer on immigrants is the key focus of multiculturalism, according to Kymlicka.

In conclusion, the debate between liberals and multiculturalists has resulted in the opening up of a space for theorists who aim to bring together what they consider to be the most important elements of both models of minority rights and citizenship. On the one hand, liberals have clarified their position on group rights, acknowledging that trying to ignore cultural and racial differences is paramount to accepting discrimination. Yet, the central role for culture and recognition argued for by liberal multiculturalists is still contested. It invokes critiques from both sides; it is not universalist enough for liberals and not contextual enough for multiculturalists. In addition, politically there is a strong tendency to turn back multiculturalist measures and to insist more on universal compliance with liberal laws. This is partly due to the increased xenophobia in Western societies and partly to relevant concerns with individual human rights being violated within minority communities. Therefore, the most promising position is to adapt a liberal model to include claims of culture with the proviso of individual human rights not being violated by extending group rights. This is a good example of the balance that can be and needs to be found between universalism and contextualism.

In order to link this argument on the balance between universalism and contextualism to the point on the interdependence of theory and practice in global ethics I will now move onto the discussion of a method of ethical reflection that again involves a mix between contextualism and universalism. Recently I showed that the implementation of the Durban agenda at the level of national laws is usefully complemented by the work of local NGOs towards combating ethnic discrimination. Politicians cannot create sustainable change without supporting NGOs that engage with (young) people in informal settings. I illustrated that the claims of multiculturalism for specific forms of group rights run into difficulties from being a top-down initiative. The groundwork of building different attitudes towards people from different ethnic backgrounds still needs to be done and especially in the region of post-communist Europe, the building of the rule of law and liberal democracy rightly takes precedence over more demanding claims of groups rights, autonomy for minorities and so on. However, there are several ways in which the local work adds the emphasis of respect and recognition for different cultures and also for the importance of preserving languages and cultures (van den Anker 2007).

The implications of this type of work for the global context of multiculturalism are potentially huge. Although this is a micro-political approach, it could influence policy outcomes exponentially once initiated in some of the larger organizations and institutions active globally. Moreover, links between multiculturalism, theories of identity and cosmopolitanism are increasingly important in global political theory, especially in areas of the fair distribution of resources and peaceful relations (Appiah 2005).

Methodological Bridges between Universalism and Contextualism

Theory and Practice

This chapter presents global ethics both as a theoretical method to debate philosophical positions and as a form of engaged activism for social transformation. In the previous section I showed that a micro-political approach of working with local actors is beneficial to implementing and interpreting universal moral and legal norms like human rights. In this section I want to elaborate on the detail of this methodological component of global ethics by elaborating on the link between an academic approaches and practitioner's engagement in intellectual and emotional reflection. The field of global ethics distinguishes itself from the existing global justice debate, not only that it is multidisciplinary, engaging with wider ethical issues in the context of globalization rather than global poverty and inequality only and in giving relevance to practitioners' and lay people's experiences as ethical reflectors as well as actors. Moreover, in many debates, academic reflection would not be relevant without input from practice and we might even argue that the theoretical and the practical are not as distinct as they are often presented, for example, in the term "applied ethics." Ethics as other theoretical perspectives are developed as a lens on practice and as such are influenced by it. We may usefully employ the term praxis to express this interdependence. Global ethics should therefore engage with practitioners and "life-experts," in order to have relevance and in the processes of ethical reflection and sense-making of a wide range of people. Historically, one form of methodology that has aimed to do this is *Action research* which intertwines community activity and research in order to make research relevant to the communities involved. This involves ensuring that communities have an input into the project so that it researches something useful to the community. Often specific injustices to communities have been the justification for action research projects. It also means that the results need to be fed back into the community in an accessible way, including guidance for action to redress the injustice researched. Action research has been used in education since the early 1970s and has created space for the active involvement of learners in creating social change. Issues of gender inequality and racial or ethnic discrimination have been at the heart of action research. Recently, some advocates of action research have incorporated the notion of a constructed reality into the approach. In a recent project, reflection on how identities are used politically and could be constructed and deconstructed was part of the research and workshop activities proposed (van den Anker 2007). Global ethics can use this approach to build local capacity, to facilitate local empowerment and to ensure relevance of projects to target groups.

A second relevant methodology to bridge the gap between theory and practice in global ethics is the basic theory of *re-evaluation counselling*. Building on an impressive amount of work done by the Re-evaluation Counselling Communities and the recently established NGO United to End Racism, I designed and implemented with a team of colleagues and practitioners a project that aimed to support existing initiatives in combating racism, xenophobia and discrimination by introducing some simple and effective tools to practitioners and others interested in ending all forms of discrimination (van den Anker 2007). These tools are based on several key insights, developed in the practice of this form of co-counselling. The main idea is that people don't function effectively and authentically when they act on the basis of old hurtful experiences. Their functioning improves dramatically when they have a chance to emotionally release these old hurts. This type of release is greatly helped by a process that starts out as simply taking turns in listening. Through practice and learning from more experienced counsellors and from the Re-evaluation counselling literature this mechanism can be made more complex and people can be even more effective in helping others to work through their emotional barriers to achieve powerful and effective functioning.

The initial process of co-counselling consists simply of taking equal length turns in listening and being listened to in pairs or small groups. If the group gets any larger than about eight people, the group can either split or people can work in pairs. The topic can be left to the speaker or can be set beforehand. Effective listening implies that the listener refrains from commenting, drawing the conversation to his or her own experiences or from asking curious questions. Instead, an attentive listener shows they are pleased with the person talking, encourages the speakers and makes eye contact. Sometimes it is found helpful if the listener touches the speaker or holds hands. This depends on the level of trust that already exists between the participants.

The speaker will, once enough trust has been built, begin to show their deeply felt feelings on the issue at hand; for example in our type of activity, when asked if they have experienced discrimination. Emotions can be expressed through energetic, non-repetitive talking but also through yawning, crying, laughing or shaking. These outwards signs of emotional release all relate to specific areas of feeling, such as sadness or loss, fear, or physical recovery. In many cultures these signs of the emotional healing process will be confused with the actual hurt and therefore interrupted. We have all been told not to cry, not to laugh too loudly, or not to be afraid. By being stopped from expressing our feelings from an early age it becomes more difficult to think clearly in particular areas. As we don't heal from hurts, we experience confusion and may fall into behavior that is not an accurate response to a new situation, which is the definition of intelligence, according to counselling theory. These cases where we react as if we are repeating an old situation are called distress patterns. For example, if someone with particular features has hurt us, we may react scared to new people who look similar to us. Or if we have been upset during a particular type of weather, this weather may make us sad in future. We may also develop behavior that seems positive to try and relive a past experience that left us feeling good. In the context of ethnic discrimination it is very important to recognize that stereotypes are not intelligent behavior, as they are not based on accurate information about the new situation.

Fortunately, we can recover from hurts and reclaim our intelligence completely even long after the initial upset. This is why encouraging people to express and release emotions are the basic approach of re-evaluation counselling. By taking turns listening while appreciating the person speaking, we can all return to our natural healing process and recover our intelligence.

This basic theory shows that some universal principles of human psychology can be used in culturally sensitive ways, as the person using the tool of listening and reflecting brings with them a particular context on which the are reflecting. In order to show that this type of approach is relevant to global ethics, let's look in more detail at the theory of how people get hurt.

In addition to this basic theory of recovering from past hurt through taking turns listening, co-counsellors developed a theory on how this process can be useful in combating oppressions. The first recognition that people did not only have individual, personal hurts, but that they were hurt systematically according to their identities, was in the context of women's oppression. Several counsellors were active in the women's movement in the early 1970s and they started to speak out about the specific ways in which they had been hurt as women. Counsellors then got together in groups based on specific identities, such as men, women, Jews, Black people, and later on owning class, middle class and working class. They discovered that a lot of the areas where they could not think freshly due to past hurt were related to these identities. In order to recover form these hurts, they developed specific questions to ask about identities that were helpful in recovering from these hurts. A specific term developed in co-counselling for the distress patterns people developed due to their identities was internalized oppression. This means that the message from the stereotype starts to be believed to be true of oneself or of others of one's group. In the words of Suzanne Lipsky:

> internalized oppression is this turning upon ourselves, upon our families, and upon our own people the distress patterns that result from the racism and oppression of the majority society. (Lipsky 1987: 3)

An example of internalized oppression is for ethnic minority children to believe that majority children are more beautiful, intelligent or attractive than they are. Another example is the criticism of members of a group on each other, which prevents them from collaborating for social change.

Another discovery was that people who acted out stereotypes were also hurt in particular ways. Although everyone has a responsibility to counteract and work towards ending oppression, the majority group that acts out discrimination is not personally to blame. Arrogance and prejudice are not natural characteristics of human beings; these attitudes are learnt behavior. It is well-known that children from families with prejudice will have more stereotypes than children from less discriminatory families. What re-evaluation counselling worked out is that in order to hurt others one must first be hurt oneself. The process of taking on board discriminatory attitudes is painful for the child itself. It means losing friends who are different because parents forbid playing with them. And it means remaining separate from the groups that one discriminates against. This in itself is a loss since the child's social circle is impoverished as a result.

A story told in *Ripples of Hope* (Weissglass 1999: 110) includes the following:

> When I was about seven, I made friends with a girl in my class who was African American. I brought her home one day. We were three playing for a while and I gave

her something to drink. After she left, my mother threw the glass away. (crying) She couldn't explain to me (pause, crying) … Other things I will forgive her for, but that I won't. She said I couldn't play with her anymore. And I guess I just gave in. I was young and didn't know what to do. She tried to say that these people lived in these projects and they had diseases. She went on and on about this kind of stuff. … It just didn't make sense to me. She was a nice child, she didn't seem any different from me. I was poor, too.

Fortunately, the counselling process also works on these so-called oppressor patterns. The same natural healing process will lead to recovery if people are effectively listened to and appreciated. This assists them to reclaim their full intelligence and allows them to make good connections to all humans. In counselling workshops we have done a lot of work on relationship building between oppressed and oppressor groups, like men and women, owning class and working class people. Outside counselling, many organizations have discovered the powerful nature of building relationships for example between a rapist and their victim, or between Jews and Germans. This is potentially very powerful in the struggle against ethnic discrimination and xenophobia. It means that when people act on stereotypes they need to be listened to with appreciation and they can be assisted in building successful relationships with the people they thought less off. In one of our workshops we had a powerful example of someone who used to hold strong prejudicial views. Everyone was moved to hear the story of this person when he showed how much better he felt now that he had let those beliefs go.

I have used this model to argue for a specific model of conflict resolution (Global society, October 2000) and for a way to work on overcoming our hesitancy to end capitalism (Globalizations, September 2005). I have also used it to develop work on ending ethnic discrimination, racism and xenophobia in former Eastern Europe and parts of the former Soviet-Union. Here I worked with local NGO trainers, pupils and teachers.

Questions asked were for example:

- For members of minorities:
  1) Who are your people?
  2) What is good/are you proud of about being x …?
  3) What is difficult …?
  4) What is difficult about being a woman x …?
  5) What do you never want to hear again?

- For members of the majority:
  1) Who are your people?
  2) What is good/are you proud of about being x?
  3) What is difficult?
  4) What do you never want to hear again
  5) How did you learn there were other people than x?
  6) What prejudices did you learn about these people?

In the case of majority members it is important to emphasize that we are not after guilt and we are not to blame. Everyone has always done the best they can; oppression is learnt behavior and it probably took some bribing and punishing before someone submitted to hurting another human being. Several members of majority groups have reported that their friendships in early life with members of minority groups have been separated forcefully. They also report fighting against the prejudice they learnt but giving in at some point.

My work with these methods is an important illustration of the need to engage with current issues, the need to give space to "altern" voices while bringing in methods and approaches that enable this. It also relates to the discussion on the requirement of a reflective equilibrium to be prepared to change one's viewpoints; the element of learning through hearing others' stories is of key importance in this work.

Global ethics will be greatly helped by people increasingly taking turns listening and being allowed to express hurtful emotions and so free up thinking and action towards creating just societies and a just world. There will be more caring expressed and more respect for difference as a result. This fits in with both contextualism and universalism. These types of practical ethical reflections in global ethics could also be a space for reflecting on what a just world would look like; despite the recent calls for minimalism, I see an important role for holding out what justice requires even if there is currently not the motivation to put it into practice.

Working as Teachers and Trainers for Justice

Our roles as educators working for social change are in itself worth addressing in our work with co-counselling tools. We play an important role in this process and it is useful to take some time to reflect on ourselves from this perspective. Our identities as academics, teachers and activists bring particular prejudice and oppression from society. These come to us through others (school leaders, parents, our families and friends) but we also carry internalized oppression. Some common distress patterns concern criticism and competition: we find it hard to be pleased with what we do, it is never good enough and we criticize others for their approach. We may not take enough rest and get angry an upset with the rest of society for not moving quickly enough. As social change activists we are described as idealistic, naive, utopian and Pollyannas. In many societies social change activists are or have been in the recent past at risk of imprisonment and violence as well as death. This creates fear and hampers our freedom of thought and expression; it puts a toll on our flexible thinking. It is important to discharge, or emotionally release, feelings about ourselves and others in this group. This is in line with Asunción St Clair's call for academic activism (see St Clair's chapter in this volume); the RC approach will prevent us from easy burn out and perpetual disappointment or even cynicism.

Conclusion

In this chapter I reflected on the role in global ethics for universalism and contextualism and held out that they are both important. By looking at the example of liberalism versus multiculturalism, I worked out the ingredients for a useful balance between the two.

In the second part of the chapter I discussed a method of ethical reflection based on re-evaluation counselling. I argued that using this method adds to the aim of global ethics to contribute to healing, self-development and social transformation in the institutional and personal spheres reminiscent of the Stoics' call for philosophy as a force for healing and social transformation.

The recent development of global ethics into a recognized field of study with its own journal and annual conference is hopeful in that awareness can be developed more widely. Yet, the responsibility of Global ethicists in academia is to ensure that their work is engaged, in that it contributes to social change, and reflexive in its awareness of who it excludes. This means that the liberal cosmopolitan agenda needs to engage more with contextualism as well as structural injustice of the current system of global politics and its disciplining discourses on politics, economics and law than it currently does.

References

Anker, C. van den (2000), "Cosmopolitanism and Impartial Conflict Resolution," *Global Society* 14(4), 611–30.

Anker, C. van den (2002), "Global Justice, Global Institutions and Global Citizenship," in Dower, N. and Williams, J. (eds) *Global Citizenship. A Critical Reader.* Edinburgh: Edinburgh University Press, 158–68.

Anker, C. van den (2005), "Cosmopolitan Justice and the Globalization of Capitalism: The UNDP and ILO Proposals," *Globalizations* 2(2), 254–70.

Anker, C. van den (2007), "Globalising Liberalism or Multiculturalism? The Durban Agenda and the Role of Local Human Rights Education in Implementing Global Norms," *Globalization, Societies and Education* 5(5)November: 287–302.

Appiah, K.A. (2005), *The Ethics of Identity.* Princeton: Princeton University Press.

Aurelius, M. (1964), *Meditations.* London: Penguin.

Barry, B. (1986), "Can States be Moral?," in Ellis, A. (ed.) *Ethics and International Relations.* Manchester: Manchester University Press, 61–84.

Barry, B. (2002), "Second Thoughts and First Thoughts Revised," in Kelly, P. (ed.) *Multiculturalism Reconsidered.* Cambridge: Polity, 204–38.

Beitz, C. (2005), "Cosmopolitanism and Global Justice," in Brock, G. and Moellendorf, D. (eds) *Current Debates in Global Justice.* Dordrecht: Springer, 11–27.

Booth, K., Dunne, T. and Cox, M. (2001), *How Might We Live? Global Ethics in a New Century.* Cambridge: Cambridge University Press.

Brock, G. (2005), "What Do We Owe Co-nationals and Non-nationals? Why the Liberal Nationalist Account Fails and How We Can Do Better," *Journal of Global Ethics* 1(2), 113–26.

Caney, S. (2002), "Equal Treatment, Exceptions and Cultural Diversity," in Kelly, P. (ed.) *Multiculturalism Reconsidered.* Cambridge: Polity, 81–101.

5

Critchley, S. (1992), *The Ethics of Deconstruction: Derrida and Levinas*. Oxford: Blackwell.

Critchley, S. (1999), *Ethics—Politics—Subjectivity: Derrida, Levinas and Contemporary French Thought*. London: Verso.

Donnelly, J. (1989), *Universal Human Rights in Theory and Practice*. Ithaca: Cornell University Press.

Donnelly, J. (1997), *International Human Rights*. Oxford: Westview Press.

Erskine, T. (2000), "Embedded Cosmopolitanism and the Case of War: Restraint, Discrimination and Overlapping Communities," in *Cosmopolitanism, Distributive Justice and Violence*. Special issue of *Global Society* 14(4).

Gills, B. and Harris, J. (eds) (2005), "Empire or Cosmopolis?" Special issue of *Globalizations* 2(1).

Grovogui, S. (1996), *Sovereigns, Quasi Sovereigns and Africans: Race and Self-determination in International Law*. University of Minnesota Press.

Grovogui, S. (2006), *Beyond Eurocentrism and Anarchy: Memories of International Order and Institutions*. Basingstoke: Palgrave.

Held, D. (2005), "Principles of Cosmopolitan Order" in Brock, G. and Brighouse, H. (eds) *The Political Philosophy of Cosmopolitanism*. Cambridge: Cambridge University Press, 10–27.

Hutchings, K. (2002), "Feminism and Global Citizenship," in Dower, N. and Williams, J. (eds) *Global Citizenship. A Reader*. Edinburgh: Edinburgh University Press, 53–62.

ILO (2004), *Fair Globalisation: Creating Opportunities for All*. Geneva: UN and WCSDG.

Jones, C. (1999), *Global Justice. Defending Cosmopolitanism*. Oxford: Oxford University Press.

Jones, D. (1999), *Cosmopolitan Mediation? Conflict Resolution and the Oslo Accords*. Manchester: Manchester University Press.

Kant, I. (1991), "Perpetual Peace," in Reiss, H. (ed.) *Kant Political Writings*. Cambridge: Cambridge University Press.

Kelly, P. (ed.) (2002), *Multiculturalism Reconsidered*. Cambridge: Polity.

Kymlicka, W. (1998), *Finding our Way. Rethinking Ethnocultural Relations in Canada*. Oxford: Oxford University Press.

Kymlicka, W. and Norman, W. (eds) (2000), *Citizenship in Diverse Societies*. Oxford: Oxford University Press.

Lipsky, S. (1987), *Internalized Racism*. Seattle: Rational Island.

Mendus, S. (ed.) (1989), *The Politics of Toleration*. Edinburgh: Edinburgh University Press.

Miller, D. (1995), *On Nationality*. Oxford: Clarendon Press.

Parekh, B. (2000), *Rethinking Multiculturalism. Cultural Diversity and Political Theory*. Basingstoke: Macmillan.

Pogge, T. (2002), *World Poverty and Human Rights*. Oxford: Polity Press.

Pradhan-Malla, S. (2001), "Gender and Racism," in Feldman, S. (ed.) *Discrimination and Human Rights. The Case of Racism*. Oxford: Oxford University Press.

Rahnema, M. and Bawtree; V. (1997), *The Post-Development Reader*. Zed Books.

Rawls, J. (1999), *The Law of Peoples*. Cambridge, MA: Harvard University Press.

Robinson, F. (2006), "Care, Gender and Global Social Justice: Rethinking Ethical Globalization," *Journal of Global Ethics* 2(1), 5–26.

Rorty, R. (1993), "Human Rights, Rationality and Sentimentality," in Shute, N. and Hurley, S. (eds) *On Human Rights: Oxford Amnesty Lectures*. New York: Basic Books, 111–34.

Seneca (ed. J.M. Cooper and J.F. Procopé) (1995), *Moral and Political Essays.* Cambridge: Cambridge University Press.

Shue, H. (1980), *Basic Rights: Subsistence, Affluence and US Foreign Policy*. Princeton: Princeton University Press, 1980).

Singer, P. (2002), *One World. The Ethics of Globalization.* New Haven and London: Yale University Press.

Smith, R.K. and Anker, C. van den (eds) (2005), *The Essentials of Human Rights.* London: Hodder.

Thucydides (transl. R. Crawley) (2004), *History of the Peloponnesian War.* New York: Dover Publications.

UNDP (1999), *Human Development Report 1999.* New York and Oxford: Oxford University Press.

Waldron, J. (1995), "Minority Cultures and the Cosmopolitan Alternative," in Kymlicka, W. (ed.) *The Rights of Minority Cultures.* Oxford: Oxford University Press.

Walzer, M. (1997), *On Toleration.* New Haven: Yale University Press.

Weissglass, J. (1999), *Ripples of Hope. Building Relationships for Educational Change.* Santa Barbara: Center for Educational Change in Mathematics and Science.

Wilson, R.A. and Mitchell, J.P. (eds) (2003), *Human Rights in Global Perspective. Anthropological Studies of Rights, Claims and Entitlements.* New York and London: Routledge.

Chapter 4

Justice in a World Gone Mad: Assessing the Ethical Landscape of Globalization

Rebecca Todd Peters

When I consider the state of our world, it is hard not to conclude that our world has gone a bit mad. A wide variety of statistics witness to the irrationality and human indifference that dominate our existence. Consider the following: in our world today, basic education for everyone would cost $6 billion while currently Americans spend $8 billion annually on cosmetics; water and sanitation for everyone in the world would cost $9 billion while Europeans annually spend $11 billion on ice cream; providing reproductive health care for all women in the world would cost $12 billion, Americans and Europeans combined currently spend that much annually on perfumes; basic health and nutrition for everyone in the world would only cost $13 billion and yet, Europeans and Americans spend $17 billion annually on pet food (UNDP 1998: 37). Currently, the quarter of the world's population who live in the developed world account for 86 per cent of total private consumption while three-quarters of the world must make due with the other 14 per cent (UNDP 1998: 2). From my perspective as a Christian social ethicist, I feel like I am living in a world gone mad.

From a moral perspective, though, can we really say there is anything wrong with eating ice cream, wearing perfume, or having a dog? Yet, clearly there is a problem when our consumer behaviors betray such moral indifference to the well-being of the majority of the world's population. While it is obvious that the money currently being spent on personal consumption reflected in these figures cannot simply be shifted to cover expenditures like basic education or water and sanitation for the world's population, what these statistics offer is a shocking glimpse into the priorities and values of our world. Any conversation about the morality of globalization or global ethics must pay attention to the lived behaviors and material realities of real people, this discourse must be at least as practical as it is theoretical.

Of course, any conversation that starts with the question of whether or not our current social, political, and economic situation is out of control begs the question as to whether or not our current situation is worse today than it has been in the past? Is life in our current era harder than life was in the Middle Ages and the time of the bubonic plague? After all, since 1990 life expectancy in the developing world has increased by two years and there are three million fewer child deaths annually (UNDP 2005: 3). What about life prior to the industrial revolution? Some people involved in the globalization debates argue that increased growth and trade have reduced poverty and increased the standard of living for millions of people around the globe (Bhagwati 2004; Wolf 2004; Sachs 2005). Others argue that the necessity of economic migration is destroying families and communities and that the repetitive nature of much industrial work is mind numbing and physically debilitating. What about life during the early days of the industrial revolution when the robber barons gained power and wealth at the expense of their workers? Some scholars argue that the current phase of globalization has increased the levels of inequality in our world in ways that damage our common humanity. Others argue that inequality is inevitable and that the rich are merely rewarded for their ingenuity, intellect, and business acumen.

The fact is life in any age is complex and full of strife, conflict, and inequality. This is not to say either that life is not worth living, or that we cannot strive to try to make it better. In fact, religious traditions are, in large part, human attempts to try to understand and make sense of life and the world around us. Many religious traditions share a common acceptance of the imperfection of the world along with a concomitant desire to try to improve not only oneself but also the world in which we live. Many religious traditions, including Christianity, accept that humans live in an imperfect world, a fallen world, "a world gone mad" if you will. Nevertheless, the moral heart of the Christian tradition does not instruct its adherents to merely sit back and accept the world as it is. Rather, the Christian calling can be understood precisely as the challenge to strive for justice *in* a world gone mad.

Globalizing forces that are shaping and transforming our world today are having a significant impact on the well-being of both the human and natural worlds. These forces are neither benign nor morally neutral. In describing the task of Christian ethics, ethicist Beverly Harrison states,

> Christian ethical discourse is not, in the first instance, language about faith. It is language about ourselves in relation to our world, our agency or action in a social context, as that action is understood from "the moral point of view." (Harrison 1985: 22)

From this perspective, the discipline of Christian ethics offers one avenue for helping to examine and parse the moral attitudes that correspond to different versions or theories of globalization that are present in our world today. This chapter will focus on two areas of interest regarding the question of "the ethics of globalization." It will begin with a descriptive analysis of the globalization debates that identifies and discusses the moral difficulties embedded in the discourse and will then discuss the contribution that religion and religious studies can make to this discourse.

Assessing the Morality of Globalization

While globalizing forces have been drawing our world together since the fifteenth century and the advent of mercantilism and sea travel, technological advances in the later part of the twentieth century have virtually eliminated the space-time gap that has traditionally separated civilizations, continents, and peoples from one another. Simultaneous with the ability of technology to knit our world together in ever tighter and more transparent ways, is the realignment of global politics and economics since the fall of the Berlin Wall in 1989 and the advent of neoliberalism as the reigning form of globalization in the twenty-first century. Globalization is not simply the proper name of a new global era we are entering, but rather globalization refers to the processes of economic and social integration that continue to accelerate in our world. It remains to be seen whether humankind has the capacity to achieve the kind of epochal transformation necessary to facilitate human and planetary flourishing for the whole world.[1] Engaging in the present challenge of developing a normative vision of justice must begin with a critical analysis of the present age and its moral challenges.

Ideological Nature of the Debates

One need not be more involved in the globalization debates than simply reading a newspaper to know that there are a multitude of disparate voices represented in the discourse around globalization. Some voices trumpet an integrated capitalist economy as the most advanced economic system humankind has ever known.[2] Others argue that increased growth and trade offer the possibility for eliminating poverty in our lifetime (Sachs 2005). Still others document the excesses and failures of the current model of globalization (Mander and Goldsmith 1996, Bello 2001). And others still see globalization as a reprisal of the colonial powers and relationships that impoverished the two-thirds world in the eighteenth and nineteenth centuries (Esteva and Prakash 1998). There is simply a cacophony of voices represented in the discourse around globalization and the din of the debate is often so muddled and confusing that it is sometimes hard to even follow what is being debated. While some scholars contend that globalization itself is morally neutral (Williams 2003: 335), I have argued elsewhere that there are four distinct globalization theories operating in our world today and that each of these theories represents a different moral vision for our world (Peters 2004a).

There is no abstract morally neutral phenomenon called "globalization" that occurs outside of human behavior. Globalization is being enacted in our world in very particular ways with very real material consequences. How people think about and understand these globalizing forces and whether they view them as beneficent or malignant largely depends on one's worldview or ideological perspective. Here I am using the term "ideology" to describe a set of beliefs

---

1   For a provocative example of just such an epochal transformation, see Berry 1999.

2   For apologetic defenses of neoliberalism see Baghwati 2004 and Wolf 2004.

and assumptions about how the world works that consequently function to shape a particular political or economic perspective or worldview. The beliefs and assumptions that make up our worldview originate from several sources including where we live, our race or ethnicity, our economic status, our gender, our educational background, and our religious tradition. Collectively these factors are often referred to as our social location or our standpoint and they have a direct effect on how we experience the world. In other words, our epistemological reality or understanding of the world is heavily influenced by our standpoint or our social location. Marx introduced the idea that material reality structures knowledge in meaningful ways that allow the disadvantaged to see the world differently from the world's elite. This is known as "situated knowledge." The fact that knowledge is situated and impacted by different experiences of the world means that acknowledging and respecting diversity is more than simply "political correctness." Respecting diversity of experience is important because of the differences in situated knowledge that different communities bring to the table. Differing opinions and ideas about globalization can be understood as representing the situated knowledge of different communities and these different perspectives offer socially valuable information to our deliberations about the morality and practicality of globalization.[3]

While it is true that globalization is unavoidable, this is not the same thing as claiming it is a natural phenomenon like a volcano or a hurricane. Globalization is enacted in particular ways in our world. In order to assess the morality of these different versions of globalization it is necessary to examine the material consequences of different ideologies and their theories of globalization. Globalization is a human creation, and, as such, the morality it exhibits will be an expression of the moral vision of the people in power. There are at least four different models or theories of globalization and each of them functions in distinctly different ways. These theories are neoliberalism, development, earthism, and post-colonial. I will briefly describe each theory and its moral vision as a way of illustrating the ideological nature of the debate.[4] In assessing the moral vision of each position, I identify each community's vision of what constitutes "the good life" by looking at how proponents of each theory understand moral agency, teleology, and human flourishing.

Four Theories of Globalization

Neoliberalism is informed by an ideology that promotes growth and profits through increased external trade between nations. The leaders of this position are

---

3   While the term "community" is used in a variety of ways, I am using the term in relation to the globalization debates to argue that there are distinct groups of people (or communities) who share an ideological orientation or worldview that represents a particular form of situated knowledge. See Bounds (1997: 1–3) for a discussion of different meanings of the term "community" under modern advanced capitalism.

4   The following summary of the four theories of globalization first appeared in Peters (2004b).

the most outspoken champions of the "free market" and are largely associated with corporations or big business. For proponents of this position, "globalization" refers to an integrated global economy that revolves around export-oriented trade best facilitated by a low barrier market (deregulation) and a highly competitive private sector (no government owned corporations).[5] For big business this represents what they believe to be a fairly straightforward globalization policy agenda that promotes economic growth, increased trade, and integration into the global economy. From this perspective, globalization is viewed as unequivocally benevolent and corporations are seen to be leading the way in spreading the benefits of globalization around the world. This view functions as the hegemonic view of globalization in our world today.

The moral vision of this position envisions the good life as a combination of hard work, a devoted and adoring family, and the rewards of success and happiness. Proponents of this position believe that the good life is accessible to everyone if only people will accept the responsibilities that maintaining such a life require—responsibility for taking care of oneself and one's family. Work is always available if one looks hard enough and diligence and efficiency in the marketplace are rewarded with wages and the potential for upward mobility. The neoliberal vision of the good is marked by the key values of individualism, prosperity, and freedom.

The second theory of globalization is mostly closely associated with development agencies like the World Bank and the United Nations Development Programme.[6] While it shares the neoclassical economic assumptions of the neoliberal position, it is more closely associated with a Keynesian approach to economic theory than the free-market approach of its rival. Proponents of the development position do not share the neoliberal belief that the invisible hand of the market will resolve the problems of poverty; nevertheless, they are convinced that it is the economic opportunities of capitalism that will eventually support

---

5   It is important to note that the neoliberal globalization dialogue has shifted, somewhat, since the anti-globalization protests held in conjunction with the WTO meeting in Seattle and the IMF/World Bank meetings in Washington. The widespread publicity that these activities generated has forced neoliberal proponents of globalization into a defensive posture that is apparent in speeches by the Director General of the WTO, Mike Moore and the Secretary General of the International Chamber of Commerce, Maria Livanos Cattaui. Recent reports released by some of the institutions of big business are also focused on justifying the neoliberal model as beneficent towards the poor. Ben-David (1999) and IMF (2000). While the neoliberal globalization rhetoric has expanded to incorporate "poverty" as a growing concern, this concern has yet to alter the position's basic view of globalization or the position's policy agenda. If anything, neoliberal concern for poverty reduction is being used as a further buttress for their argument that more rapid and widespread globalization is in order as the only viable, long-term remedy for poverty.

6   While there is much diversity of opinion within the field of development studies itself, my work has focused on those voices within the development community that are influenced by social equity liberalism and the approach of the social development of people. The phrase "social equity" liberalism is used by Johnston (1998: ch. 6).

and sustain economic development around the world. What they argue is that government intervention is sometimes necessary to mediate the potentially negative consequences of market activity. Development theorists view globalization is a knitting together of the seams that separate people. It is viewed as the way in which we will be able to improve education, health care, and other social services—by allowing the efficiency of the market to improve these sectors. The development community's sustained interaction with people and cultures in "developing" countries has taught them that global human development also incorporates other aspects of human well-being, namely—culture, education, literacy, health, and the environment. Attention to a broader array of development concerns has generated a vision of the "good life" from this perspective that upholds three primary values—responsibility, progress, and equity.[7]

While these two positions represent the dominant discourse on globalization and are the most commonly represented in the popular media, these are not the only voices present in the debate. In examining the discourse there are clearly developed voices resisting and challenging these two dominant models. There are two clear trends in the resistance movement that offer alternative visions of how globalization could be ordered. One represents an environmental perspective and the other a postcolonial perspective.

The third position in this typology is earthism, which is an ideology that is concerned with practical issues of environmental or earth justice. People who share an earthist worldview are primarily concerned about the fate of their country-people, families, and friends; the land on which they live; and the creatures with whom they share the land. Their starting point is the lived life of struggle, their own and their neighbors." A prominent theme of earthism is the perspective that humanity is not categorically different from the rest of the world, but rather that humanity represents one aspect of nature and that all in nature is interdependent. The proponents of earthism envision a different future for globalization than the one toward which we are currently headed. Their vision holds that if sustainability and caring for the earth become our central guiding concern as a human species, then our social, economic, and political policies will shift to reflect a respect for humanity's interdependence with all of nature. Their ideological perspective translates into a future that is rooted in smaller economies of scale that prioritize a turn toward local production and consumption of goods. This vision necessitates a paradigm shift away from models of globalization that promote export-oriented trade, mass produced food, and consumer products toward a model of globalization as localization. The three core values that underpin the earthist vision of the good life are mutuality, justice, and sustainability.

The fourth theory of globalization, which I have labeled post-colonial, is rooted in a worldview that identifies the current expression of globalization

---

7   Readers may note that the value of responsibility was also highlighted in the neoliberal position, but that was an *individual* responsibility to oneself and one's family, while the responsibility in the development model of globalization is a paternalistic responsibility toward those "less fortunate" than oneself.

as neo-colonialism.[8] It is a reflection of the activities of local communities of people who are mobilizing to address the powers of globalization that are destroying life for the already poor and marginalized people of the world.[9] The social location of marginalization that partially defines this position gives rise to a postcolonial ideology that is inherently political. Recognition of the deeply political nature of the transformation that is necessary to overturn dominant forms of globalization is largely what distinguishes the postcolonial position from the earthist paradigm.

Proponents of this theory argue that globalization is re-presenting the familiar threat of colonialism in a new, sophisticated, and highly seductive package that promises wealth, possessions, and comfort, but that remains neo-colonialism nonetheless. The grassroots postcolonialists argue that capitalist political economy is intrinsically a colonizing paradigm and that while the former relationships of colonization were based on extracting raw materials, the more recent move is toward an integration of the "developing" world into political and economic relationships that are dominated by the West.

A wide variety of people are involved in this form of resistance. What draws them together to form a discrete theoretical category within this study is not a common idea of what the world should be, but rather a vision of a world where individual communities of people are able to articulate their own version of the good life and where those communities possess the political, economic, and social capital to realize that goal. These communities have an alternative vision of globalization as global solidarity. In a world where global solidarity replaces neoliberal economic globalization, the focus would be an awareness of humanity's diversity rooted in respect for difference rather than the forced unity and uniformity that contemporary globalization processes promote. This approach requires and reflects a particular set of values that mold a vision of the good life, marked by community, respect for culture, and communal autonomy.

These four theories of globalization represent radically different ideological orientations and different moral visions of what the good life can look like in our world. It is the ideological nature of the debate that is ultimately causing the major tensions and disagreements between the various communities. The different lens through which these communities view the world means that they ultimately understand and define the problems in different ways. This is a vitally important element of the debate because how we define the problems is directly linked to

---

8   I will be following Elleke Boehmer's distinction between the hyphenated *post-colonial* which is used to designate the historical period after World War II and the nonhypenated *postcolonial* which is used to "denote the dynamic textual and political practices that critically examine the colonial relationship, practices through which colonized people seek to assert themselves as subjects of history." (Boehmer 1995: 3, as quoted in Ching 2000: 5).

9   While most of the people who support this position are poor and marginalized people themselves, there are also people who stand in solidarity with the poor through their own advocacy and work, privileged people who stand in resistance to the kind of future promoted by the dominant paradigm of globalization.

the solutions we are able to envision. Differing ways of seeing the world enable different moral responses. The neoliberals see the problem as one of governmental regulation and barriers to free trade, the development theorists see the problem as one of poverty, the earthists see the problem as ecological destruction, and the post-colonialists see the problem as autonomy or self-governance. When we view the problems of global dialogue and discourse in this way, it is easier to see that because different communities of people define globalization differently—they are often at odds in trying to develop strategies for dealing with problems that arise, namely because they understand them in incommensurate ways. It is this ideological clash between these different communities that we must acknowledge and examine if we hope to work toward understanding points of agreement and disagreement, not to mention trying to find compromises and solutions to global problems. In order to illustrate the moral complexities and questions embedded in each of these theories of globalization, let us examine neoliberalism in more depth.

Critiquing the Dangers of Capitalism as a Hegemonic Ideology

Economists and business leaders act as if capitalism is some kind of natural phenomenon that exists outside of human will. People speak of "the market" as if it is some kind of natural force. They talk of "market forces" as meteorologists talk of "weather patterns." In reality, these "market forces" are related to human behavior and choices, the capitalist/neoliberal market system that currently dominates our world is a human creation that reflects a particular set of moral assumptions and values. Its assumptions about human nature and human behavior are decidedly individualistic and focus on the belief that human behavior is self-centered and always oriented around maximizing personal welfare. Furthermore, the capitalist market system is not value-free as it often claims, but in fact, values efficiency and profit above all else and pursuing these two goals have become the defining markers of institutional behavior in the current economic system. What I mean by this is that the dominant institutions of the global market economy including the World Bank, IMF, WTO, and trans-national corporations now doggedly pursue efficiency and profit even at the expense of other socially valuable goods like the environment, the health and well-being of workers, and the stability and economic health of communities. It is the moral assumptions and values that are embedded in market capitalism that we must examine in a very careful light simultaneously with examining the consequences of our market system.

There are a number of proponents of the current market model who argue that the transition from poverty to advanced industrialization will inevitably be difficult for some and that the adjustment to new models of productivity may even be painful. Brian Griffiths, Vice Chairman of Goldman Sachs International has written, "The process of growth will inevitably involve change, and change is nearly always painful for some" (Griffiths 2003: 171). It is important to note that whenever I have come across sentiments similar to Griffiths that there is inevitably some amount of pain and suffering involved in the changes that come with increased development the authors are always referring to the pain and hardship that others must endure. Namely, these authors are referring to the fact that there will inevitably be pain and suffering for the poor and disenfranchised people in developing countries whose labor is currently being exploited to drive down costs for Western consumers and to drive up corporate profits. This utilitarian argument rationalizes that unfortunately there will be some casualties in the drive toward a better life for all. Remarkably, these same authors never entertain the possibility that the transitions and pain involved in addressing the problems that our world faces might also require change on the part of the developed world and the privileged classes. Indeed, given the fact that it is impossible for our planet to sustain six billion people consuming at the level of the developed world, it seems obvious that the lives, habits, and behaviors of the world's elite will have to change. What remains to be proven is that the current model of laissez-faire capitalism is indeed the best way for the human community to organize our economic and social interests.

Some scholars who support market capitalism are willing to admit that there are some problems that need to be dealt with regarding such things as environmental and labor issues, but even they are not willing to admit that these problems are inherent flaws of a capitalist model. Economist Rebecca Blank (2004: 14) argues that the predictions about how competitive markets work can only be expected to be accurate to the extent that certain assumptions are met. She identifies these as:

1) individuals are assumed to pursue only their own self-interest, with no concern for the well-being of any other actors in the market;
2) firms are assumed to pursue their own self-interest, which means that they try to maximize their profits;
3) everyone involved has "full information"—everyone knows what is being offered for sale, by whom, and at what price;
4) there exist multiple potential buyers and sellers, so nobody gains more influence on outcomes by being bigger or more powerful than anybody else;
5) all parties can choose what they want to buy and sell—none are coerced into buying something that they do not want or selling at an unattractive price.

Blank considers any problems with market capitalism the result of "market failures" by which she means the markets are not operating effectively because they have not adhered to the assumptions outlined above. This seems particularly alarming given the difficulty of actually achieving all five of her assumptions on a regular basis in the real world. Presumably her explanation of price gouging in poor neighborhoods and the dominance of firms like Wal-Mart are a result of market failures. Is it possible, however, that "market failures" are not failures at all, but simply an indication of how competitive markets *actually* work rather than how theorists think they *ought* to work? Economists readily admit that their models are theoretical—isn't it possible that actual competitive capitalist markets are inherently flawed?

It is important to note that while the hegemonic model of globalization that currently dominates our world gives the appearance that the ideology of neoliberalism is widely accepted as the only remaining viable economic paradigm—there are dissenting voices that understand and interpret the world differently. This is important not simply because it witnesses to the diversity of perspectives and lived experiences in the world to which I referred earlier, but it also offers us alternative visions of how we might organize and direct globalization and globalizing forces in the future. Since the fall of the Wall it seems as if the dominant economic discourse has written off any alternative to capitalism as impractical and impossible. The failure of state sponsored markets under the former Soviet Union has been taken as proof that laissez-faire capitalism is the only remaining possibility for the organization of our economic interests. This strain of thought has precluded meaningful dialogue about the inherent instability of neoliberal economic measures that privilege individualism and profit at the expense of the human and earth communities. My interest is in questioning whether or not capitalism might be subject to intrinsic and debilitating flaws—flaws of a moral nature—that are destroying the heart and soul of the human community, not to mention the material well-being of millions of people. Perhaps it is time to consider the possibility that market capitalism is ultimately no more sustainable than communism or socialism.

While the competitive market model has brought an increased standard of living to many people around the world, it has also generated vast economic inequality and is based on an economic model that requires cheap labor in order to thrive. What needs to be questioned is whether or not neoliberal economic globalization is indeed the *only* way forward to address the problems associated with poverty and environmental degradation in our world? While it is true that poverty rates have declined in recent years,[10] the discourse on economic globalization has not yet adequately addressed other moral issues related to the material reality that neoliberal globalization generates. Moral issues such as environmental degradation, rising inequality within and between countries, the problem of economic migration and the looming crisis of fossil fuel oil on which the economy depends are just a few. Despite prominent voices like Martin Wolf, Jagdish Bhagwati, and Jeffrey Sachs, it remains to be seen whether or not laissez-faire capitalism is truly the only or even the best path toward reducing poverty in our world (Bhagwati 2004, Wolf 2004, Sachs 2005).

The ways in which we organize our economies have significant implications for what we conceive of as our choices. Certainly capitalism is not the only example of how to organize or structure markets, and while the state sponsored experiment of communism has proven unsustainable, there also seem to be inherent flaws within the capitalist system that are not adequately acknowledged. Flaws that are perhaps so intrinsic to capitalism's very identity that the system cannot be simply "tweaked" or "corrected" by tinkering with it. The debate on global

---

10   Jeffrey Sachs (2005: 51) states that 4.9 billion people live in countries where the average income increased between 1980 and 2000 and that roughly 5.7 billion live in countries where life expectancy increased.

ethics must engage in asking if another way is possible? We must look beyond the individualistic and greed-oriented model of neoliberalism/capitalism toward a model of social capitalism or community markets that values workers and the environment as much as they value profit. While this is likely to result in lower profit margins, it does not necessarily mean the elimination of profit as a factor in the market system. Since markets are human constructions, it is possible to create a market system that does not require the exploitation of others (human or natural) in order to succeed.

We must break the ideological hold that laissez-faire capitalism has on the collective psyche of the human community and move forward toward alternative visions of the future that reflect a broader based set of moral principles. While I, as a Christian ethicist, root these principles within the Christian tradition, they transcend any particular religious identity because religious traditions represent different pathways toward understanding the sacred. Furthermore, the values of human dignity and caring for our neighbor are present in most religious traditions. In any event, religion and religious communities are an essential aspect of the debate about ethics and morality in a globalizing world.

The Role of Religion in Global Ethics[11]

There are at least three reasons why religion is an essential aspect in the debates about developing ethical norms in an increasingly globalizing world. First and most obviously, the majority of the world's people are religious; second, the resources of faith traditions can serve a prophetic role in the discourse; and third, the debates are already theological. Let's examine each of these is turn.

People desire a plausible and meaningful explanation for understanding the "madness" of the world in which we live. Whether that madness is the result of human behavior and actions or the unpredictable ravages of nature—people need a way to make sense of the world around them. Historically, religion has played the role of helping people to make meaning of an imperfect world. While it is true that different world religions define human nature and purpose in different ways—ultimately, there is a basic human need and desire to define and understand the world and what humans experience as sacred. Approximately 85 per cent of

---

11 Different faith traditions in our world each represent different and distinct approaches to ordering and understanding our world. They possess avenues toward the sacred and values that aim at helping their adherents live meaningful, fulfilling, and responsible lives. Gandhi drew on Hindu principles and philosophy in leading the Indian people to self rule, Aung San Suu Kyi invokes Buddhist ideals and teachings in her work toward promoting democracy in Burma, Ali Shariati drew on traditional Islamic principles to help explain the problems of Muslim societies in the modern world, and Abraham Joshua Heschel based his civil rights work on his reading of the Hebrew prophets. I am not simply developing an argument for *Christian* participation in dialogue and discussion about the development of global ethics, but for the participation of a wide variety of religious communities and scholars of religion in order to deepen and strengthen the discourse.

the world's people define themselves as religious in some capacity or another and many of these people look to their religious belief systems and leaders for guidance in negotiating the complex and changing world around them (Barrett et al. 2001). If for no other reason than simple pragmatism in trying to reach the majority of the world's people in an attempt to help interpret and explain the content of a global ethic—religion must be included as a partner in the ongoing dialogue about the morality of our economic and social order.

But religion is important for more than simply pragmatic reasons. While the world's religions may reflect human attempts at understanding our world and trying to make sense of our irrational and unpredictable existence, they are also reflections of profound truths that resonate in the hearts and souls of billions of people. Faith traditions have historically served as the moral centers of their respective communities in developing a common moral ground for social interaction and behavior. The resources of many faith traditions are also able to serve a prophetic role in society by challenging the status quo and holding believers and communities accountable to a higher standard of moral behavior.

This was evident most recently in relation to the global economy by the work of the Jubilee 2000 campaign that was rooted in the biblical ideal of the "jubilee year." In the book of Leviticus the Hebrew people are instructed to set aside every fiftieth year as a time of "jubilee."[12] During this year all debts are erased. Land that was sold to pay off debts reverts to its original owner and people who have become indentured servants to pay off their debts are freed. The intention behind the jubilee year is to offer a time of restoration and reconciliation for the community. The theological motivation is rooted in the value of community over property and an affirmation of human dignity. It was a way to mediate against increasing inequality within a community and to wipe the slate clean every 50 years. With land and freedom restored, even those who might have been born into poverty or subservience were regularly given a new chance. It is this theological principle that motivated people of faith to form the Jubilee 2000 campaign and to work tirelessly since 1997 organizing religious communities and their allies to fight for debt cancellation for highly indebted countries.

In the twentieth century the mobilization of religious communities was a significant factor in the success of many social justice movements and campaigns: the civil rights movement in the United States, the anti-apartheid movement in South Africa, the boycott of Nestle for its marketing of infant formula, and the challenge against repressive political regimes in Latin America in the 1970s and 1980s. In 1987 the United Church of Christ published a report entitled *Toxic Waste and Race in the United States* that prompted the start of the environmental justice movement, which examines the significant problem of environmental racism in our world. In the nineteenth century the Social Gospel movement in the United States and Christian socialism in Britain were both powerful forces in challenging the injustice wrought by the Industrial Revolution. But apart from these high profile examples, there also exist countless individual religious leaders and local religious bodies around the world who are involved in the day to day lives of their

---

12   See Leviticus 25.

communities helping people to struggle toward a more humane existence, often by helping them challenge issues of economic injustice in their midst.

Zion Hill Baptist Church in Atlanta, Georgia conducted a local assessment of community needs and found that there were no resources in their community to assist homeless women and their children and so they started a Community Development Corporation that provides comprehensive social services for these women and their children (Dassie 2006: 95–6). In Spartanburg, South Carolina, Harold Mitchell cites his faith in God as one of the motivations for his work in establishing an environmental justice organization known as ReGenesis that is cleaning up and revitalizing an African-American community that has been ravaged by industrial toxic waste (Waterhouse 2006: 83ff). Father Damian Zuerlein worked with his parish, the St Agnes Catholic Church of Omaha for a number of years to address the plight of immigrant workers in their midst who experienced low wages and oppressive working conditions in the city's meatpacking industry. With the moral and material support of Father Damian and St Agnes, the workers were eventually successful in organizing a union (Gillett 2005). Many religious communities and people of faith are already actively involved in working toward social justice, but faith communities also represent an enormous potential for even more widespread social change in society.

In addition to the formative and prophetic role that religion can play in the debate about the morality of our current global order, it must also be acknowledged that the current ideologies and theories of globalization dominant in our world are themselves products of cultures that are shaped by theological belief systems. Consequently, these ideological perspectives also embody aspects of those religious belief systems. As we have seen in our examination of the four theories, each one approaches the globalizing forces of our world with a different vision of what the good life looks like. These different visions of the good life reflect particular theological understandings of the questions of moral agency, teleology, and human flourishing that marked our inquiry. Religious perspectives are rarely univocal and a brief look at the theological perspectives embedded in each of these positions demonstrates that Christian theologians, ethicists, economists, and businesspeople often use theological resources in very different ways as justification and support for their ideological positions.

The "gospel of prosperity" represents a theological perspective that is consonant with the neoliberal position. It represents a theological agenda that promotes the idea that God desires our well-being and wants us to be successful, including being wealthy and prosperous. While this theological idea is often associated with growing evangelical mega-churches as well as televangelists who solicit money from their television viewers and often live lives of ostentation and excess, there are other versions of a similar theological vein that are more mainstream. Economist Brian Griffiths argues that wealth creation is part of the human responsibility of good Christians and that the market offers Christians an avenue to develop their full potential as productive citizens (Griffiths 2001: 3, 12ff). This theological position fits well with the vision of the good life focused on individualism and prosperity already identified with the neoliberal position and when this theology is preached from the pulpit (as it is in many churches around the world), it serves to reinforce and legitimate this ideological perspective.

Turning to the development or social equity theory we find a theological vision of compassion for the poor and downtrodden coupled with a genuine ideological commitment to the potential of the market as a salvific tool. While the proponents of neoliberalism see the market as an avenue for how they individually can be better Christians and live out their calling to be prosperous and help their neighbor, the proponents of the second theory believe in the power of market forces to raise the world's poor out of poverty and to bring them up to a level of human dignity and survival that they now lack (Black 2004b). The motivating theological understanding of moral agency is no longer focused on the behavior of the individual, but rather, it grows out of a sense of responsibility and compassion for the neighbor—a very different theological orientation from the previous position with extraordinarily different social consequences.

There is a deep and rich body of theological resources supporting the earthist position that is known as "eco-theology." It places a strong emphasis on grounding human interaction with the natural world in the creation narrative of Genesis and in emphasizing the sacred qualities of nature. Theologians and ethicists who support this position have challenged traditional Christian dualisms that have functioned to alienate humans from the natural world.[13] They seek to develop new theological attitudes toward the environment that stress human interdependence with the created order and revision our relationship with creation as one of stewardship and care rather than dominance and control. These resources provide theological depth and support for the earthist attitude that human flourishing is marked by the sustainability of the whole of creation rather than simply the well-being of the human population.

Finally, the theological underpinnings of the postcolonial position are found in "liberation theology," a theological movement that began in Latin America in the 1960s as Catholic priests worked to help address the extreme poverty and political marginalization of the poor and indigenous communities in which they worked. Liberation theology is grounded in a theological vision of Christianity that sees God's struggle in the world as one of liberating God's people. Liberation theologians emphasize the importance of local dialogue and reading the bible from the margins of history. They recognize how the standpoint of the poor and disenfranchised can shape the reading of scripture and the message of the gospel in ways that challenge the status quo. For this very reason, liberation theology has been seen as dangerous and subversive both by governments in Latin America and by the Catholic Church. Spurred by their member churches in the two-thirds world, many of whom come out of postcolonial contexts, the World Council of Churches (WCC) and the World Alliance of Reformed Churches (WARC) have been active in critiquing neoliberal globalization in recent years. This led to a controversial statement by WARC in 2004 in which they call member churches to confess as sin their participation and complicity in the "current neoliberal

---

13   For some prominent examples of eco-theology, see Rasmussen 1996, McFague 2001.

economic global system," an action that has caused some amount of tension and conflict with member churches in the first world (WARC 2004).

This example of tension and conflict between Christian churches in the first world and in the two-thirds world is rooted in their differing theological and ideological interpretations of the meaning and value of neoliberal economic globalization. Interpretations that stem out of their own encounters and personal experiences with the material realities that neoliberal globalization creates. My intention here is certainly not to imply that these four theories are Christian theories, but to begin to parse the relationships between theories of moral agency and human purpose embedded in these ideologies that find support and justification within religious teachings and communities. Beginning to understand the ways in which our political ideologies are supported and reinforced by religious attitudes in various traditions can aid scholars, politicians, and businesspeople in the very difficult and complicated process of negotiating difference in a world with collapsing borders.

Solidarity and Debate

Globalization has the potential to transform our world in positive, life-promoting ways. It offers us enormous opportunities to join together as a world community to eliminate hunger, poverty, and disease in ways that have never before been achievable. We have already seen examples of this in our world—the Marshall Plan facilitated the rebuilding of Europe after World War II, the World Health Organization has managed to eliminate small pox which previously affected 15 million people annually, the World Bank has worked with the WHO to reduce the incidence of river blindness in developing countries. However, working together on common projects of universal good will require a certain amount of self-awareness about our ideological differences and a willingness to reach beyond the narrow confines of our own comfortable worldviews. It requires thinking beyond comfortable borders and narrow nationalistic viewpoints to understand that we are citizens of the world, that our brothers and sisters, our neighbors are Ghanaian, Indonesian, Chinese, Bolivian, and everything in between. We must reorient our thinking to connection and inter-connection rather than competition, borders, and barriers.

For many years in the United States the phrase "unity in diversity" has been active in faith traditions and civil society as a way of trying to encourage people to come together in a unified way in spite of the diversity that appears to separate us. In its most generous sense, I believe that the concept of "unity in diversity" is meant to generate good will among people and to try to appeal to our common humanity as a unifying characteristic that transcends the differences that separate people in our communities. Unfortunately, unity also implies a certain amount of unanimity, a lessening of difference in the goal of striving to achieve sameness. Many of the differences that separate people are rooted in cosmological orientations to the world that arise from particular belief systems. Rather than unity, perhaps the idea of solidarity can offer a different starting point.

Solidarity is the expression of support and partnership with others. It implies a relationship that goes beyond a mere meeting of the minds or agreement about philosophical or even theological ideas. Solidarity represents a bond between people that calls for loyalty, compassion, and companionship a bond rooted in the agape love of the Christian tradition. Learning how to live in solidarity with our neighbors is an expression of our call to "love our neighbor as ourselves." Astute observers of human nature have observed that it is much easier to practice this teaching when we know our neighbor, or like our neighbor, or even feel kin to our neighbor in some way. But, in the Christian tradition, people are taught to see their neighbor even in those people whom they do not know and might not even like.[14] Embracing solidarity as a moral norm means evaluating personal and collective actions in terms of how they impact one's neighbors, those next door as well as those across the globe. Solidarity implies a respect for difference, a desire to work together with others toward a common goal, but it also reflects a desire to maintain differences because they are uniquely important to identity and to our common humanity. This implies that people learn how to understand and respect the lives of their global neighbors, a task that requires a good deal of listening. Among other things, this includes learning about different religious traditions, cosmologies, belief systems, and habits of the heart. Understanding the ideological differences that separate us also requires a deeper understanding about how those ideologies are shaped by religious beliefs and belief systems. But, the task of global ethics must go one step further than simply listening to different voices. If our greater goal is to achieve the kind of solidarity that reflects respect for human dignity, sustainability, and genuine understanding of our interdependence as a human and earth community then we must also interrogate the moral visions implicit in each community's "voice."

As important as it is to understand the many different valences present in the globalization debates, the task of global ethics must go one step further than simply striving for a greater understanding of the present situation in our world. While I have identified four different and competing theories of globalization it is not my intention to imply that all four of these are morally equivalent. In a world in which different manifestations of globalization have radically different material consequences, moral relativity is simply not a responsible option. The task of global ethics must be, in part, to compare and evaluate different theories of globalization from a moral point of view. What is necessary is for us to establish a set of reasonable standards by which we can adjudicate between the competing moral visions and claims embedded in these four theories. I have argued previously for utilizing a process of tested normativity, which allows for a moral complexity that is absent in deontological approaches that emphasize moral absolutes and in postmodern approaches that emphasize the negation of universal truths and can lead to moral relativity (Peters 2004a). The process of tested normativity requires that communities (e.g. scholars, businesspeople, religious leaders, nation-states, neighborhoods) engage in a public debate to establish a set of community negotiated moral norms. This kind of public debate

---

14   Luke 10: 25–37.

requires persuasiveness, commitment, and broad representation of the full range of voices present in the particular community. This kind of democratic discourse is challenging precisely because it can require people from differing social locations to listen to each other's stories and perspectives in a reasonable and respectful way. It forces communities to develop their own ethical standards and it refuses to provide easy answers.

In defining and describing the current cacophony of voices present in the globalization debates, it is my contention that the debates themselves are fractious and contentious precisely because there are competing theories of globalization that represent irreconcilable ideological differences among the various schools of thought. These differences have very real material consequences as the statistics of inequality I cited at the beginning of this chapter bear witness. It is not only possible, but necessary to examine the underlying moral visions of these theories because these represent the moral world we are in the process of creating. The moral world we will leave as our legacy to our descendents. In addition to interrogating the different moral visions of globalization, we need to consider new options for the organization of our global political economy. The question is, do other options allow us to more adequately address the social and moral problems that we face as a human community? Furthermore, what stands in the way of the success of alternative market models? It is my contention that a major aspect of any project of global ethics must attend to these challenges.

References

Barrett, D.A., Kurian, G.T. and Johnson, T.M. (2001), *World Christian Encyclopedia: A Comparative Survey of Churches and Religions in the Modern World*. New York: Oxford University Press.

Bello, W. (2001), *The Future in the Balance: Essays on Globalization and Resistance*. Oakland: First Food Books.

Ben-David, D., Nordstrom, H., and Winters, L.A. (1999), *Trade, Income Disparity and Poverty*. World Trade Organization Special Studies 5. Geneva: World Trade Organization.

Berry, T. (1999), *The Great Work: Our Way Into the Future*. New York: Bell Tower.

Bhagwati, J. (2004), *In Defense of Globalization*. New York: Oxford University Press.

Blank, R.M. (2004), "Viewing the Market Economy Through the Lens of Faith," in Blank, R.M. and McGurn, W. (eds) *Is the Market Moral? A Dialogue on Religion, Economics, and Justice*. Washington: Brookings Institution.

Boehmer, E. (1995), *Colonial and Postcolonial Literature*. Oxford: Oxford University Press.

Bounds, E.M. (1997), *Coming Together, Coming Apart: Religion, Community, and Modernity*. New York: Routledge.

Ching, W.W. (2000), "Negotiating for a Postcolonial Identity: Theology of 'the Poor Woman' in Asia," *Journal of Feminist Studies in Religion* 16(2).

Dassie, W. (2006), "Revitalizing Local Communities," in Brubaker, P.K., Peters, R.T., and Stivers, L. (eds) *Justice in a Global Economy*. Louisville: Westminster/John Knox Press.

Esteva, G. and Prakash, M.S. (1998), *Grassroots Post-Modernism: Remaking the Soil of Cultures*. London: Zed Books.

Gillett, R. (2005), *The New Globalization: Reclaiming the Lost Ground of Our Christian Social Tradition*. Cleveland: Pilgrim Press.

Griffiths, B. (2001), "The Culture of the Market," in Hay, D.A. and Kreider, A. (eds) *Christianity and the Culture of Economics*. Cardiff: University of Wales Press.

Griffiths, B. (2003), "The Challenge of Global Capitalism: A Christian Perspective," in Dunning, J.H. (ed.) *Making Globalization Good: The Moral Challenges of Global Capitalism*. New York: Oxford University Press.

Harrison, B.W. (1985), *Making the Connections*. Boston: Beacon Press.

IMF (2000), *Globalization: Threat or Opportunity*. Washington DC: IMF.

Johnston, C. (1998), *The Wealth or Health of Nations: Transforming Capitalism from Within*. Cleveland: Pilgrim Press.

Mander, J. and Goldsmith, E. (eds) (1996), *The Case Against the Global Economy and a Turn toward the Local*. San Francisco: Sierra Club Books.

McFague, S. (2001), *Life Abundant: Rethinking Theology and Economy for a Planet in Peril*. Minneapolis: Fortress Press.

Peters, R.T. (2004b), "The Future of Globalization: Seeking Pathways of Transformation," *Journal of the Society of Christian Ethics* 23(2).

Peters, R.T. (2004a), *In Search of the Good Life: The Ethics of Globalization*. New York: Continuum.

Rasmussen, L. (1996), *Earth Community, Earth Ethics*. Maryknoll, NY: Orbis Books.

Sachs, J.D. (2005), *The End of Poverty: Economic Possibilities for Our Time*. New York: Penguin Press.

Stiglitz, J. (2003), *Globalization and its Discontents*. New York: W.W. Norton and Company.

UNDP (1998), *The State of Human Development, Human Development Report*. New York: United Nations Development Programme.

UNDP (2005), *International Cooperation at a Crossroads, Human Development Report*. New York: United Nations Development Programme.

WARC (2004), "Covenanting for Justice: The Accra Confession," *Reformed World* 54(3–4), 169–74.

Waterhouse, C. (2006), "Engaging Environmental Justice," in Brubaker, P.K., Peters, R.T., and Stivers, L. (eds) *Justice in a Global Economy*. Louisville: Westminster/John Knox Press.

Williams, S. (2003), "Global Social Justice: The Moral Responsibilities of the Rich to the Poor," in Dunning, J.H. (ed.) *Making Globalization Good: The Moral Challenges of Global Capitalism*. New York: Oxford University Press.

Wolf, M. (2004), *Why Globalization Works*. New Haven, CT: Yale.

PART II
Is Global Ethics Possible?

Chapter 5

Global Ethics and World Citizenship

M.S. Ronald Commers

In this chapter[1] I subsequently raise four issues and deal with them as they pertain to the question on the possibility of global ethics. The first issue is whether global ethics as it is understood nowadays is a new discipline in normative ethics. The second relates to what is considered to be the ideological content of today's global ethics. The third issue is about the regulative principles of a global ethics for the future. The fourth relates to the ideal content of world citizenship for which a modest normative proposal, drawn from contemporary continental moral philosophy, is put forward.

Global Ethics: What is New in World Capitalism?

In 1908 John Dewey and James Tuft published what was to be the first version of their *Ethics*. Indeed, not long after the beginning of the Great Depression, in 1936, they edited a second version. In the 1936 version they dealt with the changing economic and social circumstances the Western world was going through. The situation they addressed was frightful. A devastating First World War provoked the downfall of European hegemony, inducing depression and poverty in Germany. In Spain a threatening civil war was approaching. Extreme right movements emerged menacing democratic governments, finally leading to the fascist seizure of power in Italy and the victory of Nazism in Germany. Writing in a general way about ethics, they conceived of situations and persons both local and global. Having an ideal normative frame of reference in mind, they were interested in practical solutions for the many problems of their day such as: generalized poverty, war, local violence, oppression, sickness, alcoholism, analphabetism, child and female labor, prostitution, unequal gender relationships. They argued in favor of an action-oriented point of view. In their opinion something very general was happening in the world and moral philosophers could not refrain from engaging in the analysis, advice, and judgment of concrete situations of misery and human need. It was their idea that humanity's realm was neither outside nor above family, community, and the state. But they nevertheless held that people are not primarily

1   I would like to thank the following people: Dr Wim Vandekerckhove for his suggestions, valuable advice and editorial comments, Dr Imke Du Ry for reading the text and for the many corrections she suggested, Dr Meins Coetsier for his encouraging words upon reading the text.

family members, cultural agents, and citizens of the state, and only secondarily persons having rights as human beings. It is within the bonds of family, culture, and state, that people live their lives as human beings. The ideal of a universal human society gains reality through the particular endeavors of human agents within these bonds. It is in this sense that one can understand the principle that humanity's realm emerges when two or three persons meet (Höffding 1888/1922: 478).

Moral philosophers such as Dewey and Tuft, writing in the Interbellum period of the twentieth century, conceived ethics as a practically oriented "science" related to the problems of a globalizing capitalist society in their time. But their moral philosophical efforts cannot be considered to be different from ours, even though political awareness and social responsiveness in their time were basically different from ours. What they had in mind was not only an ideal normative frame of reference. They were concerned with finding practical solutions to the global problems of a world capitalist society that was rapidly changing its features. They were deeply convinced that it developed into a global space-time domain, which generated disruptions and iniquities at a very fast rate. In this respect today's global ethical concerns do not look different.

Abraham Edel, somewhere in the same Interbellum period, made it clear that they—Dewey, Tuft, and himself—were focusing on the relationships between: a) current moralities—some of which were far from being ethical; b) ethics as an analytical tool; and c) the agenda of a "common ethic," what nowadays would be called a "global ethic."[2] In his book, *Ethical Judgment. The Use of Science in Ethics*, Edel (1955/1995) makes a difference between a "common ethic" and a "common human morality." The former should be derived from the intersection of moral philosophy theoretically conceived of, and practical ethics, a continuously updated and applied moral philosophy dealing with the many problems of a world capitalist society. In their research on the subject of the "current moralities," ethicists in Edel's global conception should focus on: a) the individual and the groups of individuals for which the normative rules have a mandatory force; b) the applicable conditions to be fulfilled; c) a selection of concepts and notions which serve as explanatory and regulatory tools; d) specific methods of justification and legitimization; e) a selection of measures of endorsement, rules of approval, authorizations, and sanctions; f) a selection of corresponding sensibilities; g) sets of fundamental assumptions concerning man and his world; h) a selection of relevant goals and proper measures to reach them; i) a selection of human "characteristics" (virtues as qualities).

The analytical tools of Edel—who died in 2007 after a long life of great intellectual achievement in what we call today global concern for the moral quality of universal mankind—are still far beyond what one can read in current global ethics today. One conclusion seems imperative to me, namely "not to forget" and more urgently, to step back to these earlier theoretical and practical ethical concerns with universal humankind. Global moral concern is at least as old as

---

2   Hans Küng (1990) and his "World Ethos" project is but one example of this overall endeavor. See Chapter 4, *Das Humanum als ökumenisches Grundkriterium*.

world capitalist society is.[3] This leads to the question of what the specific content of today's global ethics might be, linked to the contemporary stage of world capitalism, as well as in comparison with what happened before in the modern world-system. In my opinion this obliges us to investigate both the moral claims and the ideology of our current global ethics.

To progress in the domain of a worldwide, or global, ethics some other urgent questions should not be neglected: who are "we" when we discourse on global ethics? For whom are "we" reflecting and proposing analyses, which in the best case may result in learned and educated solutions? What are "we" writing when we write as we do? Who gave us a mandate to write about them and how do they, whom we do not see or hear, stay in control of what has been analyzed and proposed at their favor?

It is my strong conviction that in not asking these questions ethicists open the door wide to yet another ideological undertaking in normative ethics.

The Ideological Content of Today's Global Ethics

We should try to escape a perilous naïveté, common to most elaborations of global ethics of the last twenty years. The downfall of the Stalinist political and economic regime based on what turned out to be in the end a caricature of central planning of economic activities, of culture and education, of old age and health services, has also put an end to the cold war competition within the core of the capitalist world system. This competition indisputably had favored the working class at the heart of the world capitalist system to strive for a better standard of living. Politically speaking, this was necessary to win the race with what was considered as communism. In the former so-called communist states, this long period of more than 60 years led to the formation of new ruling and controlling elites. With the withering away of the limits set to capital formation and private profit they finally emerged as capitalist entrepreneurs controlling central sectors of industrial production. All this was prepared in the long period of bureaucratic state socialism, to which Gorbatsjov's perestroika and glasnost finally brought an end. In the core of the capitalist world system this major development, at the end of the "long twentieth century," stirred up a radical

---

3   In Giordano Bruno's *Spaccio de la Bestia Trionfante* (Bruno 1584/1985) one can read: "'Or dumque," disse lei, "serva a qualche sollicito Porthugese, o cursioso et avaro Britanno: accio con essa vada a discuoprir altre terre et altre regioni verso l'India occidentale, dove il capo aguzzo Genovese non ha discuoperto, e non ha messo i piedi il tenace e stipico Spagnolo; e cossi successivamente serva per l'avenire al piu curioso, sollecito e diligente investigator de nuovi continenti e terre'" (cfr. Third Dialogue). In his *La Cena de le ceneri* (first dialogue) he is even more explicit in his disapproval. He says that *conquistadores* troubled the peace of "the other" and violated the spirit of indigenous people, doubling the evil in this world by profit making and ruthless exploitation, spreading disorders, and bringing the poor under the law of the strongest. For Bruno's position concerning the brutal onset of the capitalist modern world-system (sixteenth century), I refer to the work of Giovanni Aquilecchia.

shift in socio-political discourse and analysis. It started from the 1970s onwards, accelerated as a consequence of the collapse of the bureaucratic Soviet system in 1989–1990, and continued along for the next ten years. The combined effect of the two developments introduced a new stage in the worldwide wage labor versus capital relationships, which under the name of delocalization and flexibility gave way to the reappearance of earlier forms of labor exploitation mechanisms.[4] It does not seem exaggerated to assert that "global society" is the name for this new situation. Free market ideology, regaining the strength and arrogance it had had more than a century ago, always comes into play when people mention the pros and the cons of the newly created global society.

I agree with yet another Hungarian political economist, A. Kornai, in calling the social system based on economic free entrepreneurship a free economy. For, as Kornai—reminiscent of Karl Polanyi's much earlier analyses of "trade and markets"—has repeatedly explained, markets are never free from constraints and from regulation. More precisely, markets exist only when supported and assisted by political constraints and socio-political regulation. The so-called labor market is the everlasting proof of this inescapable socio-political intervention, without which world capitalism would not be able to function as a dominant controlling social system.

The market, regulating society's economic activities, is a complex institutional system. It is based on the freedom of private profit-making enterprise, warranting the state-controlled free wage labor—capital relationships. These relationships are furthermore regulated through the world capitalist institutional framework (IMF, World Bank, the World Trade Organization, etc.), which totally escapes the "global governance" it has when it is thought of in an ideal way. There are not many reasons to disagree with Karl Polanyi's—apparently dated—analysis of this complex institutional system.

Free market, then, owes its existence to an unending regulation at the level of the nation-state and global capitalist institutions: European Union, World Bank, International Monetary Fund, Organization of Economic Cooperation and Development, World Trade Organization, supported by the nation-states which have never lost their significance for profit-making and capital accumulation. They, all together, guarantee the organized process of economic development, in which through an intricate intermingling and combination on a worldwide scale of various forms and types of labor activity organization, the dominance of capital over labor (Wallerstein 1979, 1983) is warranted.

In case we hold Western democratic nation-states responsible for global institutional violence—whether we call it structural violence or not[5]—it seems

---

4   I largely agree with Istvan Meszaros' observations on the subject. See his *Beyond Capitalism. Towards a Theory of Transition* (Meszaros 1995).

5   I refer to Thomas Pogge's thesis on "our responsibility" (see his admirable *World Poverty and Human Rights. Cosmopolitan Responsibilities and Reforms*, 2002). Contrary to Pogge, however I see no reason to drop Galtung's concept of structural violence. I find much of Kai Nielsen's philosophical vision of global justice convincing, where it bears witness to Galtung's structural violence (see Nielsen 2003). Dropping the analytical

to me a continuing task to ask how people who are living in these nation-states could possibly have the opportunity to weigh on institutional decision-making processes of the world capitalist system. How could they become dominant—or should I say hegemonic, to use a terminology which reminds us of Antonio Gramsci's analysis of political and social decision processes—actors weighing on the direction of worldwide policies? How could they be properly represented in the various international and global institutions that regulate the socio-economic processes within world capitalism?

Let us take a closer look at some of the conceptual—semantic—implications of the afore-mentioned geopolitical development in the modern world-system.[6] The people-based human development is the normative signifying concept repeatedly referred to in the various UN and UNESCO Reports and Declarations. Without any exception it is opposed to a narrow conception of economic development, which was the focus of attention of much of the post-war development programs in the South. This is also the case with the 1995 UNESCO/UN Report *Our Creative Diversity* of the *World Commission on Culture and Development* (UNESCO 1995), which in its "Introduction" mentions two views of development. The first global UN development report (UNDP 1990), addressed as its main issue the question of how economic growth translates—or fails to translate—into human development. The latter is conceived off as the way people are progressively enabled to make their own choices. The report suggested ways to measure this progression in "choice enlargement."

The 1993 report on "people's participation" (UNDP 1993) looked at means to improve the ways in which "people-friendly markets, decentralized governance and community organizations, especially non-governmental organizations (NGOs)" contribute to set free people's individual and social self-determination. In 1996 the UNDP organization published its report on economic growth and human development (UNDP 1996), in which it was argued that "if not properly managed" economic growth may equal a "jobless, voiceless, rootless and futureless" outcome for many worldwide. "Growth" is considered to be dependent on poverty reduction and sustainability, which asks for the use of human development instead of merely economic indicators of expansion.

---

concept of structural violence may provoke the loss of a critical instrument concerning the specific responsibilities actors and agencies do have in concrete situational contexts. To counter the reverse—"de-responsibilizing" ourselves confronted with world poverty situations—I suggest that an a-symmetrical point of view (cf. Jankélévitch (1981) "droits/ obligations") may be harmonized with precise empirical situational undertakings. But I agree that this altogether is not in contradiction with Pogge's stance in *World Poverty and Human Rights*.

6   For an analysis of a global ethic signifying scheme in terms of: 1) pronouns, 2) verbs, 3) actors—personal pronouns, 4) spatio-temporalities, 5) essentials, 6) audiences (assumed or real), 7) recognition (assumed or real), 8) values, 9) goals, 10) norms/ prescriptions, 11) rules, 12) regulative principles, 13) rights, 14) obligations,15) application contexts, I refer to my 2007 contribution to the *Marburger Philosophen Forum*, "On global ethics as an action-directed research discipline" (Commers 2007).

From then on, the annual global reports kept emphasizing the weight of the "human face" of growth and development indicators, advancing subjects such as: the importance of a human rights based approach to social and economic accountability, the establishment and deepening of democratic political structures at all levels of society, a singular conception of wealth, stating that human well-being is far more important than income and financial means, the significance of multicultural policies, the recognition of cultural differences, the potentialities of cultural diversity for human development, and the importance for religious freedom and tolerance. In the meantime the Millennium Development Goals had been launched, with the purpose to function as a global horizon for human development, and for the prospering of the global order.[7]

Human development, such as it was defined by the UNDP, consequently should be put alongside economic development. Human development is "about more than the rise and fall of national incomes" (UNDP 2006). It bears reference to the creation of a material, an economic, and a cultural environment in which people can develop their capabilities, are able to lead a productive and creative life in harmony with their needs and interests (UNDP 2006). The "Human Development Reports" of the UN concentrate on the enlargement of people's choices by protecting, supporting, and encouraging human capabilities, the latter broadly defined as "the range of things that people can do or be in life." Health, access to knowledge through education, opportunity to participate in community-life, cultural and political self-determination, they are all equally important for human development (UNCED 1992). It was stated from the very start that this view of development was in accordance with human rights concerns, because they both secure the "well-being and dignity of all people, building self-respect and the respect of others" (UNDP 2006).

From the 1980s onwards, it became clear that the sole attention paid to the economic side of development in the poor countries—and even in the rest of the world—was wrong at the root. Not only had many people paid with their lives, their health and well-being—with their self-determination and political sovereignty ruined or nullified—but even economic development was harmed and misdirected by this one-sidedness, as it produced some negative inverse mechanisms. One can call this the fatal and damaging paradox of early post-Second World War development programs.

Both Immanuel Wallerstein (1983) and David Korten (1995), through their work in poor countries in Africa and South-East Asia, experienced the insufficiency or inefficiency of Western views on post-colonial development of countries of the Southern hemisphere. But they were far from alone in their sudden conversion from this "developmentalist" post-war ideology. All of these

---

7   Of importance is the recently developed notion of a "global compact"—different from a "covenant" in Hobbesian terms—such as it has been defined by the UN, see http://www.unglobalcompact.org/NetworksAroundTheWorld/: ... an international initiative—the Global Compact—that would bring companies together with UN agencies, labor and civil society to support universal environmental and social principles.

critical voices agreed with the idea expressed by former UN Secretary-General, Boutros Boutros-Ghali:

> As development becomes imperative, as we approach the turn of this century, we are faced with the necessity of giving new meaning to the word. Reflecting on development is thus the most important intellectual challenge in the coming years. (UNESCO 1995: 23)

The view of human development, therefore, emphasizes other value-goal-norm sets (see Table 5.1 for an overview). For our global ethics concerns it is of importance to study them closely, to look after their factual presuppositions and the regulative principles that are implied by their actions. It ranges over signifying concepts such as: lack of opportunities, democratic institutions, participatory governance and management, quality of life, well-being, longevity, health, adequate nutrition, reasonable consumption, education, access to knowledge and to ICT, gender-based equality, decent labor conditions, child protection, dignity, human rights, justice and equity, cultural diversity, social and individual empowerment, human capabilities, sustainability, community duties, solidarity, caring, general—social—responsibility, public accountability, religious tolerance, intergenerational equity.

In the economic development view—implying a restrained economic vision on human affairs—the signifying concepts and expressions are: "open economy," "business attractive for investors," "foreign and domestic investors" (as actors), "investment opportunities," "stable macroeconomic climate" (meaning: a stable social and political situation in the investment region), "dependable property rights," "tangible investments," "tangible intellectual property," "exchange-rate convertibility."

Needless to say, this certainly is not the discourse of a human development report. No reference is made to the risks of this investment-biased approach for the social and political stability in the country soliciting the business, nor is there any concern for the freedom and the quality of life of the people who are supposed to work for the profitability of the investment. What does it mean to set "a stable macroeconomic climate" in terms of human empowerment, gender-equality, child protection against labor exploitation, avoidance of forced labor practices, health, sustainability and environmental protection, human rights defence and support, participatory governance, quality of life, etc.? All of these human development items are ignored. Indeed, the limited economic view of growth urges the economist to focus only on the allowance "to take home" profits, and on the assurance that both stability and profitability in the investment countries are guaranteed.

One of the deciding signifying differences bears on the assumed and underlying concept of governance of the two views of development. In a human development view, governance is conceived to be chiefly horizontal and decentralized, whereas an economic development view is mainly based on a vertical and centralized governance conception. The role of civil society, of grassroots organizations, and of NGOs, is highlighted in human development, whereas in economic

Table 5.1   Human development and economic development signifiers

Human development signifiers*	Economic development signifiers[†]
Reasonableness	Rationality
Human capabilities	Rational choice (social choice/ public choice)
Opportunity enlargement: social, cultural, political	Self-interest
Care and solidarity	Individual preferences
Self-determination in civil society and community life	Free trade and trade policies
Life experience at grass roots levels	Trade adjustments
Creative responsiveness	Competitiveness
Corporate social responsibility (CSR)	GDP and GNP output per capita
Stakeholdership	PPF (production-possibility frontier)
Human rights	Income
Embedding of market regulation	Human "resources"
Sustainability	Natural "resources"
Common good	Capital
Health	Technology
Education	Productivity
Knowledge access	Profitability (in terms of rates of return)
Social securization	Externalities
Well-being	Diseconomies of scale
Social and environment economy	Free market
Duty centred	Exchange rates and trade balance
Open source information	Financial and monetary accountability
Contextual adaptability	Equilibrium
Horizontal governance conception	Vertical governance conception
Spontaneous bottom-top subsidiarity guideline	Compulsory top-bottom subsidiarity guideline

Sources: * UNDP Reports; [†] Samuelson and Nordhaus, 2005, 555–79.

development governance the key agencies are multinationals, transnational professional organizations, international capitalist institutions, CEOs, etc.

Nevertheless, it seems worthwhile to me to consider in more depth the feasible relationships between the two views of development and explore the reconcilability of their signifying conceptual bases. In the UNDP reports, but recently also in the World Bank reports, the idea that human development and economic development are opposite and conflicting, has been dropped. It is a point of view to which the work of Amartya Sen (1999: 35–54) has contributed in a substantial way. I can see at least six possible relationships between the human development and the economic development view (see Table 5.2).

Table 5.2   Possible relations between human development and economic development

Human development (HD)	Economic development (ED)
1) Opposing and conflicting, without any opportunity of mediation	
2) HD enhances ED	
3) HD is enhanced by ED	
4) The economic impact of HD beyond doubt	
5) The humanizing range of ED should be endorsed and supported	
6) Extended economy (Polanyi 1944)/social economy conceptions (Etzioni 1988) are meaningful for the proper understanding of ED	

Within the ranges offered by the cases 2, 3, 4, and 5, a global ethical conception on humanity's future might be worked out. The economic impact of human development, regarded to be beyond doubt, a realistic and pragmatic endorsement of the humanizing force of economic development will be of great significance to improve the material and spiritual conditions of humankind. By following this pathway, we may transcend the narrow-minded economist inclinations to classify countries exclusively in "low-risk" and "high-risk" units for interest rates and capital investment, and we might be able to surpass both the "limits to competition" (Petrella 1995, 2006) and the pitfalls of a limited conception of the economy of human life.

On Some Regulative Principles for a Future Critical Global Ethics

In the UNESCO report on humanity's creative diversity (UNESCO 1995), which mainly addressed the subject of "a new global ethics," the expression "global ethics" appears 33 times, all of which suggest a different content. The first definition is a normative one for it states:

> We should develop a global ethics that applies equally to all those involved in world affairs. Its efficacy will depend on the ability of people and governments to transcend

narrow self-interests and agree that the interests of humanity as a whole will be best served by acceptance of a set of common rights and responsibilities. (35)

What global ethics is about can easily be grasped in rereading this definition, although its content remains far from clear. The aim is to reach shared points of reference to provide a minimal moral guidance, a purpose to which the endorsed values and principles should contribute. This is what Abraham Edel, in the Second World War period, called a "common ethic." Doubtless, global issues of concern have a say in these endeavors. Although it remains a difficult task to define the content of global ethics as a discipline it is not unachievable to raise major problems in ethical research.

Strikingly, the 1995 Report remains somewhat confused about the difference between "global ethics"—as a particular research discipline—and "global ethic." The latter pertains to a private and public agencies centred agenda for action, in which sets of value-goals-norms-principles are explicitly stated and explained from the central belief that they might have a practical significance for the future of humankind under further conditions of globalization. The meaning of "global ethics" is confused with "global ethic" in many instances in the text. Nevertheless the discourse is instructive about what the experts at UNESCO and the UN considered as vital issues:

the deeply human urge to avoid avoidable suffering and some notion of the basic moral equality of all human beings together form an indispensable point of reference and a strong pillar of support for any attempt to work out a global ethics. (UNESCO 1995: 36)

The idea of human vulnerability and the purpose of alleviating suffering is of great inspiration to the writers of the report. Mankind should combat an age-old illness of Western culture, namely its "contempt for weakness" (Ofstad 1989), and it should attempt to accept man's limitations and helplessness. Furthermore, the idea of human rights can easily be brought back to the concern for weakness and exposure, which was analyzed by twentieth-century ethicists (Lévinas 1961; Bauman 1993).

From this general value-based standpoint the UNESCO Commission suggested five principal ideas to form the core of what I think they meant to be a "global ethic" (although continually the writers kept using the expression "global ethics"): human rights and global responsibilities, democratic legitimacy linked with political autonomy and human empowerment, protection of minorities, commitment to peaceful conflict-resolution and fair negotiation, intergenerational equity. Be this as it may, it hardly seems conclusive for a reflection on the relationship between global ethical research produced by globalization, and the feasible content of a global ethic, which although neither universally accepted, nor generally applied to concrete practical matters of concern, may function as a suitable benchmark for action and policies.

In our view, a "global ethic" covers numerous factual and prescriptive domains within a wide range of concrete goal applications. These applied fields go from the spelling out of leading valuations and regulatory principles related to actual situations, to the action of recommending rules and norms:

a) from the spelling out of principles of care, to recommendations about the empowerment of local communities and individuals (see Narayan 2002, 2005);
b) from defending grassroots movements and social initiatives to impede the harmful results of a restrained and inadequate globalizing economy, to the safeguarding of men, women and children against the current re-introduction of different kinds of compulsory and forced labor relationships;[8]
c) from the uncovering of various agencies of judgment and decision, to the recognition of the many diverse audiences to which one appeals for the application of rules and recommendations of action;[9]
d) from the demand of cosmopolitan citizenship, to the request of local participatory democracy and large scale—global—democratic governance.[10]

---

8   For the more official side of this concern, see the Reports of the Director-General of the ILO Reports, more specifically: *A Global Alliance against Forced Labour* (ILO 2004, 2005). For an alternative view, see *World Social Forum* publications and declarations since 2003 (Porte Allegre, Brazil); *Post-Autistic Economics Network*, www.peacon.net. A remarkable contribution is from Jorge Buzaglio (2003), "Capabilities: From Spinoza to Sen and Beyond," 2003.

9   In this matter "dialogue" has an important notion. I refer to the UNDP handbook on democratic dialogue (UNDP 2007). See also http://www.democraticdialoguenetwork. org/ where the concept of dialogue is denoted as follows: "Dialogue is a participatory, inclusive process to help solve complex social, economic, and political issues that existing institutions and formal channels are not adequately addressing. It fosters understanding among participants and seeks to identify new options and develop shared visions while promoting a culture of participations and democracy." In this descriptive denotative definition it is acknowledged that "existing institutions and formal channels" show a "democratic deficit," a lack of democratic potentiality. Moreover the definition refers to "options" to be identified, which means that we are obliged to clarify valuational-normative-factual settings in favor of participation of civil society's participants, both agencies and individuals.

From a global ethics point of view it is important to connect this globalization context-bounded dialogue-notion with the philosophical theories on dialogue, such as Martin Buber (1962/1970), Mikhaïl Bakhtin (1970), and Chaïm Perelman (1982/2000) have developed in the twentieth century. From Perelman (2000): "... l'argumentation, qui raisonne sans contraindre, mais qui n'oblige pas davantage à renoncer à la Raison au profit de l'irrationel ou de l'indicible" (Michel Meyer, "Préface").

10   On http://glogov.org/, the Research Program of the 2001-created *Global Governance Project*, one can read a fair descriptive working definition of what global governance is alike: "... we see global governance as characterised by the increasing participation of actors other than states, ranging from private actors such as multinational corporations and (networks of) scientists and environmentalists to intergovernmental organisations ('multiactor governance'). ... we see global governance as marked by new mechanisms of organisation such as public-private and private-private partnerships, alongside the traditional system of legal treaties negotiated by states. ... we see global

The global ethical inquiry should be guided by an action and life experience oriented research on promising regulative principles and applied norms. From a theoretical point of view the global ethical inquiry—different from the formulation of a "global ethic"—should be conceived of as a Deweyian pragmatically oriented discipline (Dewey 1939/1972) answering to a radical dialogical relationalist outlook (Buber 1962/1970; Bakhtin 1970) on human interpretation and signification of man's existence:

> The core of dialogue is always a-thematic, even when the dialogue is thematically well fixed and tightened ... (Bakhtin 1970: 345)

The regulative principle of care and respect for human vulnerability—reproving "our contempt for weakness"—should remain at the centre of the "global ethic" proposals. This regulatory principle supposes the a-symmetrical relationship between rights and obligations. This can be stated as follows: the a-symmetry of rights and obligations (*droits* and *devoirs*) is the core of a all comprehensive conception of humanity. Table 5.3 offers an overview.

From a normative ethical point of view of human rights demands, raised and expressed within the many different local settings of the globalizing capitalist economy, there is quite some realism in the statement of the fundamental regulatory principle of the asymmetry between rights and obligations. Dignity is what human rights and human freedom stand for. From this standpoint we will be allowed our role of go-between researchers who attempt to match a) the never-ending danger of the "ideologization" of the concept of "global ethic," and b) the uncritical—moralistic—expression of what "global ethics" is all about.

The World Citizenship-case in Global Ethics

I argued that ethical research is relational in nature. Facing the burdens of economic crisis, depression and war, educational deficit, health deficiencies, and generalized poverty, Dewey and Edel many decades ago refused to stick to too general a moral point of reference. They exhorted ethicists to consider the intricate relations between empirical situations and generalizing values, norms, and regulatory standards. Undoubtedly, a humanistic outlook on life drove them to this stance, taking personal responsibility seriously. This way they tried to define,

---

governance as characterised by different layers and clusters of rule-making and rule-implementation, both vertically between supranational, international, national and subnational layers of authority ("multilevel governance") and horizontally between different parallel rule-making systems." Democratic governance denotes in a normative way various kinds of bottom-top people directed political interaction processes in the absence of a central political authority but in the presence of a) intergovernmental organizations, b) nongovernmental organizations, c) private sector organizations such as companies and firms, d) citizen movements and civil society actors, e) trade unions, etc. See also Rajan 2006.

Table 5.3   Rights and obligations

Rights (*droits*)	Obligations (*devoirs*)
Everyone has rights, also do "I" (revendication)	
Everyone has rights, but not "me"	"I" have only obligations
To "you" nothing but rights	To "me" nothing but obligations
Reification of rights	Non-parity of obligations
Objectivity of rights	Irreversibility of obligations
The "first person" ("I"/"We") goes the last, whereas the "second" ("Thou"/"You") goes the first	The "first person" ("I"/"We") goes the last, whereas the "second" ("Thou"/"You") goes the first
"I" am the defender of "thy" rights	"I" am not the custodian of "thy" obligations
"We" are the defenders of "your" rights	"We" are not the custodians of "your" obligations
"My" rights are not the basis of "your" obligations	"Your" obligations are not the basis of "my" rights

The opening of the eyes—for instance in understanding the challenge of world poverty and world citizenship—implies the loss of our blamelessness

The loss of one's blamelessness is the price one has to pay for keeping one's dignity

Source: based on Jankélévitch 1981.

as clear as possible, the task of the moral philosopher in a world of avoidable misery and preventable poverty.

Scholars that we are today—and such as were Dewey, Tuft and Edel in the first half of the twentieth century—we operate as uncommissioned go-betweens between policy-makers and the large public. True, sometimes we receive financial and logistical means to do our reflective work. But the concepts we invent to make it possible for us to communicate with each other on matters of human rights, global justice, world citizenship, generalizing forms of democracy, economic development related to human capacities, dignity and empowerment, are our own. The existential conditions and situations that assumed—we may as well call them the supposed ontologies—stand most of the time outside the concrete concerns of the people included in these existential or ontological assumptions. The concepts invented must be considered as tools to show, to model, and to exhort, within the assumptions of the learned, whether they are commissioned or not. Paradoxically, however, in employing these tools the learned do have existing conditions and situations in mind. For without the knowledge of other men's concerns—which ultimately transgress the learned people's specific situations and conditions—their discussions and analyses would be meaningless and trivial. Moreover their "urgent partiality" as men and women of research and advice would become meaningless without the "others" and "their problems" being there. This "urgent partiality" looks like an "encouragement."

Whenever the learned are not simply engaged in the justification of existing power relationships—which are answerable for the misery of the many who suffer from the bad consequences of to the amplification and extension of the capitalist world economy—they seem prompted by an an-archic (different from an anarchic) drive. It is in this sense that one can say they are encouraged by a "pre-original compulsion." Vladimir Jankélévitch (1981) situates it in a concrete and almost everyday event, to make it radically different from an abstract relationship in an idealized space-time domain, such as in "reflective equilibrium" thought experiments set up to legitimize a liberal societal order.[11]

On this "primeval compulsion," another French moral philosopher, Emmanuel Lévinas, states that those who speak in analyses and discourses—*thématisation où … l'être se traduit devant nous*—are motivated through the "pre-original vocation," which is the same as saying that they are incited by their own conscientiousness and responsibility. It is in this pre-original sense that a paradox may be elucidated: the "urgent partiality"—if it be sincere and genuine—is basically itself impartial. The concern ethicists have for problems of globalization make them partial in terms of the problematic issues, but leave them impartial as a consequence of the "pre-original vocation" of their concern. The global ethics interlocutors cannot avoid being taken up into this paradox again and again. It makes up the two sides—the factual and the normative—of the ethical discourses on globalization, as I shall go on to explain below.

The normative side requests the learned to speak on the subject of human rights and human obligations in terms of the human in a universal way.[12] The human being, which is the subject of our concern and which is the moral subject *par excellence*—subject of human rights and human obligations—is not this one or another concrete individual person, not the human being as it is here and now. It is—spoken of in the words of Jankélévitch—the human being "uncontaminated" and "undemanding." The moral philosopher himself, who speaks on behalf of this person who does not exist, seems excluded from the judicial and moral community he calls to mind. Paradoxically, this community extends itself to all moral subjects imaginable, and the moral philosopher hardly can accept to exclude himself from humanity. The generalized fellow citizen of the supposed

---

11   For an early and—in my opinion—convincing criticism on these "original position" thought-experiments, one should again read Karl Marx's analyses of "bourgeois-thinking robinsonades." See his *Grundrisse zur Kritik der politischen Ökonomie*, "Einleitung."

12   Cf. my free translation of Jankélévitch (1981: 43 and 45): "Let us say that the moral paradox is virtually implied in the reasonable idea of what is human in a universal way. The human being that is a moral subject of human rights and human obligations is not this or some other concrete individual person, is not the human being as it is here and now. It is the human being uncontaminated and undemanding, the human being without any further specification, and the human being without *quatenus*."

and foreseen world community has all conceivable rights before me. His rights are a-symmetrical to my obligations, for being obliged to do something does not give me any reciprocal priority whatsoever. It forbids me the opportunity to deduce my proper rights and my proper freedom to act starting from this situation.

I do agree with Jankélévitch that "their" obligations are not automatically "my" rights and that this is precisely the content of the two-sided paradox, which presides over all rights and obligations of man. The love that cares for the humaneness (= *hominité*) of the human being—and which in an urgent sense is troubled by love and not by reason[13]—that love which loves the humankind embodied in whatever human being, and which loves the enlarged person in the appearance of all humanity, is utterly paradoxical. Any community restrained to be what it is will become a clan amidst other clans, a tribe amidst other tribes. But, in the words of the French moral philosopher, the "human community" is by definition a superlative. It is the vastest community one can think about. It is this immeasurable community that offers love a maximal opening for which we do have a name: completeness. This community beyond measure is "omnilateral" and "coextensive" to humankind of which there exists only one.[14] Paradoxically, however, none of us can indicate it, nor is anyone of us able to claim ultimate knowledge of it. Our impartiality, which is the very basis of our concern will always be tainted by the way we are related to those on behalf of whom we speak.

The former, factual side, presses us to specify the situations we have in mind, the persons we care for, the particular problems we see for them. In this case we are exhorted to bear witness to the fact that the human being, who is the moral subject of human rights and human obligations, is a concrete individual person. She is a human being here and now, immersed in specific circumstances which she has difficulty examining. She is a contaminated human being who, at any time, appears to be a demanding person. She is a specific human being, a concrete and distinct person with *quatenus* (Jankélévitch 1981).

Whenever the ethicist worries about global ethics, he is not allowed to disregard the paradox. As a go-between, he gives attention to "the human" in a general way, focusing on human community in the superlative, which is the vastest community he can think about. But he will do so being hit by specific and weird demands, by pressures unforeseen, and by wretchedness unpredicted. This paradox—that Jankélévitch has succeeded to formulate so well—indicates a normative-factual continuum that is both unavoidable and "saturated with hope."

It is within this philosophical point of view, that I am suggesting we should try to explore the meaning of the very different world citizenship agendas that are linked to the endeavors of global ethics nowadays. Acknowledging the

---

13   This is what makes the difference between Misjkin and Don Quijote, the former speaking from love, the latter from reason for humanity.

14   I again refer to Jankélévitch's *Le paradoxe de la morale* (1981: 43 and 45), among the twentieth-century philosophers the one who succeeded quite well in formulating the essentials of moral thinking given modern conditions of life. For a translation in English of this crucial—and in my opinion indispensable—moral treatise, see my forthcoming book on the ethics of Vladimir Jankélévitch.

importance of civil society and possibilities of democratic governance engendered by a global awareness of environmental issues, intergenerational questions, world poverty, labor, poor countries debt problems, from a valuational-normative point of view, I am convinced of the necessity to defend a civic society perspective on cosmopolitanism. One cannot get around the fact that views of civic society based on arguments of empowerment, stakeholdership, and transparency, considerations of wage-profit equity, ideas about the common good and gender fairness, can only be made comprehensible from a relational point of view on humanity's future and its human rights and obligations, the absolute horizon of which is the asymmetrical relationship between our obligations and their rights.

In my opinion, all of our world citizen theories and agendas—which should be our concern—suggest a factual/normative continuum (F/N) which is related both to ideal conceptions of citizenship and factual or realized organizations and institutions of citizenship. None of us can ignore that the United Nations exists although we all are deeply disappointed and upset by the fact that it is not within the strict boundaries of UN that human aspirations are fully realized. The factual/normative continuum of citizenship comprises four positions:

a) factual basic citizenship (nation-states, European Union);
b) factual prospective citizenship (United Nations; International Court of The Hague; International Labor Organization);
c) normative basic citizenship (such as approached by Jankélévitch (1981), or seized by Bloch (1959, 1977a);[15]
d) normative prospective citizenship (enlarged human rights institutional measures; World Social Forum).

Factual Basic Citizenship

This is the citizenship "we" actually have in specific and described spatio-temporal circumstances or situations; For example: "we" are citizens of a nation-state in which we enjoy rights and are obliged to perform duties; "we" are citizens of larger political-institutional settings, such as the European Union, the British Commonwealth, etc. Recognition is evident.

Factual Prospective Citizenship

This is the citizenship "we" are supposed to have, in order to enjoy our rights and to fulfil our obligations, when and in so far the concrete spatio-temporal circumstances or situations in which we live have not produced the integral achievement of these rights and obligations. For example: "we" are naturalized immigrants in a country in which "we" are not yet recognized as full members, though the law and the institutions promised this to be the case as a consequence of "our" consented adoption. This is the situation full members of nation-

---

15 Bloch's *Das Prinzip Hoffnung* was published in 1959, but was written in the period of Nazist Rule in Germany and in Europe and the Second World War.

states are in, after having been given national citizenship without being able to achieve to integral membership, for example because they are not allowed to take part in elections, or they are refused jobs as government officials and representative functions in social-political networks. An interesting case is the situation nowadays (2007) of Bulgarian illegal immigrants in the core countries of the European Union. In acquiring European citizenship they acquire a factual prospective citizenship in all of the states of the European Union, while they are still seeking legal recognition as asylum seekers in these core countries. Another striking example is the case of Israeli Arab people in the state of Israel (Grossman 2003).

Normative Basic Citizenship

This is the citizenship "we" consider to be established, because the international political-institutional settings imply a virtual agreement on rights and obligations within the ruling elites, though these rights and obligations are not actually implemented at all. It is the citizenship basically implied in the international conventions on war and peace, on labor standards, on human rights, although not a few of them are constantly endangered or ignored, not to say violated. The fact that human rights standards are internationally accepted through government agencies does not mean that they are implemented in day-by-day authority relationships. We can give examples drawn from war situations, in which the rights of war victims are internationally recognized, but still frequently ignored or violated, without any possible recourse to an independent international—or better still an independent universal—court of justice under impartial jurisdiction. Nevertheless in all these cases, a similar impartial jurisdiction with its proper court of justice is basically implied in international conventions and regulations. The same can be said concerning a lot of basic human rights, the reason why they are called basic being that they are not implemented fully, or in an integral way over a period of time.

Normative Prospective Citizenship

This is the citizenship we should reclaim or defend from a "cosmopolitical" (Gould 1988/1999, 2004),[16] or a "cosmopolitan–communitarian" (Dower 1998) point of view. In arguing in favor of this citizenship "we" can rely on the philosophical "dreams"—*Träume nach Vorwärts*, such as Ernst Bloch has called them—of our scholarly ancestors, to begin with the Stoics, going to Baruch Spinoza, and gaining full philosophical strength and "evidence" both in Immanuel Kant's work on *Weltbürgerschaft* and in neokantian arguments about the "whole of humankind" (Cohen 1877/1982, 1904/1928, 1918/1994, 1994).

---

16   In Gould (2004), see 166–73 on the concepts of "cosmopolitanism," "moral" and "political," see 180–82 on the concept of "cosmopolitical democracy." In Gould (1988/1999), see Chapter 12, "Cosmopolitical Democracy: Moral Principles among Nations," 307–28.

This concept of citizenship is as old as literality itself, for we can find written arguments back as far as Mesopotamian texts of the Sumerian and Acadian period. It is a concept, which serves as an everlasting horizon of human achievement, a powerful and inviting regulatory idea (in Kantian terms). It operates as an "emancipatory acknowledgment" (in the terms of Ernst Bloch 1977a, 1977b), a conscience preceding any concrete situation of oppression and emancipation. Paradoxically, it does not lack an empirical basis for, unremittingly, it is revealed to become man's history. It is to this Ernst Bloch has drawn our attention in his *Das Prinzip Hoffnung* (Bloch 1959). Ideas, notions, and arguments about our participating in the "whole of humankind" become visible as practical principles of hope and as sensible images concerning a better future. They have "presence" both in people's and in humankind's everyday life. They are actually "everywhere people [who] are fighting for their rights" (Woody Guthrie, *Tom Joad*), giving evidence of their factual, even though ideal, content. As such they marched into the discourses of the declarations of the United Nations and they permeated the many different developmental theories related to a variety of dissimilar international organizations, ranging from the World Bank to the International Labor Organization and the World Social Forum (being the "open meeting place of groups and movements of civil society" opposed to the organized agencies of a biased capitalist globalization).[17]

Conclusion

If Abraham Edel was right in making a difference between a "common ethic" and a "common human morality"—as I think he was—we should conceive of a critical global ethics, which stands at the intersection of moral philosophy theoretically conceived of and practical ethics, a frequently updated, applied moral philosophy which confronts the many problems of world society in its development. Ethicists should focus on: a) the individual and the groups of individuals for which the normative rules have a mandatory force; b) the conditions of application to be fulfilled; c) a selection of concepts and notions which serve as explanatory and regulatory tools; d) specific methods of justification and legitimization; e) a selection of measures of endorsement, rules of approval, authorizations, and sanctions; f) a selection of corresponding sensibilities; g) sets of fundamental assumptions concerning man and his world; h) a selection of relevant goals and proper measures to reach them; i) a selection of human "characteristics" (virtues as qualities).

The regulatory standard for the factual-normative continuum of "global civil society"—connected to the ultimate horizon of a truly "human humankind" (Karl Marx in 1844)—is the asymmetrical relationship between our obligations and their rights. For this reason it is necessary and urgent to interrogate ourselves

---

17   See *World Social Forum Charter of Principles*, 2002: http://www.forum socialmundial.org.br.

in order to be as clear as possible about what "we" are doing when "we" reflect and write as "we" do and such as "we" do.[18]

References

Bakhtin, M.M. (1970), *La Poétique de Dostoïevski*. Paris: Seuil.
Bauman, Z. (1993), *Postmodern Ethics*. Oxford: Blackwell.
Bloch, E. (1959), *Das Prinzip Hoffnung*. Frankfurt aM: Suhrkamp.
Bloch, E. (1977a), *Naturrecht und mensliche Würde*. Frankfurt aM: Suhrkamp.
Bloch, E. (1977b), *Experimentum Mundi. Frage, Kategorien des Herausbringens, Praxis*. Frankfurt aM: Suhrkamp.
Bruno, G. (1584/1985), *Spaccio de la Bestia Trionfante*. Milano: Bur.
Buber, M. (1962/1970), *Das dialogische Prinzip*. Gerlingen: Lambert Schneider.
Buzaglio, J. (2003), "Capabilities: From Spinoza to Sen and Beyond," *Post-Autistic Economics Network* (http://www.peacon.net).
Cohen, H. (1877/1982), *Kants Begründung der Ethik*. Hildesheim: Olms.
Cohen, H. (1904/1928), *Ethik des reinen Willens*. Berlin: Cassirer.
Cohen, H. (1918/1994), *Religion de la Raison tirée des sources du judaïsme*. Paris: PUF
Cohen, H. (1994), *L'Ethique du judaïsme*. Paris: Cerf.
Commers, M.S.R. (2007), "On Global Ethics as an Action-directed Research Discipline," *Marburger Philosophen Forum* (http://www.philosophia-online.de/).
Dewey, J. (1939/1972), *Freedom and Culture*. New York: G.P. Putnam's Sons.
Dower, N. (1998), *World Ethics: The New Agenda*. Edinburgh: Edinburgh University Press.
Edel, A. (1955/1995), *Ethical Judgment. The Use of Science in Ethics*. New Brunswick: Transaction Publishers.
Etzioni, A. (1988), *The Moral Dimension: Toward a New Economics*. New York: The Free Press.
Gould, C.C. (1988/1999), *Rethinking Democracy. Freedom and social cooperation in politics, economy, and society*. Cambridge: Cambridge University Press.
Gould, C.C. (2004), *Globalizing Democracy and Human Rights*. Cambridge: Cambridge University Press.
Grossman, D. (2003), *Death as a Way of Life: Israel Ten Years after Oslo*. New York: Farrar, Straus, and Giroux.
Höffding, H. (1922), *Ethik. Eine Darstellung der ethischen Prinzipien und deren Anwendung auf besondere Lebensverhältnisse*. Leipzig: Reisland.
ILO (2004), *Organizing for Social Justice*. Geneva: ILO.
ILO (2005), *A Global Alliance Against Forced Labour*. Geneva: ILO.
Jankélévitch, V. (1981), *Le paradoxe de la morale*. Paris: Seuil.
Korten, D. (1995), *When Corporations Rule The World*. Bloomfield: Kumarian Press.
Küng, H. (1990), *Projekt Weltethos*. München: Piper Verlag.
Lévinas, E. (1961), *Totalité et Infini. Essai sur l'extériorité*. The Hague: M. Nijhoff.
Meszaros, I. (1995), *Beyond Capitalism. Towards a Theory of Transition*. London: The Merlin Press.

---

18 I improvise on the research orientation of the Cambridge political philosopher, Quentin Skinner, "Meaning and Context in the History of Ideas," see Tully (1988).

Narayan, D. (ed.) (2002), *Empowerment and Poverty Reduction. A Sourcebook*. Washington DC: World Bank.

Narayan, D. (ed.) (2005), *Measuring Empowerment. Cross-Disciplinary Perspectives*. Washington DC: World Bank.

Nielsen, K. (2003), *Globalization and Justice*. New York: Humanity Books.

Ofstad, H. (1989), *Our Contempt for Weakness*. Stockholm: Almqvist and Wiksell.

Polanyi, K. (1944), *The Great Transformation*. Boston: Beacon Press.

Perelman, C. (1982/2000), *Traité de l'Argumentation. La nouvelle rhétorique*. Brussels: Editions de l'Université de Bruxelles.

Petrella, R. (1995), *Limits to Competition*. Boston: The Lisbon Group/MIT Press.

Petrella, R. (2006), *The Common Good*. London: Zed Books.

Pogge, T. (2002), *World Poverty and Human Rights. Cosmopolitan Responsibilities and Reforms*. Cambridge: Polity.

Rajan, S.C. (2006), *Global Politics and Institutions*. GTI Paper Series 3. Boston: Tellus Institute.

Samuelson, P.A. and Nordhaus, W.D. (2005), *Economics*. New York: McGraw-Hill/ Irwin.

Sen, A. (1999), *Development as Freedom*. New York: Anchor Books.

Tully, J. (ed.) (1988), *Meaning and Context: Quentin Skinner and his Critics*. Cambridge: Polity.

UNCED (1992), *Agenda 21. Rio Declaration on Environment and Development*. Rio de Janerio: UNCED.

UNDP (1990), *Concept and Measurement of Human Development*. New York: UNDP.

UNDP (1993), *People's Participation*. New York: UNDP.

UNDP (1996), *Economic Growth and Human Development*. New York: UNDP.

UNDP (2006), *Beyond Scarcity: Power, Poverty and the Global Water Crisis*. New York: UNDP.

UNDP (2007), *Democratic Dialogue. A Handbook for Practitioners*. New York: UNDP.

UNESCO (1995), *Our Creative Diversity*. Paris: UNESCO.

Wallerstein, I. (1979), *The Capitalist World-Economy*. Cambridge: Cambridge University Press.

Wallerstein, I. (1983), *Historical Capitalism*. London: Verso.

Chapter 6

Why and What Global Ethics?

Heather Widdows

This chapter addresses two questions, namely, "Why global ethics?" and "What global Ethics?" At first glance these questions appear. if not unconnected. then at least separable. In this chapter I will suggest that they are necessarily related because how one answers the "What?" question fundamentally effects how one answers the "Why?" question. In particular, reasons for answering the "Why?" question depend upon one's answers to the "What global ethics?" question. This is because, one needs to know what global ethics consists of in order to endorse global ethics and give reasons to the "Why?" question. In particular, many current critics, especially those from the non-Western world, have no reasons to answer the "Why?" question positively as they consider global ethics merely an imperialist version of Western ethics.[1]

Given this connection between "What is global ethics?" and "Why global ethics?" once we answer, "What is global ethics?" in a way which is globally satisfactory and acceptable then answering "Why global ethics?" will be relatively simple. The short answer to "Why global ethics?" is that many of the ethical dilemmas in the era of globalization are of global scope and global ethical frameworks and global solutions are required to address them. This reasoning can be seen paralleled in discussions about the revival of ethics in the West and claims that there is an emergence and proliferation of new ethical disciplines in response to new ethical dilemmas: bioethics as a response to new dilemmas emerging from scientific and technological advances; environmental ethics as a response to the environmental crisis; and corporate social responsibility (CSR) and business ethics as a response to the globalization of business, organizations and IT beyond the nation state and traditional spheres of governance (Widdows 2004, 2005).

At least some of the answers to the "Why?" global ethics question are—or at least are potentially—similar to the claims regarding the revival of ethics in the West. For example, the impetus behind the emergence of CSR and business ethics—that of attempting to regulate and ethically constrain the power of transnational corporations—are of global importance; and arguably more relevant

---

1   The terms "Western" and "non-Western" have been used in this chapter, even though they are problematic. The reasons for adopting them is that the debates we are considering in this chapter (from Asian values and bioethics) divide in this way rejecting "Western" ethics and defining all other ethics as connected. However, part of the purpose of the chapter is to show that this division is a false dichotomy and greatly exaggerated.

in the developing world where ethically dubious practices and exploitation such as child labor and sweatshops are more likely to occur (Jenkins 2005). Likewise the "Why?" which has brought environmental ethics into being are the ethical dilemmas of the environmental crisis, and issues such as climate change and global warming matters of global significance which again arguably impact disproportionately upon the developing world (Caney 2006). Accordingly some of the "Why?" ethics reasons behind the revival of ethics in the West are also applicable in providing answers to the "Why global ethics?" question. In other words there are good reasons for supporting ethical frameworks which are global in scope and application and thus clear positive answers to "Why global ethics?"

However, recognizing these reasons as sufficient to justify a shared global ethics framework—as being enough to answer the "Why global ethics?" question—depends on what constitutes the global ethics which is being endorsed. The critics of global ethics we will consider in this chapter find the reasons for global ethics not sufficiently compelling for them to support the global ethics they believe to be on offer. Accordingly, those who wish to promote global ethics and convince others to do so must address these criticisms and show that global ethics is indeed global (and not, as these critics claim, simply Western ethics). If this can be done and the reply to the "What?" question is "A truly global ethics!," then all will be able to support the compelling practical reasons for global ethics and so answer the "Why global ethics?" question. For if global ethics is globally applicable and relevant then the reasons for endorsing it—that global dilemmas, such as environmental, health and economic issues, require global solutions—will fall into place automatically.[2] The need for global approaches to such issues is not contentious and is in fact already happening—shown in the ever increasing proliferation of laws, codes and guidelines on issues of global bioethics for instance (Widdows 2007b), yet until the fear regarding the imperialism of the type of ethics is resolved global cooperation on these matters and other issues of global justice will not be forthcoming. This chapter will address these issues and the claims of those who currently cannot support a global ethics—even given the obvious need for global responses (the answers to the "Why?" question)—as they consider that the current answer to "What global ethics?" is only Western ethics. For such critics global ethics is merely a "new form of cultural imperialism or an ethical version of 'neocolonisalism'"(Maklin 1999) and destructive to non-Western forms of ethics and consequently should not be endorsed globally.

In order to explore these issues we will consider first the criticisms of Western ethics (especially human rights) levelled by the Asian values movement and then, more briefly, those put forward by a group of "developing world bioethicists" who dismiss global ethics as western and imperialist. It is important to note that we are not endorsing Asian values but rather suggesting that even in this criticism of global ethics there are parallels and possibilities within Western ethics for points of immediate connection. Hence our intention is not to oppose a liberal model

---

2   Elsewhere I have discussed in detail some of these practical global issues propelling global bioethics—for instance, medical tourism, sale of body parts, genetic governance and research in the developing world (Widdows 2007a).

of global ethics with an Asian one but rather to argue that current anti-global views are not as anti as they seem.

Nothing but Western Ethics!

First then we will turn to the critique of global ethics found in the debate surrounding human rights and their supposed Western nature: in the schema of this chapter the position of those who in answer to the "What is global ethics?" respond by saying "nothing but Western ethics?" and reject it accordingly.

This critique has come perhaps most vocally from the Asian values movement –associated originally with Malaysia and Singapore, although endorsed more broadly in the non-Western world, by thinkers and politicians across Asia and Africa (Barr 2002; Bauer and Bell 1999) and it is this critique we will examine.

The roots of this critique are generally traced to Lee Kuan Yew, former Prime Minister of Singapore, who is deemed by many to be the founder of the Asian values movement. Yew attributed Singapore's speedy economic achievements to such Asian values, asserting that "we were an Asian-Oriental-type society, hardworking, thrifty and disciplined, a people with Asian Values, strong family ties and responsibility for the extended family ... a common feature of Asian cultures, whether Chinese, Malay or Indian" (Yew cited in Barr 2002.). He has continued to promote such values and as recently as 1998 he acclaimed the "Asian values of hard work, sacrifice for the future, respect for education and learning and an entrepreneurial spirit" (Yew cited in Barr 2002). In a similar manner Mahathir, former Prime Minister of Malaysia, has promoted Asian values and overtly criticized "Western values," concluding that in the West,

> the community has given way to the individual and his desires. The inevitable consequence has been the breakdown of established institutions and diminished respect for marriage, family values, elders, and important customs, conventions, and traditions. These have been replaced by a new set of values based on the rejection of all that relates to spiritual faith and communal life. (Mahathir cited in Barr 2002)

From these beginnings the Asian values movement has grown and from this standpoint Western values have been denounced. The core criticism of the Asian values movement and "the most cogent focused on the effects of excessive individualism in Western societies" (Fukuyama 1998: 26), therefore, human rights and the individualism that underlies them, have been denounced as little more than carriers of Western values. These critiques have found resonance in a number of non-Western contexts. For example, Chinese thinkers have claimed common cause with the Asian values movement and have invoked Confucianism "as the native cultural ground on which to reject human rights concepts as alien, culture-bound, Western impositions" (de Bary 1998: 6). Such opponents claim that "the West's conception of human rights is too individualistic, and out of keeping with China's communitarian traditions based on Confucianism" (de Bary 1998: 6). In addition to such content criticisms, such as those about individualism, there are also more overtly political claims that rights are used by "the West" and they have become "weapons of aggression and domination in the hands of the powerful" (Dallmayr 2002: 174). This claim is not a "value claim" as such, although it touches on the relativism-or-not of values, but rather an assertion that rights and rights-talk, is "a mere tool of Western global hegemony" (Dallmayr 2002: 174).

The popularity of Asian values, as the concepts have spread across the developing world, is testament to fact that the movement captures something which the dominant Western constructs of ethics neglect, although this is not to say that these claims should be taken at face value. The motivations of the proponents of Asian values have been criticized and it has been claimed that the lauding of Asian values is simply a means to deflect accusations of human rights abuses and to support unjust authoritarian political systems (Sen 1997). A little less critically the promotion of Asian values has been viewed suspiciously as merely a convenient way to promote economic and political progress. These criticisms undoubtedly have truth in them and clearly value rhetoric has been used for dubious means and by the powerful to bolster the unjust social and political systems which support them. However, even if it is the case that proponents of Asian values have dubious motives this does not mean that there is nothing of philosophical and ethical interest in their claims nor that there is nothing in alternative value frameworks that is neglected in human rights frameworks as they are often presented. Thus, even if we are sceptical of some of the motivations of at least some of the proponents of Asian values, we are still justified in considering their accusations regarding the Imperialism of Western ethical frameworks. In particular the claim that human rights do not express universal values, but promote a particular Western view—an individualistic, liberal view—which is incompatible with non-liberal cultures is worthy of consideration. Thus, the issue is not the motivation of the proponents of Asian values, but whether there is something Imperialist and destructive in the attempt to expand the ethical frameworks of the West into global frameworks.

Similar concerns to those expressed about human rights by proponents of Asian values have been stated in the field of bioethics, most comprehensively by a group of Filipino authors who define themselves in opposition to "Western ethics."[3] This debate will only be introduced briefly, to illustrate that this debate is paralleled by similar debates in other fields and to prevent the dismissal of the "human rights versus Asian values" as a minor or irrelevant debate. Rather the human rights and Asian values debate is just one manifestation of a large and important debate which signals a deep unease and fundamental concern about the imperialism of rights and values.[4] These developing world bioethicists use similar rhetoric to the Asian Values proponents and are explicitly suspicious of "global" ethical concepts, suggesting that those in the developing world should be

---

3   This is an argument I have addressed elsewhere. See Widdows 2007b.

4   It is particularly tempting to dismiss this debate and the claims of the Asian values movement, given some of the obviously disingenuous uses of value rhetoric by the authoritarian regimes. However, this is to miss underlying value concerns which the clearly false and agenda-ridden political assertions subvene.

"cautious about claims on behalf of a global bioethics" (Alora and Lumitao 2001: xiii). The developing world bioethicists see non-Western ethics as fundamentally different from Western ethics.

To caricature these views, the Western view is of the autonomous and isolated individual and the non-Western view is of the connected, community-defined, relational-being. The two views are presented in stark contrast and as mutually exclusive. The claim of these developing world bioethicists is that:

> The focus of Western Bioethics is individual, elsewhere it focuses on social units. Western bioethics often is orientated to principles; Filipino, on the other hand, is not articulated primarily in principles but in lived moral virtues. Whereas Western bioethics is almost always expressed in discursive terms, Filipino bioethics is part of the phenomenological world of living experience. For the West, bioethics is a framework for thought, a conceptual system. For the Philippines it is a way of life, and embodied activity of virtue. (Alora and Lumitao 2001: 4)[5]

Thus in its Western guise—defined as individualist, principlist and conceptual—bioethics is rejected.[6]

In this brief sketch of the parallel debate in bioethics it is clear that there are common themes in the criticisms of global attempts at ethics—in the instances of both human rights and bioethics. Both are regarded by the critics not as being truly global but as essentially carriers of Western values and purveyors of particular individualist models of human beings and society which threaten other ethical frameworks and understandings of the self and society. However, even in these criticisms of global there is some hope for those who wish to work within a global ethical framework and a starting point for asserting global ethical scope and content. For rejection on these grounds is not, as it at first appears, rejection of the concept of global ethics per se, but rather the rejection of the type of ethics (Western ethics) that the Asian values movement and developing world bioethicists believe constitute global ethics. Indeed explicit claims are made for "regional ethics"—of the developing world or of Asian values—for example the bioethicists claim to have "produced: an authentic vision of the lifeworld of health care and bioethics in the developing world" (Alora and Lumitao 2001: xii) and provided "grounds for supporting the regionality of moral insights" (Alora and Lumitao 2001: xiii). If such regional ethics are possible then it would suggest that wide cultural divisions can indeed be crossed in ethical theory and practice. The question then is, if these divisions in the developing world, between very different religions (including all major world religions) and cultures can be bridged could the divide between Western and non-Western ethics not equally be bridged and a truly global ethics sought?

---

5   These authors indeed "Filipino" to represent the ethics of the developing world not just "Filipino ethics."

6   Elsewhere I have discussed this argument in more detail and argued that there is some truth in these critiques of the dominant form of bioethics which is predominantly individualist and principalist focusing on issues of individual choice to the exclusion of social, economic and communal concerns (Widdows 2007b).

Alternative Ethical Frameworks

Both of these criticisms of global ethics (whether in the form of human rights or bioethics) argue that global ethics is not global at all, but Western. They reject global ethics because they answer the "What global ethics?" as Western and thus see no reason to answer the "Why global ethics?" question positively. However, it could be that these critics are only rejecting one particular (and in some senses particularly dominant) version of Western ethics. We will now consider the validity of these criticisms and attempt to show that global ethics need not be the version of Western ethics that these critics fear and indeed that Western ethics itself offers resources for providing an ethics of a very different sort which overlaps in concerns and context with at least some of the ethics and values promoted by the Asian values proponents and the developing world bioethicists. In other words we will attempt to answer the "What global ethics?" question not with the answer of "an exclusively Western ethic" (which is the current claim of these critics), but with a clear response of "a globally derived and relevant ethics!" At the very least proponents of global ethics must engage with such criticisms and attempt to assert global ethics which is representative and globally relevant and recognisable. Indeed not to do so without examination is to appear imperialistic as it denies at the outset that alternative ethical visions contain value insights worthy of exploration and recognition.

The version of Western ethics as criticized by these non-Western critics is equally under attack within the Western tradition, and for reasons which are not dissimilar to those put forward by the Asian values movement and the developing world bioethicists. We will consider two such debates within the Western tradition, those of feminist ethics and virtue ethics (predominantly focusing on feminist ethics).[7] The intention is to show that these very Western traditions of ethics are not antithetical to the ethical frameworks of the critics above and thus they provide a different answer to the "What global ethics?" question and one which those who criticize global ethics could more easily endorse. If this is the case then in asserting a particular type of global ethics (a different answer to the "What?" question), even these critiques may be able to support global ethics and answer the "Why?" question affirmatively. If this can be achieved then the force of these criticisms of global ethics will be lessened as alternative ethical frameworks will be provided as models for a global ethics and the stark contrast between Western and non-Western ethics will be eroded. It is hoped that this will provide a more globally acceptable answer to the "What global ethics?" questions, and so encourage a shared recognition of the reasons why global ethics is necessary.

---

7   The reason for focusing on the feminist debate is that it has directly addressed the issue of rights, and thus speaks more directly to the "human rights" and "Asian values" debate. However, the virtue ethics position is interesting because, even though it does not address this debate directly, as the feminist debate does, the virtue ethicists do present a picture of morality which has at its heart many of the aspects of morality which have been claimed to belong to the ethics and worldviews of the developing world; namely the importance of moral virtues embodied in the experience of moral living and as part of a way of life.

First then, let us consider the feminist critics who have critiqued the gender bias of the dominant, individualist, Western constructions of ethics, and who concur with the non-Western critics that most of "Western political philosophy has been highly individual in character" (Hampton 1997: 169). Moreover, like these critics, feminists have emphasized the importance of difference and championed the values of social justice over those of individual choice (Donchin and Purdy 1999; Okin 2000, 2002; Shacher 1998; Tong 2001; Wolf 1996).

"Feminist ethics," like other generic terms denotes a vast range of perspectives: at one end of the spectrum are "liberal feminists" who are likely to suffer from similar criticisms as those levelled at broadly speaking liberal Western ethics (at least in terms of their championing of autonomy and choice over other values); at the other end of the spectrum are radical feminists who are at least as critical of liberal individualism as the non-Western critics we have been considering. However, with the exception of the extreme libertarian end of the liberal spectrum most feminist thinkers (including liberal feminist thinkers) share some of the frustrations of the liberal rights model expressed by the developing world critics recounted above and "the basic presuppositions of liberal political theory are often seen as conflicting with much feminist theorizing" (Held 2006: 76). Consequently almost all brands of feminists suggest that, at the very least, the liberal model needs supplementing, reforming and updating. In order to explore these feminist approaches we will consider the work of Carol Gould who draws on feminist thinking (including the ethics of care), to modify and enrich human rights perspectives and then we will consider the "ethics of care" directly and its uneasiness with rights and with the liberal model in its entirety (although even this framework still has some space for rights).

We will consider the work of Gould who is critical of some forms of liberalism and rights theory, stating that "it is by now commonplace to criticize traditional liberal democracy for its abstract individualism" (Gould 2004: 7). Gould uses feminist (and other) criticisms to dismiss certain types of liberal understandings without rejecting, indeed while greatly endorsing, the theory and practice of human rights. Thus Gould is a champion of human rights, but presents human rights in a way that counters at least some of the criticisms levelled at human rights by the Asian values movement and so makes rights less alien and more supportable to non-Western thinkers.

Gould rejects the extreme individualism which characterizes certain sorts of liberal theory and which is so offensive to Asian value proponents and the developing world bioethicists. Gould, following many critics of liberal individualism asserts the relationality and connectedness of human beings which mitigates against a conception of human beings as isolated, separate individuals.[8] Thus she supports a view of human beings as social beings, a recognition which has "become a truism in social philosophy" (Gould 2004: 63). However, although a truism it is one which has not yet fully entered liberal rights theory,

---

8   Within the Western framework not only feminist thinkers but also other thinkers, such as communitarians and the virtue ethicists, considered later in this chapter, are also critical of the radical liberal rights model.

and moreover impacted sufficiently on the assumptions and practices of the rights framework as it is implemented. The social nature of human beings is still neglected and too often liberal models do not recognize that "characteristics are not only interpreted but also constructed through the concrete interactions of particular caring and choosing individuals, who are often concerned for each other and make choices together with others with whom they are engaged in common projects and interdependent networks (economic, technological, social, cultural or personal)" (Gould 2004: 63). Gould endorses a rights theory based not on individualistic grounds, but on a "distinctive social ontology, in which the basic entities that make up society are understood as individuals-in-relations or social individuals, in place of the externally related individuals characteristic of traditional liberal theory" (Gould 2004: 63). In this view of "individuals-in-relation" the individualism of liberal theory is tempered as "the characteristic mode of being of these individuals, that is, their activity, essentially involves their relations with others" (Gould 2004: 33).[9] Accordingly while the focal agents of her model are "individuals" these individuals are not the autonomous separate moral loci of liberal individualism but are "concretely existing beings who are the bearers of their relational properties" (Gould 2004: 33). By basing her philosophy and rights constructs on such understandings of the self Gould is able to recognize the related and communal nature of human beings which critics of rights models, such as the Asian values critics and the developing world bioethicists consider lacking, without denying the moral significance of the individual and subsuming the individual into the community. Thus Gould asserts that her

> conception of rights does not reduce to some atomistic distribution of rights to individuals considered as isolates—a charge sometimes brought against rights conceptions in general. Human rights are always rights of individuals, based on their valid claims to conditions for their activity, but individuals bear these rights only in relation to other individuals and to social institutions. Right is in this sense an intrinsically relational concept. (Gould 2004: 37)

Moreover, Gould considers the so-called "Western" view of rights such as the version critiqued by the Asian values movement, a flawed perspective even in the West, and she argues that "to take human rights as simply an enunciation of an Enlightenment universalism of such an abstractly individualist sort is in error" (Gould 2004: 144). Put simply, individualistic conceptions of rights are unsustainable in any framework as "without the intersubjective ties among people presupposed here, the very concept of a right as such a claim on others would make no sense" (Gould 2004: 144). For rights to work in any context, Gould would argue, requires a relational understanding, and hence she claims that "from a distinctively feminist perspective, human rights can be said to emerge

---

9   For Gould this is true not only of rights thinking but all action in the political sphere, hence she asserts that "individuals-in-relations as the basis for the extension of democratic decision making to all context of common activity, whether political, economic or social" (Gould 2004: 4).

from a practical situation of care and concern, in the following sense: If people did not tend to care about the well-being and more generally the needs of others, then the claim that each can make on the others, however valid, would remain a bare one, and people would lack the motivation needed to take these claims of others seriously and structure society in such a way as to attempt to meet them" (Gould 2004: 144–5). Gould's relational understanding of rights goes some way to addressing the earlier criticisms as, although individuals remain key moral loci as rights-bearers, they are not isolated but embedded in caring relationships.

In addition to offering a less individualist understanding of rights Gould's position also echoes other elements of the Asian values critiques of "Western models." For instance, like them, Gould is critical of universal and essentialist claims, especially when they are "put forward as a basis for development and for human rights, because they may import Western liberal conceptions of norms of development and rights under the guise of the universally human" (Gould 2004: 51). On this point feminist critics again sympathize with developing world critics in their criticisms of abstraction suggesting that the resulting conception is "not a value-free, but rather a value-laden one, that it tends to reflect the interests, needs, and prejudices of particular social groups" (Gould 2004: 57). From a feminist perspective "essentialism tends to mask the particular interests under the guise of universality and therefore is deceptive" (Gould 2004: 57). In this vein Gould argues that "various great philosophers chose those properties as universally human that the philosophers themselves either explicitly identified as male properties, or that were associated with roles and functions in which males predominated... it seems possible that contemporary theories may similarly be introducing local characteristics from a particular social context under the guise of general human ones" (Gould 2004: 57). Thus again Gould is in sympathy with criticisms made against liberal rights and she concurs regarding some of the limitations of the dominant liberal position, however, Gould's solution is not to reject universalism and embrace relativism or regionalism (as the Asian values movement and developing world bioethicists wish to do) but rather to resist the importing of such local concepts in an attempt to avoid such local frameworks. Hence, she suggests "a more refined and less philosophically demanding conception of an abstractly universal norm, such that it can be more fully cross-cultural and less biased" (Gould 2004: 61).

In this way Gould's feminist critique offers a different vision of human rights and an alternative answer to the "What global ethics?" question, an answer which recognizes relationality and culture and which the critics we considered earlier may be more able to endorse and thus answer the "Why?" question positively. Gould proposes a global and representative understanding of rights, and sees the seeds of this approach in current human rights documents. Thus, although she accepts that the concept of human rights itself "seems much less multicultural in origin" (Gould 2004: 64),

the content of the United Nations list of human rights ... in fact reflects the conceptions of developing countries as much as those of North America and Western Europe in its extensive list of rights tied to basic needs , such as means of subsistence, health care and employment, as well as certain group rights, such as that concerning development. (Gould 2004: 64)

Such documents provide resources from which to revise and enrich global understandings of rights and to temper current dominant models.

Gould has a substantive proposal for how rights should be globalized in order to move towards more culturally representative and applicable constructs. However, one does not need to endorse her programme in its entirety to recognize that her feminist perspective offers a substantially different picture of ethics and rights than that which was criticized by the proponents of Asian values. Gould believes that rights are not Western inventions but

> are claims we make on each other as inherently social individuals ... [which] ... is a more communitarian notion that goes beyond the liberal tradition in Western thought and certainly has resonances, if not also roots, in other cultural traditions. (Gould 2004: 65)

She argues for some globally shared understandings and values as underpinning such rights, for example, she suggests that "the value of feelings of empathy and solidarity have been articulated by a wide variety of cultural traditions, in a way probably more widespread than rights discourse itself" (Gould 2004: 70). Yet while endorsing common core values Gould continues to respect diversity and cultural difference as necessary if truly representative global frameworks are to be instituted. Consequently she argues that

> the sort of globalising that is required entails an expansion of democratic modes of decision making and of human rights themselves, not only internationally but also beneath the level of politics, so to speak, in social economic and even personal life. Also needed is an increased attention to differences, especially as concerns the diversity of cultural groups and their interaction. It is apparent, too, that democracy and human rights, viewed as global norms, cannot be interpreted simply along the conventional Western lines with which we have long been comfortable, if they are to win more universal assent and measure up to their universal aims. (Gould 2004: 2)

Accordingly Gould sees global rights and values—in our terms global ethics—as "emerging from such an interaction of cultures" (Gould 2004: 63). In asserting this type of global conception Gould suggests that "we are respecting these cultures and not merely privileging our own" (Gould 2004: 63). For Gould then we are left with a truly global conception—or at least the potential for and tools to develop a truly global conception—avoiding both the imperialism or neo-colonialism of imposing an ethics and the relativism or regionalism which denies the global community and sees cultures as irredeemably disconnected.

Second, although Gould's feminist inspired vision of rights provides a substantial reworking of the rights model in ways which go some way to meeting the critiques of the Asian values position, for some this model still endorses too much of the liberal critique and so-called Western assumptions. Hence we will consider a more radical feminist model of the ethics of care. In this radical model the focus shifts further from the individual, even the individual-in-relation, to a focus on caring and caring relationships themselves (Noddings 1984; Gilligan 1982). The ethics of care offers alternative constructions of persons and value frameworks in which individuals are not isolated but relational and interdependent, "enmeshed in relations with others" (Held 2006: 156). In the ethics of care framework the "moral life is populated by caring relations in which the interests of self and others and mingled and trust is crucial" (Held 2006: 157).[10]

The ethics of care in its strongest form overtly critiques the liberal models as "from the perspective of care, the person seen as a holder of individual rights is the tradition of liberal political theory is an artificial and misleading abstraction" (Held 2006: 145). Again this type of thinking shows similarities with the critics of Western ethics and shows that there are alternative voices within the Western tradition who propose very different models of ethics and rights (in other words who have very different answers to the "What global ethics?" question) which should lead critics to reconsider their blanket dismissal of Western ethics and the assertion that global ethics is Western and by definition alien to other ethical frameworks.

The ethics of care is highly critical of the dominance of the liberal model of ethics believing that this model, if left without supplement from other models, "distorts reality by leaving out vast areas of human experience that it claims to apply to but in reality cannot cover" (Held 2006: 80).[11] In particular, "it fails to address, for instance, the appropriateness, implications and effects of treating just any social relations as if they were between independent, autonomous, self-interested individuals" (Held 2006: 80). Like Gould and the non-Western critics we considered earlier, Held regards the models of isolated individuals as false. Furthermore she considers such liberal positions to be damaging and pernicious and consequently endorsing such a model (and its corresponding ethics) either globally or locally (including in the West) is morally undesirable as it

> promotes only calculated self-interest and moral indifference in the place of caring and concern that citizens often have for fellow citizens (albeit less intense than for family and friends), that members of smaller communities still more often have for each other, and that most persons could have for other persons, even in foreign places

---

10   We will focus on the recent work of Virgina Held who has attempted to systematize the ethics of care, including the seminal works in this field of Carol Gilligan and Nell Noddings.

11   While critical of the liberal model it is not dismissed in its entirety, for example Held states not "that there is no room for standard liberal individualism, but the liberal ideology has been increasingly leaving no room for anything else. My argument is that there must be room for much more than liberal individualism for either persons or societies to flourish" (Held 2006: 77). Nor are the insights of the liberal model, such as the importance of individual autonomy abandoned: "This does not mean that we must choose between the ethics of care and due regard to autonomy. Many feminist moral theorists ... have been showing how autonomy as self-governance is compatible with (not antagonistic to) the ethics of care" (Held 2006: 83–4).

and distant lands ... Adopting the assumptions of liberalism contributes to making actual indifference to others more pervasive. (Held 2006: 83)

From this perspective the liberal model should be resisted and tempered as it

is not a morally good model for relations between persons ... To encourage morally better social relations we should limit rather than expand the use of the liberal, contractual model, both in our institutions and practices and in the ways we think about social issues. (Held 2006: 81)

Those who assert the ethics of care do not abandon autonomy as a key moral concept nor do they deny the moral significance of the individual. Rather they argue that

thinking of persons as relational does not mean that we cannot make autonomous choices to resist various of the social ties we grew up with or find ourselves in and to reshape any relations we maintain. (Held 2006: 84).

On the contrary, conceiving of persons relationally provides a far richer understanding of human being than the isolated liberal model as it recognizes that

we maintain some relations, revise others, and create new ones, but we do not see these as the choices of independent individuals acting in the world as though social ties did not exist prior to our creating them. (Held 2006: 84)

Unlike the abstract ideals of liberal theory the ethics of care also allows us to address social and economic issues so often regarded as secondary in liberal models, as it

requires us to pay attention to, rather than ignore, the material, psychological, and social prerequisites for autonomy. Persons without adequate resources cannot adequately exercise autonomous choices. Autonomy is exercised within social relations, not by abstractly, independent, free and equal individuals. (Held 2006: 84)

Thus from an ethics of care perspective (and again in accord with non-Western traditions) social and economic issues fundamentally underlie and connect with other questions of rights and justice, and thus dismissing social and economic rights and prioritizing civil and political liberal rights is nonsensical.

Feminist theorists are critical of liberal models of rights. Held (2006: 87) noted that many feminists were struck by how fully rights reflect masculine interests and how much the very concept of a "right" seems to clash with the approach of caring. For instance, Gilligan suggests that "a morality of rights and non-interference may appear frightening to women in its potential justification of indifference and concern" (Gilligan 1982: 22). However they have not rejected rights but suggested them be revised to include the values of care, difference and relationality. Such feminists while clearly recognizing the problems inherent in rights also grasp their usefulness and that "women and oppressed groups have used the language of rights to redress their grievances and will probably need to do so for the foreseeable future" (Held 2006: 140) and consequently "most feminists ... have come to accept the necessity of rights for feminist aims" (Held 2006: 88).

Given this staunch critique substantial effort is required to rehabilitate rights in a way which brings it into the ethics of care framework and counters the criticisms of the liberal conception of persons. Held argues that such reworking is possible and that rights

> can be interpreted as (1) demands for reformulations of existing schemes of rights, (2) calls to reconstruct the concept of rights, and (3) moral recommendations for limiting the reach of law to its appropriate domain and placing that domain in the appropriate context. (Held 2006: 142)

Thus, for Held it is not rights that are the problem but the way they have been presented and implemented. She argues that rights are not, or should not be, individualist in the way they have often been presented but that in fact, and in a not dissimilar claim to Gould, that rights presuppose care.

> Respecting rights within a society requires that persons care enough about each other to be willing to think of each other as fellow members of whatever groups or political entity is asserting or recognising such rights. (Held 2006: 159)

Such a picture has much in common with the approach of the developing world bioethicists and counters the criticisms of Western ethics levelled by the Asian values movement and for all these perspectives moral agents are regarded as "encumbered" and "embedded" in relations with actual other persons" (Held 2006: 84). Given these similarities such feminist thinkers argue that

> the ethics of care has resources to understand group and cultural ties and relations between groups sharing histories or colonial domination or interests in nonmarket economic development. (Held 2006: 157)

An approach of this sort they claim draws "on the understanding of care that can be developed from actual experiences of caring and being cared for, often across divergent cultures" (Held 2006: 158). Thus it forms an obvious base for global ethics as "the ethics of care is more suited than the ethics of justice for understanding the particularities of different situations, groups and cultures, to see what really will improve the lives of children, women and men" (Held 2006: 164). Therefore like Gould's feminist rethinking of rights, the ethics of care criticism of the liberal model and understanding of persons as characterized by their relationships is an ethical framework which has more in common with the models put forward by the Asian values movement and by the developing world bioethicists. Consequently if the answer to the "What global ethics?" question embodied these values it would be more difficult for the non-Western critics to reject global ethics as Western and alien. In feminist ethics we have seen alternative proposals of how to construct and revise ethics and rights and thus have gone a long way to proving that the criticisms levelled at Western ethics at best only apply to a particular version of such ethics and should not be levelled at Western ethics or global ethics per se. Such a discussion has shown that even within the West there are different answers to the "What?" question, hence there may be common ground between these alternatives and the views of non-Western thinkers and thus a possible global ethics.

Third, in addition to feminist traditions there are other schools of thought within Western ethics which offer alternative ethical frameworks and ones which have resonance with the frameworks and values put forward by the non-Western thinkers such as the virtue ethicists. We will briefly consider the virtue ethics position in order to show that this debate is not limited to this field but occurring in many fields.[12]

The beginnings of the virtue ethics movement—or more accurately its revival, as authors look to Aristotle and Plato for inspiration—are found in the last century. Its (re)birth is often traced to an article by Elizabeth Anscombe, published in 1958, in which she criticizes post-Enlightenment ethical theory and calls for moral philosophy to return to issues of moral psychology and human flourishing (Anscombe 1997 [1958]). Such an approach was championed by Iris Murdoch who termed the reductionism of post-Enlightenment moral theories—as a "void in present-day moral philosophy" (Murdoch 1970: 46)—now a standard criticism of dominant Western ethics.

Like the non-Western critics and the feminist critics the virtue ethicists are critical of the individualism of dominant liberal ethics. For example, Murdoch claims that post-Enlightenment moral philosophy has left us not with a more realistic, more complex, relational and historical account of the self, which accords with our experience, but with an over-simplistic and unrealistic picture which negates all thick theories of the self (Murdoch 1992: 150). This individualistic picture of the self excludes historical and relational aspects of human experience and is a view Murdoch believes represents "the ideal citizen of the liberal state" (Murdoch 1970: 80); it is the "democratic view" (Murdoch 1970: 9); "the liberal theory of personality" (Murdoch 1997 [1959]: 262); and the "natural mode of being of the capitalist era" (Murdoch 1997 [1970]: 224) a picture she regards as reductionist, unrealistic and simplistic.

Moreover, virtue ethicists do not focus on right acts or principles, but like Asian values proponents and the developing world bioethicists, in embodied and relational virtues and values. For example, Murdoch claims that morality is part of every aspect of human life—"morality must engage the whole man" (Murdoch 1992: 457)—a fact which should be reflected by philosophy and she asserts that:

> Any moral philosopher must (should) appeal to our general knowledge of human nature. Morality is and ought to be connected with the whole of our being...The

---

12   The virtue ethics position is only considered very briefly here to show the ubiquitous nature of these concerns, however, more detailed discussion of this debate is found elsewhere (Widdows 2007a, 2007b).

moral life is not intermittent, or specialised, it is not a peculiar separate area of our existence. (Murdoch 1992: 495)

This broad vision of morality as embedded in everyday life has been continued by contemporary virtue ethicists who have emphasized character, habit and virtue. For example, Charles Taylor has criticized the reductionism and destructive nature of post-Enlightenment predominantly liberal ethics and suggested, in a similar vein to those in the developing world, that "what is really going on is that some forms of ethical reasoning are being privileged over others" (Taylor 1999 [1982]: 139–40). Other thinkers making similar claims are Alasdair MacIntyre and his highly influential attempts to reclaim the virtues (MacIntyre 1982, 1988) and John McDowell and his work on virtues and moral realism (McDowell 1978, 1983, 1985, 2003 [1979]). However it is not necessary to discuss these theories in detail, suffice to say that like the feminist ethicists the virtue ethicists are promoting a type of Western ethics that does not fit with the model presented by non-Western critics. Moreover, considering virtue ethics and feminist ethicists shows that the criticisms of Western ethics put forward by the non-Western world are not alien to Western ethics, but are echoed by critiques from within the Western tradition. This is not to suggest that virtue ethics presents the same position as those critiques from the non-Western world, nor that a global ethic should be a form of virtue ethics any more than an exclusively feminist ethics.[13] What this discussion does suggest is that the gap between the ethics of "the west and the rest" has been greatly exaggerated. In fact, the concerns of these internal critics—for virtues, for a holistic picture of morality and about the reductionist nature of the dominant forms of Western ethics—are shared with the external critics.

Towards a Truly Global Ethics

Given these similarities it is clear that Western ethics is not necessarily alien to non-Western cultures and indeed there are many shared understandings. Therefore global ethics need not be an imperialist ethics but could arise from shared and truly global insights. Accordingly it is not too great a claim to say that the Western ethics, so criticized by the Asian values movement and the developing world bioethicists, is only one version of Western ethics and one which is regarded with suspicion and even fear within the Western system too, for example, in the feminist and virtue traditions. If this is the case then global ethics need not be the highly individualist and mechanistic ethics that currently dominates and moreover there are schools of thought even within the Western tradition, feminist ethics and virtue ethics being only two examples, that provide resources for reforming Western ethics and common cause with the non-Western critics.

---

13   Indeed MacIntyre and Taylor exhibit some of the wariness suggested by the developing world critiques: MacIntyre in his rooting of values in community (MacIntyre 1982) and Taylor's fear of "particularism masquerading as the universal" (Taylor 1994: 44).

Hence the debate on "what ethics" in the West suggests that the Asian values movement and the developing world bioethicists have a point when they criticize a particular liberal Western ethics. However, the same debate shows that the problem of "What global ethics?" lies not in an unbridgeable gap between the West and the non-West, but rather with a particular liberal discourse on rights that overemphasizes an individualistic and atomic notion of self and which is, because of that overemphasis, under attack even in the West.

Of course, feminist ethics, ethics of care and virtue ethics have, as philosophical positions also met their share of criticism—which due to space limits we have not touched upon. We can nevertheless offer the following important conclusion: The question "What global ethics?" will continue to feed a discussion, but that what needs to be discussed is whether to base a global ethical framework on individualistic or on relational notions of the individual and rights, rather than allow that discussion to run along geographical, cultural or religious demarcation. We hope that this chapter has contributed to show that the latter discussion is a false one. If we can avoid such a false discussion, then fears about imperialism and neo-colonialism can be allayed allowing the "Why?" question to be easily answered: "Why global ethics?" because "the problems and dilemmas we face are global and require global solutions!"

References

Alora, A.T. and Lumitao, J.M. (2001), *Beyond a Western Bioethics: Voices from the Developing World*. Washington: Georgetown University Press.

Anscombe, G.E.M. (1997 [1958]), "Modern Moral Philosophy," in Crisp, R. and Slote, M. (eds) *Virtue Ethics*. Oxford: Oxford University Press, 26–44.

Barr, M.D. (2002), *Cultural Politics and Asian Values—The Tepid War*. London and New York: Routledge.

Bary, W.T. de (1998), *Asian Values and Human Rights: A Confucian Communitarian Perspective*. London: Harvard University Press.

Bauer, J.R. and Bell, D.A. (1999), *The East Asian Challenge for Human Rights*. Cambridge: Cambridge University Press.

Caney, S. (2006), "Environmental Degradation, Reparations, and the Moral Significance of History," *Journal of Social Philosophy* 37(3), 464–82.

Dallmayr, F. (2002), "Asian Values and Global Human Rights," *Philosophy East and West* 52(2), p173ff.

Donchin, A. and Purdy, L. (1999), *Embodying bioethics. recent feminist advances*. Oxford: Rowman and Littlefield Publishers.

Fukuyama, F. (1998), "Asian Values and the Asian Crisis," *Commentary*, 23–7.

Gilligan, C. (1982), *In a Different Voice*. Cambridge MA: Harvard University Press.

Gould, C.C. (2004), *Globalising Democracy and Human Rights*. Cambridge: Cambridge University Press.

Hampton, J. (1997), *Political Philosophy*. Boulder, CO: Westview Press.

Held, V. (2006), *The Ethics of Care: Personal, Political and Global*. Oxford: Oxford University Press.

MacIntyre, A. (1982), *After Virtue: A Study in Moral Theory*. London: Gerald Duckworth and Co. Ltd.

MacIntyre, A. (1988), *Whose Justice? Which Rationality?* London: Gerald Duckworth and Co. Ltd.

Macklin, R. (1999), *Against Relativism: Cultural Diversity and the Search for Ethical Universals in Medicine*. Oxford: Oxford University Press.

McDowell, J. (1978), "Are Moral Requirements Hypothetical Imperatives?," *Proceedings of the Aristotelian Society* 52, 13–42.

McDowell, J. (1983), "Aesthetic Value, Objectivity and the Fabric of the World," in Schaper, E. (ed.) *Pleasure, Preference and Value: Studies in Philosophical Aesthetics*. Cambridge: Cambridge University Press, 1–16.

McDowell, J. (1985), "Values and Secondary Qualities," in Honderich, T. (ed.) *Morality and Objectivity: A Tribute to J.L. Mackie*. London: Routledge and Kegan Paul, 110–29.

McDowell, J. (2003 [1979]), "Virtue and Reason," in Darwell S. (ed.) *Virtue Ethics*. Oxford: Blackwell Publishing.

Murdoch, I. (1997 [1959]), "The Sublime and the Beautiful Revisited," in Conradi, P. (ed.) *Existentialists and Mystics: Iris Murdoch's Writings on Philosophy and Literature*. London, Chatto and Windus, 261–86.

Murdoch, I. (1970), *The Sovereignty of Good*. London: Routledge and Kegan Paul.

Murdoch, I. (1992), *Metaphysics as a Guide to Morals*. London: Chatto and Windus.

Noddings, N. (1984), *Caring: A Feminine Approach to Ethics*. Berkley and London: University of California Press.

Okin, S.M. (2000), "Feminism, Women's Human Rights and Cultural Differences," in Narayan, U. and Harding, S. (eds) *Decentering the Center: Philosophy for a Multicultural, Postcolonial and Feminist World*. Bloomington: Indiana University Press.

Okin S.M. (2002), "Mistresses of Their Own Destiny: Group Rights, Gender and Realistic Rights of Exit," *Ethics* 112(2), 205–30.

Jenkins, R. (2005), "Globalization, Corporate Social Responsibility and Poverty," *International Affairs* 81(3), 525–40.

Shachar, A. (1998), "Group Identity and Women's Rights in Family Law: The Perils of Multicultural Accommodation," *Journal of Political Philosophy* 6, 285–305.

Sen, A. (1997), "Human Rights and Asian Values," *The New Republic* (July), 33–40.

Taylor, C. (1994), *Multiculturalism*. Chichester: Princeton University Press.

Taylor, C. (1999 [1982]), "The Diversity of Goods," in Sen, A. and Williams, B. (eds) *Utilitarianism and Beyond*. Cambridge: Cambridge University Press, 129–44.

Tong, R. (2001), "Towards a Feminist Global Bioethics," *Healthcare Analysis* 9, 229–46.

Widdows, H. (2004), "Religion as a Source of Moral Authority," *Heythrop Journal* XLV (April), 197–208.

Widdows, H. (2005), "Why Global Ethics?," in Eade, J. and O'Byrne, D. (eds) *Global Ethics and Civil Society*. Aldershot: Ashgate.

Widdows, H. (2007a), "The Self in the Genetic Era," *Health Care Analysis* 15 (March), 5–12.

Widdows, H. (2007b), "Moral Neocolonialism and Global Ethics: An Investigation of the Issue in the Context of Bioethics," *Bioethics* 21(6), 305–15.

Wolf, S. (1996), *Feminism and Bioethics. Beyond Reproduction*. New York: Oxford University Press.

Chapter 7

Cosmopolitanism and Community[1]

Nigel Dower

There are a number of cosmopolitan theories. What they have in common—hence what makes these theories cosmopolitan theories—two aspects. First, a set of values is postulated as values to be accepted everywhere. Second, though there may be different views taken about the appropriate means to adopt, there is some notion of *active* responsibility to further these values and to oppose those who frustrate them, either through wilful wrongdoing or through commitment to inappropriate moral values. In this chapter I will argue for a specific kind of cosmopolitanism which I call solidarist-pluralist. This position will be arrived at after considering some of the objections to the *whole idea* of universal values and global responsibilities. Finally, a notion of global citizenship will be derived from the solidarist-pluralist position through discussing how cosmopolitanism is opposed but could be combined with communitarianism.

Objections from Non-Cosmopolitan Perspectives

While different theories of cosmopolitanism can be criticized on the relative emphasis they put on one of the two aspects characteristic to cosmopolitan theories (postulating universal values and how to further these values), there are also important objections to the *whole idea* of universal values and global responsibilities. I will briefly sketch out these objections and then formulate replies.

The Tendency towards Hegemony and World Government

The argument here is that the inner logic of the cosmopolitan theory would lead, if followed, towards world government, but before that the development of international institutions which would concentrate power in the hands of powerful nations, or perhaps at the present time just one—the USA. This has been the theme of a recent book by Zolo, entitled *Cosmopolis* (Zolo 1997).[2] It is significant that the title says "cosmopolis" rather than "cosmopolitan," that is putting emphasis upon the idea of a world "polis" or political institution rather

---

1   This chapter is taken from Chapter 5 of the second edition of *World Ethics—the New Agenda* (2007), with new introductory paragraphs and minor changes elsewhere.
2   Toulmin's earlier book *Cosmopolis* (1992) also criticizes the tendencies of modernity.

than on the idea of being a "world citizen." World government and indeed hegemony by a super-power are dangerous for various reasons but also lead to the following difficulty. [3]

The Projection of Universal Values and the Tendency towards Homogenization of Cultures

The danger is that those in positions of power project the values important to them as if they were universal values equally applicable to all peoples, whereas in fact values vary from culture to culture. What is in fact occurring, as writers such as Sachs and others argue, in that the development of the global economy is undermining local cultures in ways which are disastrous for human flourishing (Sachs 1992). We can call this the thesis of cultural pluralism, which is often associated with what the relativist claims (though as we shall see this is not necessary).

Inappropriateness of Idealism

A somewhat different argument is that the tendency of cosmopolitanism is to introduce ideals into decision-making and thus insofar as politicians or others are influenced by them, they may be led to do things which are inappropriate in the real world. Thus so-called Wilsonian Idealism is often criticized (by Carr and others) as leading to a disastrous peace settlement after the First World War. Woodrow Wilson's idealistic principles led to punitive action against Germany and the setting up of the unrealistic League of Nations, both of which arguably contributed to the return to war twenty years on. Analogously Anscombe criticizes pacifism on the grounds that by setting too high a standard, it sets all forms of violence on the wrong side of the moral fence and this in fact encourages the abandonment of ethical constraints in warfare (Anscombe 1970: 48).

The Prosecution of Holy War/Ideological Conflicts

Another related danger of cosmopolitanism is that in the name of particular religious or political ideals or ideologies which are seen by their adherents as universally applicable in a world which does not share those ideas, engagement with other countries in the world in order to "convert" them leads to conflicts of a military kind, and thus in the past to holy wars like the crusades, and more recently ideological conflicts between East and West, often through so called "proxy" wars in the Third World. There are dangers that conflicts between Western liberalism and Islamic theocratic ideals may lead increasingly to such conflicts in the future, as we are now witnessing in the polarization implicit in the "war against terror."

---

3   See also Chapter 9 in Dower 2007 for discussion of world government.

The Undermining of Loyalty to the State as Citizens

Another line of argument will be that insofar as ordinary citizens are concerned, the spread and strengthening of cosmopolitan ideals will lead to a weakening of respect for and loyalty to the state. Apart from pacifism, which has always been seen as in some sense subversive of the state because of a refusal to defend it in ways required (and because it provides a view of the world in which the state's legitimacy, premised on the right of military defence, is challenged), other forms of cosmopolitanism may lead to challenges to state authority. Someone who smuggled in refugees or gave sanctuary to them may do so inspired by a global ethic which certainly challenges state authority. If we are world citizens, can we still be state citizens, at least in the sense we have always assumed?

Replies

First, none of the theories as set out earlier strictly entails any of these consequences. As theories about a universal ethical domain, they leave open in many ways the issue of how these are to be translated into policies in the real world. Certainly certain theories are more likely to have some of these consequences. Marxism is more likely to endorse conflict, as are certain more proselytizing forms of religious faith. Libertarianism is likely in view of its robust defence of individual liberty as a universal value to lead to economic processes in the world which do indeed undermine local cultures. Any of the theories may lead a thinker, given her more detailed interpretation and development of the theory and her view of what changes in the world will most effectively realize these values, to advocate things which will lead to these consequences. A vigorous champion of human rights may well advocate intervention leading to conflict and may well promote ideals which lead to unintended unfortunate results.

One response of the cosmopolitan may be of course a *robust* defence of these consequences as acceptable. Yes, world government is something to be aimed at; modernization does require the transformation of traditional cultures; idealism may sometimes lead to bad consequences but sometimes that is the cost of acting on principle;[4] sometimes wars have to be fought in order to promote values not yet accepted elsewhere (because these values are after all right); and transformations in our attitude towards the state are exactly what we need.

The strategy adopted here however is that of accepting that the objections pick out some real dangers, but to argue for a version of cosmopolitanism which avoid these dangers. Not all cosmopolitan theories or normative positions are equally acceptable. Indeed the challenge in world ethics is as much to engage with alternative cosmopolitan theories and positions on norms to be advocated as to argue against those who would deny a global ethic altogether.

---

4   Note the deontological theme, illustrated by the Latin tag "fiat iustitia ruat coelum" i.e. "let justice be and the heavens fall."

Types of cosmopolitan approach

The kind of cosmopolitan ethic which I give next would I think not generally have the dangers we are considering (though it does involve a re-evaluation of the nature of citizenship, which I return to shortly).

Outline of a Normative Approach

Briefly the kind of cosmopolitan ethic I commend is as follows. An analysis of human nature shows that there are a number of main elements of human well-being or flourishing: nutrition, health, shelter, security, family, community, liberty/autonomy, recreation, exercise of (other) rational capacities.[5] Because of their tendencies towards selfishness human beings need to live in society, which is an intrinsic good as well. To live in a society certain basic rules are needed: non-deception, non-coercion, respect for life, liberty and property, benevolence. But this recognition of the need for society requires us, on rational reflection, to accept all of humanity as part of society, as susceptible to the good and bad impacts of our actions, including omissions, for which we are responsible. It also requires us to extend concern to non-human life as well. But our responsibility towards others is coupled with a recognition that the ways people interpret the basic goods and the basic rules may be somewhat varied, and it is not our business to impose our conception of the good and the right on others. Responsibility requires us, in accepting a value such as truth or justice, not only to act justly or truthfully but also to promote these values. This responsibility is extensive but not exhaustive, since the right to pursue our own lives and to have particular attachments and relationships is also to be sustained.

What is important to the kind of world ethic qua set of agreed principles which I am trying to develop and which both expressed the above values and would be supported by a range of theoretical approaches, is this: (i) it is sufficiently broad to allow for diverse manifestations of value in different contexts and to allow for diverse intellectual sources of support; (ii) its main elements of global responsibility will be (a) commitment to maintain (and promote) the conditions of well-being, peace, justice and environmental care, that is commitment to not harming others and helping them in respect to the primary elements of human well-being; along with (b) commitment to respect for diversity, both in relation to life-style and culture and with regard to beliefs including beliefs about moral values.

The distinctive nature of the approach which I call "solidarist-pluralist" will become clearer if we contrast it to two other approaches. All these approaches are cosmopolitan in both the respects indicated earlier. First, a set of values is postulated as values to be accepted everywhere. Second, there is some notion of *active* responsibility to further these values and to oppose those who frustrate them, either through wilful wrongdoing or through commitment to inappropriate moral values, though there may be different views taken about the appropriate

---

    5   But note that not all have to be satisfied in any one life for that life to go well.

means to adopt. Indeed one of the hallmarks of any global ethic which is presented as cosmopolitan is precisely the emphasis upon positive responsibility to further what is valuable. Put formally, if x is a basic value (truth, liberty, peace, reverence for nature), then ethically we are not merely committed to expressing these values in our own behavior (acting x-ly) but also to promoting x in appropriate ways.[6]

It must be stressed that there are no sharp divisions: the different elements of each position could be combined in different ways. In any case perceptions will vary. A libertarian who vigorously promoted individual liberty by opposing other illiberal cultures would merge into a form of idealist-dogmatism (and would be perceived by others as such), but if he stressed the liberty of others in other cultures to choose a non-individualist way of life, his position would merge into pluralism. Likewise in the pursuit of social justice and human rights someone who saw himself as a solidarist-pluralist may be seen as a dogmatist by others. What follows is a kind of framework for interpreting approaches, it does not provide a simple or agreed analysis.

Idealist-Dogmatic

First, there is what I shall call, somewhat stipulatively, an idealist-dogmatic cosmopolitanism which asserts a fairly specific and definite set of moral norms or ideals, which it sees as emanating from the specific worldview, religious or metaphysical, which it also asserts. What is important to this kind of view is not only the set of values which is recognized as not generally accepted elsewhere in the world, but also the worldview from which the values emanate, which it also sees as important that other people and societies, with other worldviews, ought to accept. Such was the basis of much religious crusading and proselytizing in the past. It is currently a feature of fundamentalist Christianity, as well as of militant Islam (though we must note that this is not as such a general characterization of Islam or Christianity in the modern world). It is also a feature of some modern worldviews of a non-traditional religious kind. A militant humanism or atheism which saw the suppression of religion as important to its goals would be one such, but so too would a radical ecological outlook which saw it as more important that other people give up their anthropocentric *views* than that they give up environmentally destructive lifestyles, whatever their reason for doing so. Whilst the passionate pursuit of an ideal may well be done through negotiation and dialogue, there is a greater tendency within this approach than within the others to let the end justify the means in terms of the use of coercion and manipulation.[7]

With regard to the type of world ethic which is a proselytizing world ethic, where the goal is projecting one's own specific values (seen as universal) and

---

6   A "global" ethic could assert certain universal values but make light of or deny any duty to promote these values worldwide, but it would hardly be called "cosmopolitan." See "Introduction" in Dower 2007.

7   See Ceadel 1987: ch. 4 for discussion of "crusading" approach. He distinguishes five approaches, militarism, crusading, defencism, pacific-ism and pacifism which, whilst not the same as my distinction, are sensitive to the same kinds of issues of ends and means.

thus converting the rest of the world to it, two issues can be raised. Practically, one has to argue that this approach, especially if it comes up against alternative proselytizing approaches, simply results in antagonism at various levels, wasted energy and at worst destructive conflict and states of affairs which undermine other universally accepted goods which the different worldviews would include as desirable. Theoretically, the issue is also raised as to whether it is even desirable that the worldviews of all peoples should be the same or that people should behave the same ways. So long as a common framework is observed that enables people to lead fulfilled lives, the variety of ways of living should be no problem, and similarly though with a qualification the variety of worldviews is no problem.

The qualification is this: worldviews, whether religious or otherwise, have a "truth" component, as indeed many views of ethics, ethical beliefs and theories have themselves. Am I saying then that it does not matter whether different individuals or groups hold different beliefs about what is true and hence that some hold false views? I am not arguing this nor am I saying that disagreement about truth matters in other areas but not in respect what is important in ethics, because that prejudges the issue as to whether there are ethical truths which matter, as opposed to certain patterns of satisfactory behavior. But there is an issue concerning the relative importance of the correctness of intellectual formulations, in religion or ethics, as compared with certain patterns of articulated practice. If we accept the importance of the latter, we may be in a position to see the issue of intellectual disagreement in a context that shows that the need to make everyone else believe what I believe does not have such great importance.

Libertarian-Minimalist

Second, there is what may be called the libertarian forms of cosmopolitanism. This on the face of it is at the other extreme in that it precisely does not advocate a specific set of values, but rather stresses the value of freedom or choice, coupled with a rejection of intervention, aid or generally the positive *promotion* of goods. There is no general duty of doing this, as opposed to the duty not to harm others, though action to establish freedoms and oppose illiberal practices may be seen as right, and in terms of the ethics of the means, there will be a general preference for the way of consent. However organized attempts to come to the aid of others generally represent a form of interference which is contrary to the principle of liberty. The trouble with extensive aid is that it requires bureaucratic structures which are invasive of liberty, privacy and so on. Such a view tends to be supportive of the society of states and the more limited "morality of states" and of course to be supportive of the global economy and the principles of the global free market.

Theoretically in allowing people to do their own thing, to pursue their own conception of the good, this view allows not only for personal diversity but also cultural diversity, since the way a group lives should be up to them as well. However, although it is opposed to the dogmatic forms of cosmopolitanism, there is a danger that it assumes its own forms of dogmatism, insofar as its stress on the free choice of individual agents is not neutral between different value conceptions in different parts of the world but is a specific value of a liberal Northern culture and therefore insofar as it is present to or projected onto the rest of the world, it becomes a value to be promoted elsewhere where it is not already accepted. The current dominance of the Western market model of economic development as the key to the good life can be seen as a combination of a minimalist approach in some aspects with an attempt to proselytize for a dominant image of the good life on the other.

Both the acceptance of the global free market and the acceptance of the morality of states can be seen as expressions of this libertarian approach. As such this approach may be supported by a number of different theories, and thus constitutes an important form of consensus or agreed global ethic. There is however another kind of agreed global ethic and that is the one which I have characterized as "solidarist-pluralist," to which we now return.[8]

Solidarist-Pluralist

Third, there is the cosmopolitanism in the middle, which can be called solidarist-pluralist, and takes its starting point to be the observation that if ethics is about enabling people to flourish and to flourish as far as possible consistent with other people doing so, we need to be clear what the basic conditions of flourishing are (cf. the idea of responsible pluralism, e.g. in Drydyk 2003). The basic values of peace, reliable access to elements of well-being (food, shelter and so), a healthy and resource-full environment to live in, stable community and relationships, autonomy (in the sense of a level of self-direction which enables a person to have dignity) need to be affirmed. Of course a libertarian or an idealist cosmopolitan may by and large agree with this list. But whereas the idealist thinker will see this as only the starting point for a wider set of objectives to be pursued (the acceptance of specific values and beliefs), and the libertarian will in stressing liberty as the value sustained by the other goods, downplay the level of obligation needed to make it possible for all to enjoy these values, the solidarist-pluralist cosmopolitan will deny the importance of promoting these other values and beliefs but assert the importance of obligations at the global level to bring these values into existence. That is, he or she will combine the twin values of plurality or diversity and global solidarity or global responsibility; solidarity because we need a firm basis of positive obligation to promote these goods, and plurality because in not being as concerned about whether other people's beliefs and values are the same as her own, she is saying in effect "differences of values and beliefs between individuals and cultures do not matter as much as the promotion of common and indeed commonly agreed values." She will almost certainly have her own more complex set of values plus supporting theory, but the promoting of these is not seen as of overriding importance or indeed relevance. Up to a certain point diversity of belief and practice is something to celebrate anyway.

---

8   My criticism of the conventional "morality of states" has already been given in Chapter 3 of Dower 2007. My criticisms of the libertarian basis of the global economy are given in Chapter 7 of Dower 2007.

There are two abiding motivations for the kind of approach I have advocated. First, we need desperately an ethic of global responsibility (reflected in changed state priorities) for dealing with the evils in the world—poverty, environmental degradation, lack of peace and so on. Second, we need a humble recognition, at least for those of us coming from Northern cultures, that in discharging this global responsibility we should not be in the business of promoting or projecting values—ideas of the good life and ways of living in society—which are actually culturally specific to our own cultures. There is a great need to respect the great cultural diversity in the world, to allow for significant variations in the ways people pursue development and so on. One of the great dangers, to be explored later, is precisely that in the name of development we are projecting a specifically Eurocentric model of development on the rest of the world, which for a variety of reasons may not be appropriate.[9]

What matters then to the cosmopolitan position I am advocating is the building of consensus of agreed values, not the finding of or the creation of agreed fundamental beliefs. This does not mean that she is not opposed to other beliefs. She is certainly not seeking the lowest common denominator. She is opposed to dogmatic cosmopolitanism as much as to denials of cosmopolitanism altogether, as she will be opposed to libertarian versions which deny extensive global obligations and endorse models of development that actually make things worse for the poor. But she is seeking alliances of convergence for practical principles and policies, in order to build a world ethic as a social reality of genuinely shared values. In many ways the position I am developing is similar to that put forward by Arne Naess, since he recognizes that what is important in the environmental movement is agreement in practice to oppose the dominant economic paradigm, not agreement on the "ecosophies" themselves which are diverse.[10] Whilst the position does not rule out the use of force *in extremis*, its strong preference will be for the way of peace, dialogue and negotiation.

The Issue of Pluralism

More needs to be said about pluralism in order to distinguish it from the relativism which I criticized earlier. The three main differences are that the assertion of pluralism is linked first to the assertion of global responsibility; second there is still assumed to be a common value framework but one which allows variable interpretations; and third, there are limits to what is seen as acceptable. The following remarks will bring out the differences.[11]

First, however we characterize universal human goods, this needs to be done with a sufficient degree of flexibility and sensitivity to significant variations in

---

9   For a balanced survey of different cultural values see Laszlo 1993.

10   Naess 1989: ch. 2. Hans Küng argues similarly for peace values (Küng 1990). See Chapter 6 of Dower 2007.

11   For a useful discussion of pluralism, see Kekes 1993. He also sees pluralism as a middle way between traditional objectivism and relativism. The general upshot is similar, but the theory somewhat different.

interpretation. These variations according to cultural or personal factors may be, for instance, in the values associated with liberty or autonomy, with stable relationships, and with community and participation in it. The duty of others to respect these ways of living depends on the general value of these things like liberty and relationships, even though there may be variations in how these things are interpreted both between and within societies.

Second, the fact that some moral rules or principles are seen as universal does not entail that all such rules have to be seen as universal. Some rules and customs within a society may simply have local significance and validity. One of the reasons for this is that part of the moral force of rules (the cosmopolitan cannot accept "all") derives from what is established and customary and thus, because agreed upon, has the moral force which agreements as such, as a universal value, carry. That is, promising, contracting, agreement or consent are not merely acts, states or processes which create obligations in otherwise neutral individual acts but can also create obligations which inhere in new social structures and rules of behavior.

Third, whatever the variations in non-universal culturally specific norms and in expressing universal values, it remains true that certain goods and rules have a universal validity, because they are preconditions for the more specific forms of life and the moral culture which depend on them. Access to subsistence and adequate means to a range of actions which make up a meaningful life, generally good health, a healthy environment, freedom from arbitrary attack (basic security), along with the basic ground rules of not lying, killing, attacking, breaking promises, can all be seen as universal features of any society, and therefore give rise to obligations, in principle if not in practice, in others in other societies not to undermine those preconditions.

The acceptance of diversity of values is not meant to be an "anything goes" approach, amounting to a *de facto* relativism of values. If one is to avoid being shipwrecked on the Scylla of the traditional objective of proselytizing or missionizing promotion of values, there is of course the danger of hitting the other rock, the Charybdis of relativism. The need to steer a middle course between these two extremes is part of the challenge for anyone advocating a sensitive but radical world ethic. My view is not meant to be, and I hope is not perceived to be, an admission of relativism. This is for two reasons. Global obligations are a central part of the story, and they are what are denied by relativists. More to the point, the argument is not that all values—all ways of thinking of the good or of moral rules—are equally valid and are simply to be accepted because they are dominant in a given culture.

Some values are to be seen as universal, even if needing to be characterized in fairly non-specific terms, and it may well be the case that what is dominant or practised in a society simply is not acceptable from this universal point of view. This may be both because certain elementary rules are simply ignored or distorted in established practice, as when there are violations of the kinds of human rights which concern Amnesty International, or because what is established may well be a reflection of a certain power structure which simply does not reflect the perceptions and values of other groups in society. These may be majorities, like blacks in Apartheid South Africa, or minorities such as persecuted religious sects or ethnic groups, or just half of a population, in the case of women in a male-dominated society.[12] Discrimination, persecution, exploitation and slavery are all extreme examples of the more general phenomenon of voices not heard which should be heard.

No one, least of all me, is pretending that deciding what is legitimate cultural variation and what is not is an easy business. It is not. Many controversies will exist over these issues. But the framework has to be acknowledged in which these dilemmas arise. It would be a false escape either to retreat into an old-fashioned "we know what is right and good and the rest of the world had better change" or to retreat into a relativist "whatever is thought good or right is good or right," which apart from anything else undermines the whole idea of global responsibility anyway.

Cosmopolitanism and Communitarianism

Underlying communitarianism (and this is what makes it problematic to go hand-in-hand with cosmopolitanism) is the general idea of morality arising from socially constituted community and the implications it has for the relations which *individuals* have to others in the rest of the world (see Sandel 1982; Taylor 1989). The idea is a more general one partly because there may be many kinds of community, small or large, linked to a geographical area or made of up members geographically spread out, none of which are communities corresponding to political units. The same issues concerning the relationships between members of such communities and those outside them arise.

Communitarianism

The communitarian position entails two claims: first a descriptive claim, then a theoretical/normative claim.

Descriptive   Ethical relations as a matter of fact exist in terms of how they are perceived to be and are embedded in social practices and traditions. Conceptions of well-being and identity are not given in the abstract but grounded in concrete cultural particularities of time and place. The relations which people have with the community or society as a whole, to the "nation" or the "state" are of central significance in their lives. It is in the context of shared values and social sanctions

---

12   One of the biggest gaps in this work is a lack of discussion of feminism's contribution to thinking about international relations. Some though not all feminist themes are I believe reflected in my approach and may have influenced it indirectly—questioning hierarchical models, celebrating difference, and valuing caring and the way of peace and negotiation. These values are all supported by feminism, as indeed postmodernism and ecological visions, but I do not see them as essentially depending on such theories. See Peterson 1992 and Robinson 1999.

that most people are adequately motivated to act in accordance with the agreed norms.

Theoretical/normative What is important however to the communitarian approach is usually the theoretical understanding that goes with the above analysis, namely that these facts about the social constitution of ethical norms provide us with the key to their justification. Ethical norms are justified precisely by being embedded in custom, convention and tradition. The values of people's identities are indeed constituted by the social context of their lives. The society, the nation or the state do provide the context in which the nature and scope of ethical norms and values are to be located. One of the key elements in this style of thought is the recognition of the importance of the *contingent* in the formation of people's identities and moral values. That is, what is important is the particular time and place one lives in, the particular traditions one is part of, the national group one happens to be born into and so on. These are "non-rational" elements, because in a sense they are arbitrary and not something equally relevant to any rational agent.

On the face of it, the general thrust of communitarianism seems to be in conflict with the general thrust of cosmopolitanism and to give support for a global scepticism and for either internationalism or international scepticism. The communitarian is saying that moral values arise out of actual community and shared traditions, whereas the cosmopolitan goes back to a basic theory which his own reasoning supports and says in effect, "given my reading of human nature, the human situation, what reason requires, and so on, these are the values which apply to human relationships generally." However the conflict is not direct nor, as we shall see, necessary. Although communitarian thinking can support and be linked with ethical relativism, it need not be. Whereas relativism precisely denies what the cosmopolitan theory asserts, communitarianism has a different primary agenda, and allows for various possible account of values in the world as a whole. What follows is a somewhat schematic consideration of different logical possibilities, and how one might respond to each.

Why is There a Conflict?

In fact the opposition between communitarianism and cosmopolitanism can be seen potentially in several different respects. First, they may be in conflict over the *source* of moral values, as I have just indicated. Second, they may in conflict over the *nature* of moral values. If the cosmopolitan says that there are moral values which are universal and obligations which are global in scope, the communitarian may say that because there is no relevant global community, such values and obligations do not exist. Or as a variation, there may be a conflict over the *strength* or *importance* of global norms, if the communitarian says they are weak because that is the extent to which they are accepted in a weaker global community, whereas the cosmopolitan claims that they apply in principle and with a strength in practical terms that is not generally acknowledged.

Clearly the conflict will be most conspicuous if the first two bases of conflict are combined. That is, there is a disagreement both about the source or validation of moral norms and about whether they exist at all at the global level. Elsewhere I have used arguments against relativism as arguments against communitarianism (Dower 2007). Briefly, it conflicts with deep intuitions that we do stand in some kind of ethical relations to all human beings simply in virtue of our common human-ness, it undermines the idea of progress measured by any common yardstick, renders unintelligible internal minority dissent, and makes external assessment of social practices problematic.

The disagreement would not be as intense if for one reason or another the communitarian did acknowledge the existence of global values in some form. This might arise in a number of different ways. First, if he thought that some kind of global moral community already exists, as evidenced by levels of agreement about core values and duties of mutual aid. Second, if he recognized that many global organizations are made up of individuals who share global ideals, that is moral values internal to the organizations in question and thus part of their globally shared traditions and agreed norms. Third, if people generally within one's own community shared concerns for the outside world, cosmopolitan values could become part of the traditions of that society.

Let us suppose that sometime in the future there emerged a world in which all these features above were *well* established—well established global community, many people endorsing global values through the organizations they belong to, and a strong sense of commitment to other human beings internal to most communities throughout the world. If this happened, the strength of commitment to global responsibility would not be weaker than what a cosmopolitan advocates. Indeed, such an outcome would be exactly what a cosmopolitan wanted. For reason to be developed below, the best hope for any cosmopolitan theorist to get what his theory recommended actually done is to create the characteristics of community just indicated. So the eventual convergence of what the communitarian stresses as necessary to morality and what the cosmopolitan recognizes as the necessary means to what she advocates would be recognized.

However, even in these cases where it is recognized that the world as it is now has actual levels of moral concern for the rest of the world, and that in the future such concerns might be well established (to the heart's content of a cosmopolitan), there would still be a fundamental area of disagreement, namely about the nature of the source of those values. The existence or strength of cosmopolitan values do not depend upon what is already established in a global community. Nor are cosmopolitan values contingent upon what a community happens to care about. If people in a country happened to care about distant poverty but what made that valuable was the fact that the values are shared and accepted, then if that community ceased to care or never had cared, it would no longer be or would not have been a value. Such contingency is contrary to the cosmopolitan position. Third, the moral conventions within a country may be no more right, in the last analysis, than the morality of states, and the fact that they are in either case accepted does not cut off the question: are the norms acceptable or adequate? Convention, custom and tradition are neither necessary nor sufficient for valid moral claims to be made. What is customary even at the global level may be wrong and something that ought to be done may not be accepted as a duty. On its own then communitarianism would seem to be seriously inadequate.

Can We Combine Them?

Do we have to take communitarianism on its own though. Perhaps there is some way in which we can combine the strengths and insights of communitarian's thinking with some form of cosmopolitan theory? After all many of the values in a society, to do with conceptions of well-being and social norms, do seem to vary, as we noted in the section on pluralism, and their being valuable in the way they are can be accounted for by the fact that they are shaped and accepted in the traditions of that society. The fact that they are contingent does not necessarily make them ethically questionable. Communitarianism also provides useful insights about the conditions necessary for the general observance of moral norms.

There are three ways in which one can respond to the disagreement between the two positions. The first is to accept the conflict as fundamental, and argue for one against the other. The second is to adopt a strategy of *mutual accommodation*, and argue that both theories have part of the truth about the nature and source of ethical values. The third approach is one of *assimilation*, that is of taking one approach as fundamentally correct but interpreting various features of the other approach as *derivative* from the basic theory (and mistaken by its advocates as being fundamental).

Both the latter two strategies seem promising. Although the kinds of ethical theory—Kantianism, Utilitarianism, Natural Law—associated with cosmopolitanism tend to be presented as *the* bases of morality, thus excluding any other type of theory as well as each other, there is no reason why morality could not be seen as deriving from a variety of sources. Certainly, communitarianism can readily be seen as open to the possibility of there being a layer of obligation we have towards fellow human beings in virtue of our human-ness, *alongside* the values which arise from established society. This is one reason why communitarianism cannot be identified with relativism. Part of the attraction of pluralism is that there may be a variety of ways in which moral values arise.

But it is one form of the third strategy which I adopt here, that is to argue that cosmopolitanism is basic and that many of the things which the communitarian stresses can be seen as applications or expressions of universal values. But we need to recognize that it is possible to adopt a "communitarian cosmopolitanism" too. Thus a communitarian might argue that idea of universal values and global responsibilities arise naturally out of the traditions of societies and increasingly in the modern world out of the shared values of the "society of societies" (Thompson 1992).[13]

---

13 Nagel discusses these issues of strategy in several papers in Nagel 1979. His distinction between agent-centred ethics and outcome-centred ethics, both of which he argues have some validity, is similar to but not the same as the distinction between communitarianism and cosmopolitanism respectively.

Why do I prefer my form of cosmopolitan thinking? First, since agreement and consent are universal values (they are not valuable merely because people have agreed to value them), many practices and ways of life peculiar to local domains are indeed valuable. Second, the existence of a political order and participation in it are indeed important both because such arrangements are necessary means to the fulfilment of universal values but also because, as Aristotle stressed, such participation is an intrinsic and important good (Aristotle 1988: esp. bks 1 and 2). Third, apart from the political order, living in communities is both valuable in its own right and a vital source of motivation for moral agency. Thus a cosmopolitan might say that the values internal to living in a particular community are to be derived from a fundamental theory as expressions of it.

My reasons for preferring this strategy are twofold. First, it is theoretically sound. Whatever the practical importance of values established in community, we will not seek to *create* them, unless we have moral reason to do so, prior to and independent of their creation. Second, unless we have a fundamental ethical basis, we will not be able to argue for significantly progressive cosmopolitan obligations. Without this we will not counterbalance the tendency in practice for communitarian arguments to resist active expressions of global citizenship.

In the mid-1990s there was an interesting and important exchange between Martha Nussbaum and her critics in a special edition of *The Boston Review*, in which she defended cosmopolitanism and the need for a cosmopolitan education (Nussbaum 1994; see also Cohen 1996). It is very striking that in this debate very few of the respondents actually reject a framework of a global ethical kind in which it is acknowledged that there are duties towards the world's poor, to protect our common environment and defend human rights. But most of the writers nevertheless reject Nussbaum's call for "cosmopolitan education" which would take seriously the *teaching* of the idea that we are citizens of the world. Their reasons for rejecting this are various but many were ringing the communitarian bell that identities have to be primarily national. In another context Alasdair MacIntyre, whilst he is not hostile to some framework of common values in the background (after all he is deeply influenced by the natural law approach) nevertheless rejects strongly the idea of world citizenship on the grounds that makes us rootless citizens of nowhere lacking any real identity in a particular culture (quoted in Almond 1990: 102).

What the responses to Nussbaum's article showed was not only great resistance to cosmopolitan education in the American context but also, more positively, the point that the issue is not simply between good cosmopolitan education and bad national citizenship education. Both cosmopolitanism and patriotism can have their pathologies as well as wholesome forms. If the cosmopolitan education was informed by a less than satisfactory set of values like a form of fundamentalism, as discussed earlier, that would not be better than an education which taught a pride in national identity and loyalty but with a "live and let live" approach to other cultures and countries. If an education in citizenship stressed, as officially the American way of life or constitution reflects, the ethical values of liberty, democracy and respect for rights and these are seen as universal values, then in principle such a citizenship could inform enlightened foreign policy. But if that education was based on the idea of the superiority of one's own nation or country and the legitimacy of putting one's own country's interest before all others, then that would be unsatisfactory because it was inconsistent with reasonable cosmopolitan values. There is therefore a false tension between the two kinds of citizenship, and cosmopolitanism needs to acknowledge the importance of ordinary citizenship and indeed the values of established community (see also Tamir 1993 and Tan 2004 on the complex relationship between cosmopolitanism and nationalism).

Although I have indicated my reasons for preferring a cosmopolitan theoretical basis and seeing communitarian values as both expressions of this and means towards its fuller realization, it remains important to stress the two senses of global/world ethic discussed earlier. If a global ethic is an ethic widely shared across the world, then in effect we have a community of shared values and if that shared-ness is not merely coincidental but the product of negotiation, consultation and transnational dialogue, then even more evident is the emergence of global community. As Parekh notes, an emerging global ethic should be one we can both assent to and consent to (Parekh 2005: 27). I have already stressed the importance of assent—which each one of us can give, given our (different) comprehensive intellectual/spiritual standpoints. But part of the rapprochement between communitarianism and cosmopolitanism is precisely the recognition that an ethic needs consent too and the wider the better, consistent with fidelity to our own starting points, and that this consent is also part of what gives the shared values their validity.

Global Citizenship

We can now return to the idea of global citizenship and consider what the appropriate form of implementation is. Does global citizenship really exist in the world today? If so, is it in competition with or complementary to the citizenship we have as members of particular nation-states? We can state the position as follows. The idea of global citizenship as something strictly analogous to ordinary citizenship simply has no application in the world as it is. The idea of global citizenship as the assertion that we have duties in principle towards all fellow human-beings is of course both intelligible and, if the arguments of this book are sound, valid. It does not however depend at all on whether or to what extent global institutions exist to give it expression. What we need to recognize is that there is something between the two interpretations which is important to advocate and for which the nature of international institutions is important and critical.

To be a global citizen in this sense is first to accept the moral thesis above that one has duties in principle towards anyone in the world; second, to believe that there are a range of ways in which individuals can act so as to make a difference towards what happens in the world; third, to engage to some extent in patterns of action which one believes to be an exercise of one's global responsibility, patterns of action which one would not have engaged in but for this belief. What any individual does may of course vary considerably from private acts of, say, recycling glass, not using one's car when one could have done, giving donations to a third world charity, to active engagement in NGOs campaigning for change on global issues, engaging in the education of others, or taking part in political parties in order to influence their foreign policy priorities.

For such activities to be engaged in (and the idea of global citizenship is not to remain an unactualized ideal), there needs of course to be a backcloth of institutions through which one's actions can take effect. Without a charity like Oxfam, donations to help the poor in distant lands could not readily take place. Without environmental organizations, neither action in solidarity with others (who are doing the same) nor appropriate political influence would be possible. Without democratic institutions within countries the capacity of ordinary citizens to influence foreign policy decisions, through voting, lobbying or whatever, would be lost.

A good example of global citizenship engagement was the Jubilee 2000 campaign—a campaign that is ongoing—to get the debt of the poorest countries cancelled (Jubilee Campaign 2006), along with commitment by many to "fair trade" and "ethical consuming." Another recent example of the exercise of global citizenship, and of the importance of the influence of international NGOs is the World Court Project which I shall focus on because it is less well known. On July 8th 1996 the World Court in the Hague delivered an advisory opinion on the legality, in international law, of not only using but also possessing and thus threatening the use of nuclear weapons. It ruled that the threat or use of nuclear weapons would generally be contrary to the rules of international law applicable in armed conflict and also clearly stated that there was an obligation for nuclear disarmament negotiations to be pursued and concluded. This was the culmination of a number of years' work by many activists in a citizens' movement called the "World Court Project." The Project organized the collection of a large number of "declarations of public conscience" by ordinary citizens throughout the world, which the "de Martens" clause of the World Court constitution requires it to take heed of. This led eventually a motion in the UN General Assembly in 1994 which asked for an advisory opinion.[14]

There are a number of interesting issues raised by this case. First, is it helpful or relevant? Experts have dismissed it as irrelevant to the real challenges of checking nuclear proliferation. Certainly it has to be acknowledged that as an advisory opinion, this judgment, like other "soft" parts of international law is not enforceable. On the other hand, it may well contribute towards the building up of a pressure for the reduction of nuclear arsenals. It is important to remember that the whole process would not have taken place at all but for the development of groundswell of public opinion, as expressed in the declarations of public conscience. It is difficult to see how this now activated level of public awareness can simply be dismissed as having no effect.

Second, this was an exercise of world citizen power or global civil society. That a body like the World Court can be responsive to such influences is of course, from a cosmopolitan point of view, much to be welcomed. The fact that a lot

---

14   For an account of the background to this, see Mothersson 1992 and World Court 1996.

of people think the threat and use of nuclear weapons is wrong or the fact that a judgment tends to confirm a position in international law, do not, either of them, actually establish that the possession or use of nuclear weapons is wrong. People, even judges, are fallible. Nevertheless for any thinker who for reasons other than the fact that it is already accepted by others or embodied in a public and authoritative advisory opinion, believes reliance on nuclear weapons to be wrong, such influential processes in global civil society are encouraging signs for the future.

But global citizenship, if it is to be an effective idea, does not merely involve a range of activities which the committed person engages in for the sake of some global good. It must also involve, to some extent, a change of attitude towards his own society and political order. Recognition of a meaningful membership of a global community of humankind may not lead one to questioning one's general loyalty to the state or to question the special place membership of one's own community or society has, any more than recognizing the value of the wider society undermines family loyalties, but it must involve some reordering of priorities. At the very least, if one gives generously to Oxfam, it is reasonable counterfactually to suppose that had one not been ethically concerned about distant poverty, one would have given more to some domestic charity. If one had not campaigned for the saving of whales, one would have campaigned for something else closer to home. At a deeper level, one may in terms of one's concerns, be led to break the law in acts of civil disobedience. It is not merely that commitment to some moral or religious ideal can lead one to defy the state—this can always be the case, whether the ethic is global or not—it is rather that the claims of community and state may have quite generally less of a pull, if one really does think of oneself as having an identity as a citizen of the world and one sees a significant part of one's responsibility as a moral agent being exercised at this level rather than at a more local level. The development of international institutions, aided of course by the recent massive explosion of global communications, all contribute towards these trends, so that global citizenship becomes more a practical reality, as the institutions which embody its ideals are themselves developed (see Carter 2001; Hutchings and Dannreuther 1999; Parekh 2002).

One example which illustrates what the implications might be of this revised perspective is that of refugees. The flood of refugees has grown dramatically in the last few years and now stands, according to official and therefore conservative estimates at over 20 million people (UNHCR 2006). The refugee crisis is one of the major issues facing the world today. Many countries, especially the wealthy countries, have very strict and unhelpful procedures for admitting political refugees and countries generally do not accept "economic" refugees at all. Many cosmopolitans would argue that the rights of individuals to escape persecution or extreme poverty should lead to a relaxation of the tight frontier controls which are maintained. To be sure, such relaxation will have effects on existing citizens, who may prefer not to undergo possible reduction in economic well-being or not to have others who are not part of their community entering the country, and these preferences may well be seen as democratic justifications for not doing so. But it is not clear why these considerations should take precedence over meeting the basic needs of others. In many ways our attitude towards refugees is a litmus test of how far we accept a cosmopolitan way of thinking and how far we retain a traditional communitarian approach and support for internationalism.

Nevertheless the importance of community for cosmopolitanism in the sense that the communitarians stress can be underlined if we recall the distinction between a world ethic as theory and as social reality. In this sense it is a truism, but an important if neglected one, that a cosmopolitan ethic, like any other ethical code, is more likely to be realized, the more people accept it. Therefore the development of a public ethical culture which embodies the values in question is clearly crucial to the more effective realization of the values involved (see e.g. Boulding 1990). For instance, if one's theory says that the rich ought to be generous toward reducing extreme poverty, then the more people who believe this, the more individuals will be motivated ethically to do, the more such behavior will be strengthened by the perception of like behavior and the more governments are likely to reflect such electoral preferences in aid programmes. So whilst a cosmopolitan may actually be more interested in the normative/theoretical part of his claim, it is clearly important that this ethic becomes more fully represented in the "global social reality."

So the argument must be to create the appropriate kinds of social structure to embed the idea of global citizenship, so that it is not either membership of a global political order or merely membership of a moral domain. What those structures are is the challenge. "We are global citizens with tribal souls," as Piet Hein once remarked (quoted in Barnaby 1988: 192). The challenge is: how can we acquire our global souls? Bradley, the English political idealist, once suggested that a morality has both body and soul, the body being the social institutions and public practices and the soul being the individual moral wills which breathe life into that body (Bradley 1878: 177–81). If a global ethic is to exist in the fullest sense then it will need both body, the public social embodiment in shared norms and institutions, and soul, the beliefs of sufficient number of moral agent who believe that ethics is global in character. Cosmopolitan theories provide us with the soul of that morality. Communitarian thinking provides us with the insight as to what must also exist for that morality to be embodied. We cannot do without either.

References

Almond, B. (1990), "Alasdair MacIntyre: The Virtue of Tradition," *Journal of Applied Philosophy*, 7(1).

Anscombe, G.E.M. (1970), "War and Murder," in Wasserstrom, R. (ed.), *War and Morality*, Belmont, CA: Wadsworth Publishing Co.

Aristotle (c. 350 BC), *The Politics*, e.g. in Everson, S. (ed.), (1988). Cambridge: Cambridge University Press.

Barnaby, F. (ed.), (1988), *The Gaia Peace Atlas*. London: Pan Books.

Boulding, E. (1990), *Building a Global Civic Culture—Education for an Interdependent World*. Syracuse: Syracuse University Press.

Bradley, F.H. (1878), *Ethical Studies*. Oxford: Oxford University Press.

Carter, A. (2001), *The Political Theory of Global Citizenship*. London: Routledge.

Ceadel, M. (1987), *Thinking about Peace and War*. Oxford: Oxford University Press.

Cohen J. (ed.) (1996), *For Love of Country: Debating the Limits of Patriotism*. Boston: Beacon Books.

Dower, N. (2007). *World Ethics*. Edinburgh: Edinburgh University Press.

Drydyk, J. (2003), "How to Make Global Ethics Credible: Beyond Minimalism." Ottawa: Department of Philosophy, Carleton University.

Hutchings, K. and Dannreuther, R. (eds) (1999), *Cosmopolitan Citizenship*. Basingstoke: Macmillan.

Jubilee Debt Campaign (2006), accessed on 10 November 2006 at www.jubileedebtcampaign. org.uk/.

Kekes, J. (1993), *The Morality of Pluralism*. Princeton: Princeton University Press.

Küng, H. (1990), *Global Responsibility—In Search of a New World Ethic*. London: SCM Press.

Laszlo, E. (ed.), (1993), *The Multicultural Planet* (UNESCO Report). Oxford: Oneworld Publ.

Mothersson, K. (1992), *From Hiroshima to the Hague: A Guide to the World Court Project*. Geneva: International Peace Bureau.

Naess, A. (1989), *Ecology, Community and Life-style: Outline of an Ecosophy*, trans. Rothenberg, D. Cambridge: Cambridge University Press.

Nagel, T. (1979), *Mortal Questions*. Cambridge: Cambridge University Press.

Nussbaum, M. (1994), "Patriotism and Cosmopolitanism," *The Boston Review*, October.

Parekh, B. (2002), "Cosmopolitanism and Global Citizenship," *Review of International Studies*, 31(2).

Parekh, B. (2005), "Principles of a Global Ethic," in Eade, J. and O'Byrne, D. (eds) *Global Ethics and Civil Society*. Aldershot: Ashgate.

Peterson, V.S. (ed.), (1992), *Gendered States: Feminist (Re) Visions of International Relations Theory*. London: Lynne Rienner Publishers.

Robinson, F. (1999), *Globalizing Care: Ethics, Feminist Theory, and International Relations*. Boulder, CO: Westview Press.

Sachs, W. (ed.), (1992), *The Development Dictionary*. London: Zed Books.

Sandel, M. (1982), *Liberalism and the Limits of Justice*. Cambridge: Cambridge University Press.

Tamir, Y. (1993), *Liberal Nationalism*. Princeton NJ: Princeton University Press.

Tan, K.-Ch. (2004), *Justice without Borders Cosmopolitanism, Nationalism, and Patriotism*. Cambridge: Cambridge University Press.

Taylor, C. (1989), *Sources of the Self: the Making of Modern Identity*. Cambridge, MA: Harvard University Press.

Thompson, J. (1992), *Justice and World Order*. London: Routledge.

Toulmin, S. (1992), *Cosmopolis—The Hidden Agenda of Modernity*. New York: Free Press.

UNHCR (2006), accessed on 10 November 2006 at www.unhcr.ch/.

World Court (1996), *Advisory Judgement*, General List No. 95, 8 July.

Zolo, D. (1997), *Cosmopolis—Prospects for World Government*. Cambridge: Polity Press.

Chapter 8

Community and Society on a Transnational Scale

Peter Caws

Globalization—"the closer integration of the countries and peoples of the world which has been brought about by the enormous reduction of costs of transportation and communication, and the breaking down of artificial barriers to the flows of goods, services, capital, knowledge, and (to a lesser extent) people across borders" (Stiglitz 2003: 9)—has been a progressive feature of human development for a very long time, though it has been named and explicitly conceptualized only in the last half century or so. It has largely been analyzed in economic terms. While its cultural impact has not been entirely neglected the situation of displaced and disadvantaged individuals who have borne its costs has not been a matter of primary concern, and nor (more seriously perhaps) has the responsibility and complicity of those who have stood to profit from it. In the last few years ethics has been showing up sporadically in the discourse of globalization, from a number of different disciplinary directions—international relations, economics, political science, sociology. It deserves to engage the explicit interest of moral philosophers.

Globalization and Morality

One reason why ethical interests map awkwardly on to economic ones is that economic units, whether producers or consumers or managers or other intermediaries, are not considered, as such, to have moral standing. Even *per capita* data do not take specific heads into account—economic calculations deal with aggregates, not with persons. Ethical or moral concerns, on the other hand, are inescapably personal. Moral agency and moral responsibility go hand in hand, but both are strictly individual. As Kierkegaard (1975: 310) put it, "the crowd has no hands"—and it has no obligations either. Ethics, or morality (I will deal with the distinction shortly), comes into play when the actions of one individual have consequences for the situation of another (or others). Moral or ethical principles are learned in the first instance in domestic or local contexts, when my actions or those of my peers have an effect on the circumstances of proximate others, whose reactions, or the reactions of bystanders—especially parents and other authority figures—teach me what is acceptable. (What is culturally acceptable, and what is acceptable to me, may come to diverge.) Life in society widens the range of those possibly affected by my actions, either directly or in virtue of what I call "secondary accumulation."

Secondary accumulation comes into play when the effect of my act, taken by itself, falls below the threshold of moral concern, but the cumulative effect of my act along with the similar acts of many others rises above it. My act is still mine alone, but I bear the responsibility for the whole effect to which it contributes. Sartre offers a vivid and relevant image: if I along with ninety-nine others storm the Bastille, each of us acts with the strength of a hundred. Whether the act is for good or ill, the moral arithmetic remains the same. Globalization means that the range of the effects of my action becomes co-extensive with the human race. As a moral agent I am now obliged to think beyond the familial or ethnic or national or regional to remote others whose welfare, thanks to the global interpenetration of chains of causation, is henceforth inextricably connected with my own. What changes, if anything, when the reach of my action extends from known associates to whom I have affective ties to strangers in different cultures in distant parts of the world?

Theory and Practice

This, then, will be an exercise in speculative moral philosophy. Moral philosophy may be perceived, particularly by those who are mainly concerned with what they think of as practical real-world interests, as remote and theoretical. It *is* mostly theoretical. But this does not mean that it cannot be put to work in practice. As I shall argue, some of its conclusions in this area are of intense practical relevance. I think here not only of Marx's somewhat ambiguous claim that "the *practice* of philosophy ... is itself *theoretical*" (Marx 1967: 61) but also of the argument of Kant's essay "On the Common Saying: 'This May Be True in Theory, but It Does Not Apply in Practice.'" This essay serves my purpose in two ways: not just because of its defense of theorizing but also because, along with his works on universal history and on perpetual peace, Kant can now be seen as a major precursor of globalization, who remains strikingly relevant in our own day. (Marx's more internationalist views—which gave insufficient credit to the force of the nationalist idea—have fared on the whole less well.) Kant deals with the relation between theory and practice under three heads—morality in general, political right, and (most germane for our purposes) international right, "considered from a universally philanthropic, i.e. cosmopolitan point of view"—and concludes firmly "that whatever reason shows to be valid in theory, is also valid in practice" (Kant 1970a: 92).

To claim that a theory would work if it were applied in practice does not mean that it will actually *be* applied. For example, if Kant's "first definitive article of perpetual peace," namely that "the civil constitution of every state shall be republican" (Kant 1970b: 99) (understanding *republicanism* as "that political principle whereby the executive power ... is separated from the legislative power") (Kant 1970b: 101), had in fact been observed everywhere, and if the legislative processes had everywhere been sufficiently democratic, it does seem likely that world peace would be closer than it is. But these conditions have so far not been generally met, and at the present time it is tempting to draw the pessimistic conclusion that they never will be. This is no argument against the validity of the theory. And Kant will not give up the hope of an eventually satisfactory outcome. "Not giving up hope" is a basic principle for him.

> History may well give rise to endless doubts about my hopes, and if these doubts could be proved, they might persuade me to desist from an apparently futile task. But so long as they do not have the force of certainty, I cannot exchange my duty ... for a rule of expediency which says that I ought not to attempt the impracticable. (Kant 1970a: 89)

"What may I hope?" was one of the three questions that Kant, in the *Critique of Pure Reason* itself, took to combine "all the interests of ... reason" (Kant 1956: 635). This eighteenth-century optimism was shared by Jefferson, who was writing during the same period (though I know of no evidence that either was aware of the other, a question that deserves closer inquiry). We may still learn something from it today. Jefferson too (like the other American Founders) thought in universal terms, though without global ambitions as we might now understand them; his hope was in democracy, while Kant's lay in the realization of pure republics, one state at a time. Kant feared the dictatorship of the people, and does not seem to have envisaged the possibility that the representative institutions he advocated could also be democratic, whereas Jefferson considered just this combination, representative democracy, to be his greatest contribution to political enlightenment. The issue is important for questions of globalization considered as a cultural and political development. Jefferson's challenge was to secure the participation of the people in a government that would nevertheless be centralized and efficient. The underlying problem here has never been satisfactorily solved: real participation is likely to mean real conflict, but delegation to a representative reduces participation to an occasional formality. One thing Jefferson was sure about, though, was the imperative need for an educated electorate: "Educate and inform the whole mass of the people ... They are the only sure reliance for the preservation of our liberty" (Jefferson 1903: 392).

Another way of approaching this fairly intractable situation is through Rousseau's distinction between particular wills and the general will (Rousseau 1968: 63). One reading of this distinction makes both kinds of will functions of the individual: each of us has particular wills but each has also a general will, that is, a conception of and a desire for what would be best for the whole. Following up this point would take me too far afield, but it does reflect the concern that permeates the discussion: how to enlarge the sense of this "whole," to take account of the situation of the moral agent as he or she operates on a series of different levels, from the personal all the way up to the global. Confronting this multiplicity of contexts challenges the individual to emerge from a primitive identification with the domestic and local—confines within which perhaps the majority of human beings have always lived, hardly arriving until recently even at a resilient sense of personal identity—and to rise to a vision of worldwide human equality, in which each citizen disposes reflectively of what might be called a "global general will." But again—though Rousseau makes the connection less directly than Jefferson does—it will clearly require an educated population if individuals are freely to bring their private wills into conformity with such a general will.

Political History

As current events are demonstrating, it is much harder to export democratic republicanism than many naive statesmen have thought, and even in places where it is already supposed to obtain it is often not put into practice. The recent history of the United States is a striking illustration of this inconsistency. The original genius of the American representative system, which gave elected representatives the power of the purse, required them to contest their seats afresh every two years, and also provided that no appropriation of funds for military purposes could be made for longer than a similar period of two years. But it did not anticipate the venality of power and the vested interest in incumbency that would eventually corrupt it. Kant's optimism meets a serious challenge here—but history may yet vindicate it. He thinks that human nature will eventually "*compel* us to follow a course that we would not readily adopt by choice" (Kant 1970a: 90), and goes on in an unexpectedly Hobbesian vein (unexpected because part of the essay on practice is subtitled "against Hobbes") to say

> On the one hand, universal violence and the distress it produces must eventually make a people decide to submit to the coercion which reason itself prescribes (i.e. the coercion of public law), and to enter into a *civil* constitution. And on the other hand, the distress produced by the constant wars in which the states try to subjugate or engulf each other must finally lead them, even against their will, to enter into a *cosmopolitan* constitution .... Thus sheer exhaustion must eventually perform what goodwill ought to have done but failed to do: each state must be organised internally in such a way that the head of state, for whom the war actually costs nothing (for he wages it at the expense of others, i.e. the people), must no longer have the deciding vote on whether war is to be declared or not, for the people who pay for it must decide. (Kant 1970a: 90–91)

I am already allowing myself to be turned away from a central focus on globalization towards a topical preoccupation with the current foreign policy of the United States, which seems to be presciently encapsulated in Kant's last remark, conducted as it is by a "head of state, for whom the war actually costs nothing." This is a tendency that is hard to resist in the political climate of the day. At the same time it is not without its relevance: that policy has global repercussions, and the individual human beings who suffer from it are among the distant strangers I referred to earlier, whose freedom cannot be a matter of indifference for me. The crucial concept in Kant's text is "the people," who must decide and who must therefore bear responsibility (including the responsibility of failing to decide, or of failing to insist on their right to decide). This is the sort of responsibility (and not only on the part of citizens of a particular state) that cannot, as I have been suggesting, be displaced to an anonymous collective but must be borne by each of us individually. But how do individuals constitute "the people," and how is moral responsibility assigned?

Minimal Consequentialism

Kant does not clarify the connection between the pure rational will in the kingdom of ends on the one hand, and the actions of the citizen in the thick of political affairs on the other.

I follow him in his cosmopolitan but not in his moral theory, because his moral theory rests on an unrealistic claim about the paramount status of duty. In moral theory I take a radically consequentialist position, though not quite in the generally accepted sense, which tends to conflate consequentialism with utilitarianism. I call this view "minimal consequentialism" (Caws 1995). The minimalism is a crucial part of the position and will apply in what follows as well. Neither the minimalism nor the consequentialism, however, are incompatible with a broad conception of virtue—a disclaimer I find necessary in view of the frequent misrepresentation of consequentialism by deontologists and virtue ethicists. Consequentialism as I understand it entails basic virtues, because it insists on concern for others—and that means *all* others, everywhere around the globe.

Here I offer the barest sketch of the theory. Agency I define as the appropriation, by a subject (in Sartre's sense rather than Foucault's), of a bodily action as an act of his or her own. The moral weight of an act lies not in its being the kind of act it is (deontology), or in its being intended to produce some end (teleology), or in its ministering to some calculated general good (utilitarianism), or in its realising a potentiality of the agent (virtue ethics), but in its foreseeable consequences for the freedom of some other subject or subjects. "Foreseeable" is to be taken as strictly as possible—that a given consequence was not in fact foreseen (when with sufficient diligence it might have been) does not excuse the act that led to it. Moral theories are distinct from, and need to be complemented by, theories of value. The corresponding theory of value in my case requires the familiar distinction between instrumental and end values, and makes two basic claims: (a) there is no universal end value; and (b) there is one and only one universal instrumental value, namely freedom. This last claim rests on an argument which in its stripped-down form says that any agent who values anything as an end must also, on pain of inconsistency, value as an instrument the freedom to pursue it.

However the freedom in question is what I call "complex freedom." According to this conception an act is free if and only if the agent (a) means to do it (b) is not restrained from doing it (or constrained to do something else) (c) and has at his or her disposal: (i) the energy, skill, and material resources to do it; (ii) sufficient information about the context in which it is done; and (iii) sufficient knowledge of the world to be able to foresee its consequences. My act takes on moral significance just to the extent that it has an effect on the freedom of others, against whom I can offend in various ways corresponding to the elements of complex freedom—namely by restraining them, constraining them, depriving them, deceiving them, or keeping them in ignorance. And it follows that my moral obligations do not consist merely in negative avoidances (not getting in the way, not compelling) but also in positive helps (providing, informing, educating).

The Moral Community

Only those actions of individual agents that have an effect, positively or negatively, on other individuals are to be judged by moral criteria. It is therefore essential to introduce the concept of a "moral community." By this I understand the domain within which mutual relations of obligation and respect are taken to hold. The concept of "community" is an inspiring one, evoking lives and interests in common. It covers the domain of the "moral sentiments" to be found in Hume and in Adam Smith, a domain held together by mutual recognition and concern. Membership in a community is affective rather than contractual—I am bound to the other members by lively fellow-feeling and by shared commitments. A pressing question is whether any such community can be realized on a global scale. In spite of calls for planetary solidarity there appear to be good reasons, cultural and geopolitical, to suggest a negative answer to this question.

Ideally each of us would be bound by community to all other human beings, feeling compassion for strangers as well as familiars, something implicit in the Christian notion of the Good Samaritan. But the victim on whom the Good Samaritan took pity was on the other side of the road, not the other side of the world. Community involves a degree of proximity, and even for Christians affect can reach only so far. The comment of an Anglican divine, William Inge, has always seemed to me to reflect a kind of wisdom: "I do not love the human race. I have loved just a few of them—the rest are a pretty mixed lot" (Inge 1954: 73). If we could take on (as Christ is supposed to have done) the suffering of the world, we would find the emotional burden intolerable. That is no doubt why, preposterous as this may seem to sensitive consciences, so many people can sleep at night when so many others—in Iraq, in Rwanda, in Darfur, in the sweatshops and ghettos of the world—live from day to day in fear and deprivation.

I do not wish here to make excuses for indifference, only to acknowledge a reality—and an impotence. Cases differ, of course—it is not so easy for those of us who are citizens of the United States, whether by birth or naturalization, to ignore what is being done in our name in Iraq, but nor, given the breakdown of the practice of democratic republicanism, is it so easy for us to do anything effective about it. (All honor to those who have tried, in these or other historical circumstances.) But there is a rhetoric of sympathetic indignation about the state of the world that sometimes risks crossing the line that separates the moral sentiments from moralizing sentimentality. Community beyond what we might think of as its organic bounds may be an unrealistic goal.

The concept of community has been hijacked for political purposes twice in modern times, once by "communism" and once by "communitarianism." We all know what passion and commitment went into the former, and to what futile ends (even as we may admit that the need for a struggle, not between classes but against the conditions that feed their inequalities worldwide, is as great as it ever was in Marx's day). About the latter it may be too early to tell, though my impression is that the tone of much popular communitarian writing is *moralistic*, that is hortatory rather than reflectively argued, and what I have been suggesting so far is that moral appeals are of limited effectiveness in a global context.

Morals and Ethics

Here however I remind myself that my topic in this essay is not "global morality" but "global ethics," a difference I now wish to explore and sharpen. I note in the literature of this subject a tendency to conflate ethics and morals—I on the other hand see them as potentially distinct. If moral communities are essentially local, might it be possible to envisage a global arrangement that would enable them to meet and interact? Might we devise a set of second-order principles covering first-order acts and consequences? These would have to appeal, not to proximity or personal sentiment, but to the rational interests of the community as a whole. An available name for them would be, precisely, ethics, and the name for the global arrangement under which they would operate might well be "society" as distinct from "community."

There is, and I freely admit it, something stipulative about all this. But it is connected, in the second case rather obviously, with the work of others. The distinction between morals and ethics I take from some aspects of contemporary usage, and the distinction between community and society from Ferdinand Tönnies in his classic work *Gemeinschaft und Gesellschaft* (Tönnies 1940). In neither case, however, do I really need the authority, either of ordinary language or of German sociology, in order to make my point—the distinctions I draw are independent of these sources, can be understood without them, and need not use just these names, though the names are available and convenient. The elements distinguished do not map exactly on to their originals, but they do so closely enough to make clarification sufficiently simple and the invention of a whole new vocabulary unnecessarily cumbersome.

The tendency to use "ethical" and "moral" interchangeably is understandable enough, given that they both have roots meaning (in Latin and Greek respectively) "customary behavior." It is hardly necessary to point out that "ordinary language philosophy" as practiced in English does not necessarily translate in any straightforward way into other languages. The difference between "moral" and "ethical" corresponds lexically to similar differences in French and German, complicated in the latter case by the addition of a third term, *sittlich*, with a similar meaning (from another root), but what follows strictly applies only to English.

In English, then, there has come to be a *de facto* division of labor between the two terms, according to which "moral" tends to apply more to personal, and "ethical" more to institutional, principles and decisions. The separating out of special subdisciplines like "medical ethics" or "business ethics" suggests the possibility of codifying rules, for application in special circumstances, the following of which may have little to do with the moral principles subscribed to by those who apply the rules under those circumstances. There is nothing inconsistent in the idea that a thoroughly immoral person might behave ethically. By the same token, two or more persons whose moral intuitions were at variance with one another might agree on a set of ethical standards.

The point can be brought home by asking what would happen if we substituted "morals" for "ethics" in the names of the subdisciplines referred to above, speaking of "medical morals" and "business morals." The result is semantically counterintuitive—the doctor and the business executive, *in their official capacities*, are expected to follow the ethical guidelines of their professions, discussion of which has been the staple of journals of medical and business ethics, but their private moral convictions and judgments are not at issue. We may hope that they are also guided by the deepest moral sensibilities, but as long as they observe the ethical code that is not our affair—insisting on the point would, we feel, involve some sort of category mistake.

I take advantage of this observation to press my stipulative restriction of "moral" to private behavior in the light of personal values, and of "ethical" to public behavior in the light of institutional values. This picture can be complicated by adding the category of the "legal," as applying to conduct that falls under requirements or sanctions imposed by the state, normally as a direct or indirect result of legislation. Although my attention here is not focused on international law, the concept of law is bound up with the concepts of morals and of ethics. It cannot be made a legal obligation to behave morally, but we might claim (at a domestic level) that it is a *prima facie* moral obligation to obey the law, in so far as the community comes under its rule *(prima facie* because the law may order me to do something immoral, and in such cases my moral obligation to others in the community outranks my obligation to obey the law).

Given this prior moral obligation it would seem odd to ask whether it might also be an *ethical* duty to obey the law, and yet there is a subtle change of modality as I move from a private moral to a public ethical context. As a private person I wish to be law-abiding within the constraints of my conscience, but in cases of moral conflict my refusal to obey normally affects no one but myself, whereas in discharging a public duty I am obliged to conform to the relevant laws, and failure to do so will implicate others also. *Once I have subscribed to the code of ethics* I no longer have the luxury of dissent, short of resigning from the position which requires me to conform. This is a strategy that should probably be followed more often than it is.

From Community to Society

Perhaps these cases will begin to illuminate the contrast I am trying to establish, with a view to its usefulness when we get to global ethics as such. I wish now, however, having paid so much attention to "community," at least in its relation to the idea of the "moral," to turn to the other term of Tönnies's opposition, namely "society," which the argument of this chapter is clearly going to pair up with the "ethical." It remains to be seen what mileage we can get out of this. It is worth saying at once that this term also has been appropriated for political purposes, in the form of "socialism," but in this case I will not say "hijacked," because socialists—partly because of their political diversity—have by and large not had quite as aggressive or moralizing tendencies as communists or communitarians. I realize the vulnerability of this claim—socialists have sometimes been just as pious and Utopian, perhaps, but my point is that they have had better grounds for hope, given known tendencies of human beings in groups. As we saw in the case of Dean Inge, it is hard to whip up sentiment for all and sundry, but to envisage contractual, rather than affective, relations to the rest of the world seems more realistic.

Gemeinschaft and *Gesellschaft* oppose and complement one another, as nature and family on the one hand, reason and contract on the other. Community was originally rooted in the land, and in the affective relations between those who inhabited and worked it; society detaches itself from these roots, and its relations become more formal and economic. To a first approximation the two categories tend respectively towards the local and the global. The complication that presents itself is that the concept of locality can no longer be limited to contiguous areas of land; in an age of global communication individuals can discover neighbors at great distances, and be practically and affectively closer to them than to others living in greater proximity. This idea of widely distributed "localities" goes back at least to Marshall McLuhan and his "global village" (McLuhan 1962: 31), and has been explored under another name, in an academic context, in work on "invisible colleges" (see Crane 1972). There may thus be overlapping virtual localities on a global scale, conflicts between the inhabitants of which may reproduce themselves at disparate real localities around the world. Some of the most venerable avatars of this idea, going back for centuries, are the world religions. (We might argue, for example, that Catholic and Protestant Christians inhabit such overlapping virtual localities—but the Belfast in which they clash is real enough.)

There is a tendency to see *Gemeinschaft* and *Gesellschaft* as diachronically related, so that the slow transition of one into the other accompanies the emergence of modernity. Tönnies himself seems to have thought in this way. I on the other hand see them as synchronically coexistent, as representing different ways in which the same subject and agent can relate to his or her contemporaries. We all begin in communities; what societies we emerge into will depend on opportunity, enterprise, mobility, education etc. Our moral bonds with the other members of the community need not be broken when we develop ethical understandings with other agents whom we meet in society.

There is also a tendency to see Tönnies's two forms of grouping as synchronically exclusive—for example Roland Robertson (1992) in his rich and provocative "images of world order" takes care not to mix them up—whereas I on the other hand think they interpenetrate. I find Robertson's images useful primarily because they form so many stages on which I can place my moral and ethical players—or rather player, in the singular, committed as I am to a radical individualism in these matters. He distinguishes four main positions:

Global Gemeinschaft 1: the world should and can be ordered only in the form of a series of relatively closed societal communities;
Global Gemeinschaft 2: only in terms of a fully globewide community per se can there be global order;
Global Gesellschaft 1: the global circumstance [is] a series of open societies, with considerable sociocultural exchange among them;
Global Gesellschaft 2: world order ... can only be obtained on the basis of formal, planned world organization. (Robertson 1992: 78–9)

The main problem with these formulations is the repetition of "only," which suggests that no two models can obtain at the same time. I am aware that these categories have been around for a while and I do not know where Robertson stands with respect to them now—I suspect indeed that in their original formulation their stark contrasts arose more from formalism than from conviction. But I see no difficulty in envisaging a world in which these arrangements overlap, and in which the agent, belonging to multiple communities and multiple societies, has the freedom but also the burden of being in his or her own person an autonomous actor on the world stage.

This agent, you may feel, is a rare specimen. So is Jefferson's educated voter. The success of global society is conceptually tied to the success of national democracy. My point for the moment is this: that while moral bonds may hold preferentially between inhabitants of the *same* locality, ethical constraints might, given a degree of mutual understanding, govern the relations between the inhabitants of *different* localities. The question is whether, and how, people with passionate "local" attachments (to religions, for example) can be brought to see themselves as having global responsibilities—how they can be members at the same time of local communities and of a global society. This means having at least two levels of understanding and at least two allegiances—which may be beyond the psychological capacity of most of the inhabitants of the world, particularly those who have been indoctrinated into one or another form of religious or nationalist fanaticism.

On the other hand, if it is within the psychological capacity of any, it is in principle within the psychological capacity of all. As with Jefferson's educated electorate—an idea that has never been fully tried out, even in Jefferson's own country—there is no reason to think that such a plan could not work in practice, given appropriate conditions. At this point another consideration enters, to which I cannot do full justice here. It derives from work I have been doing on fanatical belief, and involves a distinction between credal *de dicto* beliefs and fideist *de re* beliefs—the latter requiring conceptual insight and commitment, the former requiring nothing more than blind acceptance and the learning of slogans. The willingness of mindless followers to repeat and act upon the formulaic instructions of often cunning leaders is depressing—but at the same time suggests that in the hands of the right leaders things might turn around more quickly than we might otherwise hope.

If the idea of persuading Osama bin Laden to share in the promulgation of global ethical standards, in return for a guarantee of genuine respect for the local moral standards he seeks to defend, strikes you as wildly funny, I certainly cannot blame you. But perhaps you will at least understand me if I say that, whatever his morals may be, I regard George W. Bush as one of the most unethical players to have appeared on the world stage in the last half-century. For there is in a sense already available a set of ethical principles, a sort of global code, set out in the Charter of the United Nations. Unlike the Constitution of the United States, which Bush also misunderstands and openly flouts, the UN Charter is not a legal document. Nor is it a moral one. But its signatories deserve credit for having had a vision of global ethics more than 60 years ago (and of course they were not the first even then). I cite as I work towards a conclusion just two texts from the Charter: first from the Preamble, a commitment "to ensure by the acceptance of principles and the institution of methods, that armed force shall not be used, save in the common interest," and then from Chapter 1, article 2, a provision that "all Members shall settle their international disputes by peaceful means in such a manner that international peace and security, and justice, are not endangered." As in the case of an earlier quotation from Kant it is pertinent to consider the current policies of the United States in the light of these citations.

Autonomy

One last remark as to what we might want the ethics of a global society to achieve. In addition to the mutual accommodation of local moral communities and respect for their differences, we should surely also be concerned for the freedom of members of such communities to exercise individual autonomy. This is a crucial and difficult point, on which the whole enterprise may founder. The two desiderata may in fact contradict one another. There is massive and dramatic evidence, and not only in what we are accustomed to think of as repressive communities, of the fierce and ruthless opposition on the part of powerful members to independent thought, or failure to conform to the local mores: the ostracism or even killing of women who contract relations with members of other communities (or resist coercive relations with members of their own), the cutting off of men and women who reject the communal faith. Part of the necessary respect for communities involves allowing them to follow traditional observances, but part of the doctrine of freedom for individuals involves their protection from forced membership in any community.

I cannot insist on membership in any community of my choice—I may not qualify. But I can, or ought to be able to, leave my community for a larger society if I find it stultifying or restrictive. In other words I may choose to associate myself with a body of fellow human beings who have a larger and freer conception of life than those among whom I was raised or find myself. The possibility of this choice needs to be codified in an ethical *principle of free association*, which would guarantee the right of the individual to opt out of any community affiliation without penalty (other than exclusion from the community opted out of, if it should be so ungenerous as to insist on such a policy). It is another interesting feature of English that it provides no analogue, on the side of "community," for the concept of association—"communication" functions quite differently. I can of course freely associate, in the ordinary sense of that term, with members of my own community

Raising these considerations to a global level requires much more research. Before closing I will evoke a dormant project, which I proposed to UNESCO some years ago, though it met with no encouragement and I did not follow it up. It was to have been a field inquiry into the attitudes of members of communities to one another, with the idea of delimiting the concept of "moral community" empirically. Individual subjects would have been asked to whom they felt moral allegiance and from whom they expected moral support, what behavior they could tolerate on the part of other members of the community, which other communities they felt were friendly and which antagonistic, how far they would sacrifice their own interests to the collective interest, etc. This inquiry would have looked into national communities (bearing in mind Benedict Anderson's (1991) concept of the nation) but also into ethnic and tribal communities, religious communities, communities of common interest in sport, culture, the professions, etc. I think that we do not know enough about these things, and that we need to find out more before we can move confidently toward the construction of ethics for a global society. But we do not have to wait for the former project to be completed before the we move further forward with the latter.

Thinking Globally

What is crucially needed is a sub-population, distributed around the world, that is willing to think moral implications beyond its own communities, so as to draw up specifications for an ethics with global reach. I remarked at the beginning that ethical concerns map awkwardly on to economic ones, as an implicit explanation of the lag of global ethics behind economic globalization. But the fact that economic relations have gone before may help to pave the way for the penetration of ethical concerns. Corporate global structures are in place; they provide overarching links between nations and cultures, outside diplomatic and military channels, and staffed by individuals who may be open to re-thinking their own practices in the light of ethical theory. (Some of them may very well already be far ahead of anything I could propose along these lines.) If we consider how codes of ethics have evolved in other professions—medicine, business, etc.—it becomes apparent that they were not responses to moralizing from without, but to disquiet within: some practices were perceived, by the professionals themselves, to be dubious, some standards too low, some individuals unscrupulous. It is when something is manifestly wrong that self-examination begins.

And something is manifestly wrong, at the economic level, with the global distribution of power and resources. If we follow the money, along the channels from the industrial nations to the Third World and back, we will find ready-made pointers to the consequences of our joint actions. I have been suggesting that it may be impractical for us to embrace those who suffer such consequences as members of a *moral* community to which we all belong—we do not have ready access to them, we may not know enough about their cultural conditioning and expectations, well-meaning intervention might prove to be disastrous. But those same channels are potential conduits for *ethical* remedies. Our thwarted moral sense of what would be right for affected populations can be translated into an insistence that the multinational corporations which are exploiting or oppressing them should observe ethical standards in their dealings. We can refuse to buy what they sell, we can divest ourselves and the institutions we support of our holdings in their stocks. We can refuse to work for them, and insist that those who do acknowledge their role in the secondary accumulation of adverse effects. This does not mean loving the human race—Dean Inge was probably right about the difficulty of that—but it means respecting all its members wherever they may be. That is surely one of the conditions of the ethical life.

References

Anderson, B. (1991), *Imagined Communities: Reflections on the Origin and Spread of Nationalism*. New York: Verso.

Caws, P. (1995), "Minimal Consequentialism," *Philosophy* 70(273).

Crane, D. (1972), *Invisible Colleges: Diffusion of Knowledge in Scientific Communities*. Chicago: University of Chicago Press.

Inge, W.R. (1954), Dean of Westminster, quoted in *Newsweek*, 8 March, 73.

Jefferson, T. (1903), "Thomas Jefferson to James Madison, Paris, 20 December 1787," in Lipscomb, A.A. and Bergh, A.E. (eds) *The Writings of Thomas Jefferson, Memorial Edition, Vol. 6*. Washington, DC: The Thomas Jefferson Memorial Association.

Kant, I. (1956) (transl. Norman Kemp Smith), *Critique of Pure Reason*. London: Macmillan and Co.

Kant, I. (1970a) (transl. H.B. Nisbet), "On the Common Saying: 'This May be True in Theory, but it does not Apply in Practice'," in Reiss, H. (ed.), *Kant: Political Writings*. Cambridge: Cambridge University Press.

Kant, I. (1970b) (transl. H.B. Nisbet), "Perpetual Peace: A Philosophical Sketch," in Reiss, H. (ed.), *Kant: Political Writings*. Cambridge: Cambridge University Press.

Kierkegaard, S. (1975) (ed. and transl. Howard V. Hong and Edna H. Hong), *Søren Kierkegaard's Journals and Papers, Vol. 3*. Bloomington: Indiana University Press.

Marx, K. (1967), "Notes to the Doctoral Dissertation," in Easton, L.D. and Guddat, K.H. (eds and transl.), *Writings of the Young Marx on Philosophy and Society*. New York: Doubleday Anchor Books.

McLuhan, M. (1962), *The Gutenberg Galaxy: The Making of Typographic Man*. Toronto: University of Toronto Press.

Robertson, R. (1992), *Globalization: Social Theory and Global Culture*. London: Sage Publications.

Rousseau, J.-J. (1968) (transl. Maurice Cranston), *The Social Contract*. New York: Viking Penguin.

Stiglitz, E. (2003), *Globalization and Its Discontents*. New York: W. W. Norton.

Tönnies, F. (1940) (transl. Charles P. Loomis), *Fundamental Concepts of Sociology (Gemeinschaft und Gesellschaft)*. New York: American Book Company.

PART III
How Can We "Do" Global Ethics?

Chapter 9

Global Poverty: Development Ethics Meets Global Justice[1]

Asunción Lera St Clair

Severe poverty, together with climate change, are the two most important moral problems facing our present generation. The choices we make in the next few years will decide the life chances of billions of human beings; the inhabitability of large areas of the planet, and the survival or demise of numerous ecosystems. We now face choices that people only two generations ago could not even contemplate, and we now have the power to address these threats and thus the choice "to do or not to do." Our generation can in fact eradicate the most severe global poverty and reduce other types of poverty as well as protect many vulnerable people from the miseries of deprivation. We have the economic means to do so. In the same way, our generation has the ability to arrest environmental crisis and even to reverse some of the already visible damage to the balance of global ecosystems. We have the technological and economic means to do so. The question remains, however, do we also have the will to do it?

The current development aid framework is legitimized as the tool to make globalization work for the poor. But the relations between global poverty and globalization are very complex, not only because of causal relations of various kinds, but also because the ways in which people perceive and theorize poverty tend to be related to specific views about what globalization processes actually are and how, and which alternatives, to envision for the future.[2] One of the fundamental drivers between contrasting views on globalization are value disagreements of various kinds; ethical ideas of what is worthy, who and why, and also cognitive values such as quantification or simplicity that leads us to focus either on aggregate data and abstract indicators or on people's actual lives. Our moral awareness of poverty tends to shape how we perceive views on globalization, its essence, main drives, dangers or hopes for the future: matters that shape the will to act. On the other hand, theories and conceptions of poverty and strategies for reducing it or to protect the poor can either promote awareness for the need for a "fair(er)

---

1   This chapter is a reprint from "Global Poverty: Development Ethics Meets Global Justice" by Asunción St Clair in *Globalizations* Vol 3 (2006), 139–58. Reprinted by permission of the publisher (Taylor and Francis Ltd).
2   I do not address here the question of climate change, yet the arguments put forward in this chapter may serve to promote a rethink of climate change as well.

globalization"[3] or can be blind to questions of (global) justice and fairness for the poor. The presumed neutrality of orthodox economics (the primary source of knowledge about poverty as it is produced by development aid agents) leads to normative blindness and a pretense of fairness, while a proper unveiling of what is and what is not valued reveals that cognitive (that is instrumental) values are given more weight than concerns for the intrinsic worth and dignity of all human beings. In general, moral awareness of poverty and explicit ethical concerns for the dignity of all people leads to more critical views on the dominant form of neoliberal economic globalization and to viewing transnational processes of all kinds as being under the control of human agency. We can change the future.

In this chapter I argue that the ethical aspects of global poverty lead to redefining both development and globalization. In addition, as the "global" impinges increasingly on every field of knowledge (and praxis) so too development, philosophy and ethics and the relations among these fields of knowledge are forced to redefine their scope and subject matter. This, in turn, has consequences for the ways in which globalization is treated, and in particular, for the emergent field of globalization studies. My main point is that the ethical aspects of globalization are interrelated with an ethical perspective on knowledge and policy for poverty reduction, and moral understandings of poverty; perspectives—among others—investigated by the fields of development ethics and global justice. In addition, I suggest that poverty needs to be treated globally, and not as a social fact that occurs only in developing countries. This entails a re-engagement with literature and theories within the field of development studies—including critical engagement with the ideas and policies generated and defended by development actors—as poverty research is dominated by the knowledge and policies elaborated and espoused by development actors. Much can be learned from the merging of development ethics and global justice, but these also have lessons to draw from globalization studies and vice versa. The first section reflects upon the entanglement between development and globalization. The second section argues that it is precisely a re-framing of poverty as a global question, as well as a moral matter that leads to a rethinking of both fields. In the third section, I outline some of the main ideas currently investigated by development ethics and global justice and argue for a merging of goals and scope. The study concludes by suggesting that research may be a form of activism and that what matters is collaborative rather than competing views. Cross-fertilization between these fields may lead to stronger theoretical formulations for alternative globalizations, for a better understanding of the paths towards fairer development aid policies and global relations more responsive to global poverty.

---

3   See the forum section "Towards Fair Globalization?" in *Globalizations*, 2(2), pp. 241–82.

The Entanglement of Globalization and Development

The characteristics and scope of development have changed substantially in the past 20 years. One of the important consequences of the increasing dominance of neoliberal economic globalization and the globalization of (unfettered) capitalism is that development is increasingly becoming, conceptually and practically, a matter of "relief," perhaps too close to the goals of humanitarian intervention; a tendency that reinforces the already common "charity" aspect of development aid (Gasper 1999; Glennie 2006). Meanwhile, progress and social improvement are increasingly left to the forces of free markets led by neoliberal ideology and the self-interest of a global elite. At the same time, powerful development actors such as the World Bank and donors state their goals for aid in terms of a rhetoric of socially sustainable and pro-poor development, often emphasizing local solutions and the strengthening of the poor's entrepreneurship. Themes of empowerment and participation are now commonplace in mainstream development aid discourse. Such rhetoric serves to legitimize the neoliberal restructuring produced through aid.

Although a focus on poverty and the provision of social services through the Millennium Development Goals (MDGs) and its targets is welcome, this has also been an opportunity to narrow the conception of development to a form of collective charity. At the same time, these strategies tend to put the burden of responsibility on individuals and local groups to cope with the negative effects of global socio-economic change. For example, certain preconditions for sustainable livelihoods or entrepreneurship require much more than access to small amounts of funds because of the immense influence of global finance capital or the dominance of agricultural businesses. At the same time, the rhetoric of global development actors and even many international NGOs fails miserably "to engage with the subtleties of structural conditions, comprising power and inequality, and the constraints they place on human agency" (Wood 2000: 2).

There is now a tendency to target development aid money as a tool for providing social safety nets, while the traditionally core matter of increasing economic growth is dependent on countries being globalized. Increases in living standards are dependent on the privatization of social services and availability of private funds, through either foreign direct investment and transnational corporations, regional transnational elites, or public–private partnerships— matters regulated and permitted by states. And as global institutions themselves interact increasingly with the private sector, they themselves may be in the process of becoming privatized (Bull and McNeill 2006).

The way in which neoliberal economic globalization is shaping development aid can be related to Cowen and Shenton's (1996) depiction of intentional development: as it seeks to impose order on the disruptive consequences of global dynamics, while legitimizing itself because aid aims to reduce poverty and help the vulnerable. The dominance of technocratic-bureaucratic thinking in development aid (Bøas and McNeill 2003) reinforces the intentional aspects of development, while disrupting and often preventing what may be positive bottom-up processes of social change (Hickey and Mohan 2005). At the same time, this specific meaning of development as technocratic, bureaucratic and intentional, is in itself the main justification for current neoliberal economic globalization. For example, according to the liberal economist Jagdish Bhagwati (2004), the world is already on the right track to reduce poverty and suffering. There is only one single "scientific" view as regards economic development, Bhagwati (2004: 53) argues "that trade enhances growth, and that growth reduces poverty." Development agents, he explains, would do best to keep themselves busy with questions of relief (and allow the free market to take care of the economy).

The belief that further neoliberal economic globalization is the sole source of increased living standards and that, at the most, we simply need to widen its scope so it benefits those so far left behind, overlaps in its entirety with what has been the most powerful myth of the past century: the image of development as securing affluence and fulfilling lives for all, an image driven by rationality and technological advance (Goulet 2005). Whereas "modernization" was the developmental myth of the second half of the twentieth century, globalization has emerged as the new developmental myth of the early twenty-first century. As Patomäki (2006) argues, this myth constitutes also a dominant conception of global justice. At the same time, development is being discursively transformed into a tool for "helping out" those left out of the presumed economic bonanza of free trade and liberalization, and the means for appeasing our conscience (or our sense of guilt). It thus tends to act as a legitimizing strategy for neoliberal restructuring.

Defenders of the ways in which the planet and its people are presently being globalized rely upon the ubiquitous claim amongst powerful development agencies that there is a positive relation between the main tenets of the Washington Consensus—or its more recent revisionist "post-Washington Consensus" version (see Broad 2004)—and the reduction of global poverty. Often, the linkages between globalization and development are made through data on poverty reduction as one of the fundamental justifications for the well-functioning of current globalization processes. Within this framing, development means something very specific: to follow the call for increasingly globalized markets and the privatization of social services; to prioritize economic concerns above anything else; to measure every aspect of social life with a monetary metric. "Globalization friendly" policies are held to lead to more "development," defenders argue, and the proof is often presented in the guise of poverty data, showing decreases in poverty over time as evidence of the fairness. Yet central questions about the forces that produce or cause poverty, and the possibility that global processes as presently constituted may have no need for attending to the poor—as the extreme poor are often neither producers nor consumers—remain unaddressed from this perspective.

Critics of such positive views of globalization tend to agree on the need to redefine the meaning of development, they disagree fundamentally with a positive correlation between poverty reduction, development and globalization, and are reclaiming multiple meanings of the global. The field of critical globalization studies has emerged from authors that pioneered what is today known as "new political economy" or new international political economy, but also include a variety of authors discontented with mainstream development and international relations. Although this is not the place to outline in detail what are critical globalization studies, I wish to pinpoint how most authors seem to converge on viewing the relations between globalization and development within their historical contexts and from a political economy perspective.

For many critical globalization scholars development funds and their attached conditionalities and discourses are ways of disciplining developing countries into joining the ranks of the globalized in a way that perpetuates a hierarchical and unequal world (Appelbaum and Robinson 2005; Gills 2005; Patomäki 2006; Robinson 2002; Sklair 2002). They unanimously argue that neither development as it is currently practiced by global institutions nor neoliberal economic globalization is leading towards increased well-being across and within countries, nor to environmental sustainability, whereas alternative globalizations may lead toward a fairer future. Often, critics point to the ways in which these global forces actually *produce and perpetuate poverty*.

Critics tend to focus their attention not on the success stories, but on evidence that persistent deepening severe poverty and increases in inequalities are occurring in virtually all countries, advanced as well as "less developed." Those unconvinced by the often fallacious correlations between neoliberal economic globalization, development, increased growth, and the reduction of poverty, look at China and India's remarkable economic performance in recent years with some skepticism. Socio-economic improvement has not reached many of the rural poor; in urban settings this new "development" is creating an upper class coexisting with all shades of poverty; radical inequalities are emerging that could threaten the country's future; a forthcoming crisis of natural resources, land, and water, as well as increasing environmental degradation are apparent; issues that are already of serious concern for China. India's replicas of Silicon Valley coexist with millions of the most destitute people in the world; whose lives are but a shadow of humanness, and for whom neither effort nor talent can apparently help them to achieve a better life. Likewise, gender inequalities remain worryingly unaddressed, and thus may threaten any kind of long-term social stability. According to a recent report by the United Nations Children's Fund (UNICEF 2006) up to 50 million girls and women are "missing" from India's population, probably the result of the middle classes' use of ultrasound techniques for fetal sex detection that leads to the (mass scale) selective abortion of female fetuses. Those without access to such technologies simply commit infanticide. UNICEF's report is evidence of systematic gender discrimination in India. Thus, rather than global poverty eradication through development, we are witnessing that persistent inequality between the world's individuals is simply staggering. As Milanovic (2005) argues, "Inequality among individuals is astonishing and likely to grow. Today, five percent of the population control one third of the world's assets." And this "gap" translates into all sorts of mechanisms that perpetuate poverty and inequality, as both are path dependent.

Critics also focus attention on what is happening in advanced economies, where these cycles of inequality perpetuation are also common and where no one except a small elite is safe from falling from grace (Newman 1999). The "working poor" are now the fastest growing social class in many European countries, and a well known fact in the United States (Krugman 2002; Shipler 2004). One of the most rigorous and well researched studies on poverty and social exclusion in Britain shows that at the beginning of the twenty-first century there are more people living in or on the margins of poverty in Britain than at any other time in history (Pantazis et al. 2006). Yet these poor people from "rich" countries are often left out of the global poverty count, as the defenders of neoliberal globalization look only to the South for such data, and mainstream development research ignores patterns of poverty in advanced economies. Besides being a serious academic flaw (Townsend 2002), the unwillingness to draw links between poverty research in advanced economies and the developing world is a way to avoid having to engage in a self-reflection that may reveal too many homeless at home, too many destitute in the lands of plenty and opportunity.

There are serious scientific disagreements over the ways data and trends are interpreted or deemed to be reliable, and on what constitutes evidence for poverty policies, but also over fundamental values related to views of human life and the future, and to the meanings attached to the notion of development. As I have argued elsewhere, knowledge for the reduction of poverty is dominated by the World Bank, a state-like transnational expertised institution, which under the pretension of scientific certainty leads the public to believe that its account of what is poverty, how many poor people are in the world, and what to do about it is value free and apolitical expert scientific knowledge (St Clair 2006a). But these views are fundamentally outdated in discussions about scientific knowledge in general. It is much more accurate to describe knowledge for the reduction of poverty as inhabiting a shifting divide between knowledge in the making and global politics in the making (St Clair 2006b). The disagreements regarding the reliability of poverty data, where and how to look at the problems, and what to count as evidence, risks or costs, are neither coincidence nor mere scientific disagreements. They are also the result of complex sets of values, both moral and non-moral assumptions, part of diverse perceptions of social processes and underpinned by political ideologies that surround the construction of knowledge. The disagreements are related to views of human life and the possible futures, to the meanings attached to the notions of development and globalization, to what constitutes progress, descriptively and normatively. As argued earlier, these disagreements are also related to the level of importance attached to the cognitive values of policy and economic thinking. Although I have no time to address this issue here, the fact that a narrow dominant view prevails is also due to the power of a particular conception and practice of orthodox economics, itself the result of the unequal power and influence of an elite in the education sector.[4]

It is important to notice how defenders of neoliberal globalization, who use an unjustified faith in scientific knowledge on poverty and economic growth to justify their views, scrutinize and dismiss the scientific knowledge that shows human actions related to progress and technology are leading to climate change

---

4   See for example the Post Autistic Economic Review at http://www.paecon.net/ PAEReview/issue36/contents36.htm.

that threatens the sustainability of the planet. Technological advances that have led to many of the positive aspects of global processes have transformed the atmosphere into a dangerously unstable environment (Oosthoek and Gills 2005). The consequences of climate change would affect mostly poor countries, as the Inter Governmental Panel on Climate Change (IPCC)'s forthcoming report will show. In addition, the patterns of environmental racism already visible in advanced economies point towards the poor and vulnerable in advanced economies as the most likely victims of climatic change, as hurricane Katrina showed the world in 2005. Yet climate change science is dismissed by those same individuals and groups that put all their faith in an economic science that promises riches to all while ignoring the costs to the poor and vulnerable. As I have argued elsewhere, scientific knowledge on climate change is the result of processes of knowledge production much more scrutinized than economic advice and certainly much more democratic than views on poverty trends and poverty reduction offered by an expertised institution that draws its legitimacy through a circular process between the knowledge it produces and the audiences that legitimize that knowledge (St Clair 2006a, 2006b).

Defenders of alternative globalizations (both activists and academics) often refuse, though wrongly in my view, to directly engage with the dominant views produced within the governing global institutions, even if in the end these are part of the problem. It is simply not enough to dismiss the scientific claims of such institutions as fallacious or merely "political." These problems of knowledge creation and the flaws and shortcomings of orthodox economics and its influence on all knowledge for development policy deserve more serious scrutiny and active critical engagement as they directly affect the lives of millions of people. It is precisely by better understanding (from direct experience where possible) the forces that shape knowledge about global poverty and development in the most powerful and influential institutions that it may be possible to offer fresh critical views contributing to alternative globalizations. It is of utmost importance to understand these organizations' cultures, and the ways in which they permit or hinder alternatives that may lead towards accepting responsibilities for the production and perpetuation of global poverty (McNeill and St Clair 2006). Some authors do understand such a challenge. For example, Ray Kiely (2005) argues convincingly that the relation between poverty and global integration is far from straightforward, and he does so precisely by engaging in debates and discussions driven by data produced by the World Bank. Yet the task is even larger that Kiely's work leads us to believe.

In my view, the tasks of development research and critical globalization studies overlap, if our definitions of these two issues are consistent. Critical globalization studies must include regenerated development studies (Robinson 2002). The conceptual tools of the latter, such as the notion of methodological territorialism, the idea that the overarching category shaping socioeconomic, cultural and political aspects of societies and peoples is the territorial boundaries of the nation state (Scholte 2000), may help unveil what are often fallacious correlations between poverty and growth. For example, the pervasive methodological territorialism in development research keeps local problems "local" and blind to questions of global socio-economic justice.⁵ Also, the blindness towards increasing deprivation and the slow demise of the middle classes in advanced economies is also the result of methodological territorialism in development research. I want to suggest that alternative views on globalization are dependent upon the rethinking of development. The task is to reclaim development, not as more global integration and economic growth, but as a meaningful process for all. There are various ways to reinvent development, some already practiced by social movements worldwide. According to Alf Nilsen, the discourses of resistance crafted by social movements articulate an ethics of praxis grounded in the assertion of needs and capacities that are not met or allowed to develop within the structural parameters of the current social order (Nilsen 2005). Alternatives always entail a rethinking of the meaning of development, and posing the questions: Development for what? Development for whom? (Gasper 2004). Such are the tasks of ethical thinking on both development and globalization. Re-framing poverty—as a global and a moral problem—and looking into its structural causes, leads to a re-framing of both development and globalization. Even if often misguided and having caused much distress, I believe that a path toward alternative globalizations passes through the improvement of the development aid system and its institutions, elements needed to regulate the global, no matter how one defines it.

Re-framing Poverty as a Global and a Moral Problem

The death and suffering that millions of people face everyday in the world goes against any moral standard of Western values no matter the ethical theory one chooses to defend, no matter the religious code we espouse. The main problem is often that there are all sorts of mechanisms that hinder rather than stimulate moral awareness, leading to complacency and even legitimating of such gross unfairness. It may be the case that our wealth and that of others may in the end depend on the misery of many. This has been the case for centuries, and still remains one of the missing pages in development and globalization writings. As historian Mike Davis reminds us in his sobering *Late Victorian Holocausts: El Niñõ Famines and the Making of the Third World* (2001), the British Empire was built on top of many bodies, the bodies of those who died from famines caused by agricultural and trade policies, by manufactured environmental degradation directly linked to the Empire's achieved wealth. While politicians blamed bad weather and people's own lack of moral behavior for the deaths of millions of people, the British public knew little about the lives lost far away, and even less about their own involvement. It is a human trait; we describe complex facts in ways that do not incriminate us. But the millions of deaths and the resulting unequal balance of power and means that resulted from the Victorian era were, as Davis clearly argues and documents, policy choices. "Millions die" was "ultimately a policy-

---

5   The notion of methodological territorialism was advanced by Erik Wolf in his study about the spatial assumptions proper to the social sciences, *Europe and the People without History* (1982). For an extended analysis see Nilsen (2005).

choice: to accomplish such decimation required (in Brecht's sardonic phrase) a "brilliant way of organizing famine" (Davis 2001: 11). The fatal meshing of the world climate system, commercialized agriculture, and Victorian world economic policies led to millions of deaths, (ostensibly) morally justified and legitimized by political and knowledge variables. The thesis that severe poverty and famines were caused by climate freed the colonizers' consciousness and protected them from being accountable towards their constituencies. Countries of the South affected by disadvantaged weather conditions were described as lands of poverty and famines. The lesson the British drew from these catastrophes, Davis explains and documents, was that relief could have prevented some deaths, but that "the cost could have been such as no country would bear or should be called upon to bear" (Davis 2001: 175). The death, destruction, poverty and inequalities caused by a combination of faith in a particular version of economic science, systems of moral legitimization and justification, and a complete lack of moral awareness for the suffering and destitution of human beings, led to policies that were "the exact moral equivalents of bombs dropped from 18,000 feet" (Davis 2001: 22). At the beginning of the twenty-first century, we ought to draw better lessons, and a strategy may be to conceptualize and treat poverty in a way that raises moral awareness for the lives of the poor and the forces that produce and perpetuate poverty.

I suggest that development and globalization studies need to reframe poverty as a global and a moral problem while embedded in local contexts, value systems and shared norms. Rethinking both development and globalization requires addressing the ways that poor and vulnerable people's agency and dignity is impacted by transnational practices as well as by local culture, beliefs, moral and religious principles and practices and the role that development aid may play. The poor and vulnerable may serve no purpose after all. Economic globalization may in the end have little or no need for those bypassed by their benefits, either in the South or in the North, and development aid as relief may simply serve to hide from view such unfairness by making us believe we do something for the vulnerable and thus legitimizing a system that harms millions of human beings. Those global "losers" may be characterized, as Zygmunt Bauman argues, as "outcasts;" the poor and the very poor, the refugees, the illegal migrants, those ill with HIV/AIDS, children and women. Some may argue that Bauman's characterization ignores that the free market needs those at the very bottom anyway. Such critique is relevant to a certain extent, as there seems to be a new category of people emerging in many poor countries, the severe working poor, men, women, and children who suffer the vicious circle of long working hours without being able to meet their basic needs or having any hope of ever improving their situation. These human beings may be but the "waste" of economic progress, of modernity and globalization; their "wasted lives" serving no global purpose (Bauman 2004) or simply being necessary parts of a machinery blind to human needs; based on false promises and hopes. These represent the emergence of a transnational fourth world; not a spatial but rather a social cartography of social relations between the poor and the non-poor; relations that are increasingly characterized by structural irrelevance (Castells 1998; Hoogvelt 1997; Robinson 2002). Associated with this is the increasing concern to control these outcasts, evidenced by the emerging dominance of a governance agenda focused on controlling corruption and imposing the rule of law. As security concerns dominate the agenda of powerful players, aid has become a tool for "securing" neoliberal restructuring through networks of marketization and privatization (Duffield 2002). Privatization also reaches morality. Contemporary development aid, furthermore, privatizes responsibility by placing the burden of personal improvement and coping upon people's own shoulders, while it shifts and diffuses away any kind of political responsibility from development aid agents (McNeill and St Clair 2006).

Framing poverty as a global and a moral problem focuses our attention on political economy processes of poverty production and perpetuation while bringing stronger and better informed criticisms against dominant development theories and pro-globalization arguments. It may help the reframing of the scope of development to include self-reflection on the impact of free market capitalism on people's lives in advanced economies as well as in the South. Such re-framing may also help unveil how relief and charity may go hand in hand with increasing and perpetuating severe and chronic poverty, and focus our attention on a needed agenda addressing the politics of justice (Hickey and Bracking 2005).

Alternative globalizations will emerge as the poor become agents of their own destinies, as they resist and reframe problems in their own terms, according to their own values and reinvent their own meanings of development. On the one hand, poor countries need to regain a "policy space" severely limited today by the prevailing rules of the global economy (Gallagher 2005; Wade 2005). Similarly, poor groups need to regain an ethical space, a space for the deliberation needed to sort out how to cope with the often cruel choices posed by progress. Complementary to this, nevertheless, explicit ethical analysis is also needed on how to transform global rules and institutions into just systems, including the formulation of mechanisms and practical proposals that would lead to more fair globalization(s) (Patomäki and Teivanen 2004; Pogge 2002; Caney 2006).

The search for and justification of alternative globalizations cannot avoid engaging with normative, fundamental thinking as to what matters and why in relation to socio-economic, cultural, and political structural changes. Such fundamental research includes, as Patomäki (2006) rightly argues, the unveiling of what sorts of practices of justice are already common and why they are just, or not. Yet engaged normative theorizing, the explicit investigation of the ethical dilemmas and value questions posed by globalization processes, is still wanting in globalization studies, and is often taken for granted in many claims made by activist groups or individuals, or too scattered, under-theorized, and unclear. Paradoxically, the globalization debate would thin out without the moral legitimacy of each side's arguments overflowing and dressing up empirical data and predictions for the future, justifying in a veiled way why such or such position (whether open markets or grassroots views of global relations) are better, more humane, more ethical choices. It may be argued that activism is a form of ethical praxis, of seeking explicitly normative alternatives. Similarly, it may be argued that new political economy analyses that address questions of power are a form of normative theorizing. Yet these are not sufficient contra the pervasive normative blindness promoted by dominant views on development and globalization (Busch 2000; St Clair 2006a, 2006b). Unquestioned scientific knowledge together with the self-righteousness of the faith in markets as the fairest way to allocate resources legitimizes undetected sources of gross unfairness disguised as moral choices. It is thus of utmost importance to frame questions of global poverty from an ethical perspective. Similarly, there is also a serious need to engage on the value choices promoted by relevant global actors, in particular the global institutions responsible for the knowledge and the policies that dictate the futures of poor people and poor countries.

An enriched critical globalization studies which explicitly embraces moral and value questions related to progress, development and poverty and that engages with the ways in which lack of moral awareness blinds experts, politicians and the public from the negative consequences of many transnational processes is thus needed. Given that development ethics and global justice writers have already addressed some of these complex matters, much can be learned, many dead ends avoided, and fundamental yet often invisible problems properly identified by seeking synergies and complementarities with these disciplines. Development ethics and global justice may help us rethink alternative globalizations, and vice versa. These two fields can also be strengthened by cross-fertilization, both among themselves and with theoretical frameworks and political economy analyses developed by critical globalization scholars. Otherwise, proponents of ethical or justice frameworks may reach simplistic arguments, disembedded from actual practices. As I shall argue, I disagree with several of Simon Caney's proposals (2006), as they take for granted that all poverty reduction strategies are ways towards increased fairness.

Development Ethics and Global Justice

Development ethics draws its intellectual underpinnings from historical figures that fought for alternative meanings of modernity, such as Marx or Gandhi, and critics of orthodox economic development such as Franz Fanon, Raul Prebish, and dependistas (Crocker 1991). Development ethics emerges as a discipline with the work of Denis Goulet, whose early writings dating from the 1960s draw insights from various critics of mainstream development and proponents of alternative economics. Inspired by French economist Louis-Joseph Lebret, the work of Paolo Freire on education as liberation and struggle, Gunnar Myrdal's normative social theory, and insights from Liberation Theology, Goulet argues that development theory, policy, and practices must be assessed ethically, as mainstream meanings of development may be bad for people, which may simply be maldevelopment (Goulet 1971, 1995). Goulet, an activist himself, has engaged with the ideas proposed by development agencies, and in the past 50 years has explored many of the ethical dilemmas that development practitioners find themselves in, and many of the ethical components of what may be a fairer system of global relations.[6] His recent work engages with questions of globalization and draws important lessons from the value added between both fields (Goulet 2000, 2005). Critics of globalization will find in the extensive body of Goulet's writings many rich arguments for the transformative power of activism and engaged research.[7]

Building from Goulet's work, in the past 40 years an increasingly visible group of scholars from various disciplines have offered insights to understand processes of development "beyond economics," and the importance of a focus on human beings and human well-being. The efforts of Anglo-American philosophers in the late 1970s and the 1980s to deepen and broaden the philosophical debate about famine relief and food aid, such as Peter Singer (1972), were followed by a transition from an "ethic of aid" to an "ethic of development," including the elaboration of human rights-based views (Aiken and LaFollete 1995; Crocker 1991, 1995; Dower 1988; O'Neill 1986; Shue 1980).

The capabilities approach elaborated by Amartya Sen and by Martha Nussbaum is perhaps the best known development ethic. Sen's work represents an alternative conception of development economics and poverty that expands their dominant informational basis to include concerns for the quality of life, well-being, agency, social justice, entitlements, freedoms and rights. Sen's approach to development originates from a critique of the reductionism and hegemony of utilitarianism in both moral philosophy and in economics. His multidimensional view of well-being and poverty places the emphasis not on goods and consumption, nor on preference satisfaction or happiness, but rather on opening people's choices to live productive and creative lives according to their needs and interests; or, as Sen often formulates it, to focus on the lives that people have reason to value (Sen 1985, 1999). Martha Nussbaum's elaboration of the "capabilities approach," which is perhaps best viewed as a capability ethic, elaborates on the need to define a specific list of capabilities and on how these ought to be transformed into constitutional guarantees by all countries (Nussbaum 2001). Many development ethicists are engaged with the work of Sen and Nussbaum, leading to a very wide and relevant body of literature reframing the meaning and the practices of development and addressing many of the complex normative aspects of development.[8]

---

6   Many of the ideas currently defended by proponents of alternative conceptions of development, such as Amartya Sen, have been explored by Goulet, who also draws on Lebret's conception of human development. Goulet's work, however, is much more interdisciplinary, and insists on the role that moral awareness plays in the ways in which we perceive progress, the promises of technology and science, and the rethinking of social and political activism.

7   Routledge is in the process of publishing a set of essays by Denis Goulet collecting the evolution of his work, *Development Ethics at work: Explorations—1960–2002*.

8   It is beyond the scope of this chapter to offer a full revision of all these approaches. For an updated bibliography of development ethics see Crocker (2008). For a full bibliography of Sen and Nussbaum's work as well as the emerging body of writings on the capabilities approach see the Human Development and Capability Association (http://www.fas.harvard.edu/_freedoms/).

The engagement of Amartya Sen with Mahbuh ul Haq and the United Nations Development Program (UNDP) led to the creation of a special unit, the Human Development Report Office, and to an annual publication, the Human Development Report (HDR) that has popularized and partially operationalized Sen's capability approach. Sen's reframing of the capability approach in terms of "freedoms" has led to an increasing amount of scholarship and influence (Sen 1999). Today, many donors define their work using Sen's terminology. But the capabilities approach also has critics who deserve attention, as they question the coexistence of an increasing rhetoric in terms of freedoms and capabilities with an unfair global system (Pogge 2004a). Such coexistence may be a misinterpretation of the work of Sen, yet the warning is important, as I believe that the most substantial problem with the rapid widespread use of the freedom and capability terminology may lead to narrow interpretations that could indeed coexist with a grossly unfair global system of unequal power and resources. Freedom is a powerful term, but fuzzy and unclear. As current global politics clearly show, there are many actions that can be justified as promoting "freedom," yet unethical. Also, and although beyond the scope of this study, it is important that capabilities and freedom do not hinder other alternatives resulting from collective action and resistance movements. The risk of philosopher kings replacing technocrats is not an enticing option. Nevertheless it is important not to throw the baby out with the bath water; there is much in the capabilities and human development literature upon which to build.

Development ethics is much broader than the capabilities and freedom approach. Des Gasper's definition captures the fundamental drivers of development ethics as looking

> at meanings given to societal "development" in the broad sense of progress or desirable change, at the types, distribution and significance of the costs and gains from major socio-economic change, and at value conscious ways of thinking about and choosing between alternative paths and destinations. It aims to help in identifying, considering, and making ethical choices about societal "development," and in identifying and assessing the explicit and implicit ethical theories. (Gasper 2004: xi)

And although poverty has been a main focus of development ethicists, other important aspects include reflection on the role of human rights, investigations on the ways in which bottom-up development may be achieved through deepening democratic processes, or more specific issues such as the ethical dilemmas entailed by development-induced displacement, global citizenship and cosmopolitanism, or the synergies with other global normative discourses such as human rights and human security, virtue ethics and more instrumental views such as global public goods (Chatterjee 2004; Crocker 2005; Dower 2003; Drydyk 2005; Gasper 2005; IDEA Newsletter; St Clair 2006c; Young 2004). Development ethics overlaps increasingly with concerns for global ethics, and as globalization changes the scope and meanings of development, many authors are engaged with global issues and the role of a global ethic (Dower 1998). In parallel a small group of Western scholars are engaged with reframing questions of justice and producing important work on the emergent field of global justice. This work, as I shall argue, complements development ethics and challenges narrow interpretations of capabilities and freedom.

Global Justice

Calls for global justice are very common amongst critics of globalization, yet explicit academic work under this label is relatively new. Rethinking justice as global is not only about justice for all but a reframing of justice's scope and character. I choose to focus on one of the most relevant authors of this emerging field, German sociologist and philosopher Thomas Pogge, because he takes poverty as his central concern; also, because his work represents a critique of the methodological territorialism pervasive in Western moral and political philosophy and social theory.[9] It is not sufficient to bring in moral and political theory to critical globalization studies. Ethical ideas per se may not lead to a satisfactory answer to Patomäki's question: are worldwide actions, relations, practices and institutions fair? Moral discourse may reflect the same biases and blind spots one encounters in orthodox development theories proposed by global institutions. As Thomas Pogge illustrates in his work, even the best-known Western philosopher on questions of justice, John Rawls, seems blind to the global forces that may affect the moral scope of human action, and puts the blame for a lack of global fairness on the poor's political culture (Pogge 2004b: 261). Pogge quotes relevant passages from Rawls' later work where such moral methodological territorialism is evident:

> the causes of the wealth of a people and the forms it takes lie in their political culture and in the religious, philosophical, and moral traditions that support the basic structure of their political and social institutions, as well as in the industriousness and cooperative talents of its members, all supported by their political virtues ... the political culture of a burdened society is all-important ... Crucial also is the country's population policy. (Rawls 1999, p. 108)

> When societies fail to thrive ... "the problem is commonly the nature of the public political culture and the religious and philosophical traditions that underlie its institutions. The great social evils in poorer societies are likely to be oppressive government and corrupt elites. (Rawls 1993: 77)

These views have a remarkable similarity with those espoused by sociologists like Anthony Giddens, as Ray Kiely wisely observes (2005) and demonstrate a structural bias towards blaming the poor and poor countries for their own problems while ignoring the important causal and moral relations between global rules and institutions and the life chances of people in the South.

Global justice, in Pogge's account, does have a very important intellectual framework distinguishable from international or from social justice conceptions.

---

9   For Pogge's extensive body of writings see http://www.columbia.edu/_tp6/index. html.

Although a thorough exposition of Pogge's ideas is beyond the scope of this study, I wish to briefly outline that global justice mainly refers to viewing events in our social world not simply from a global perspective, but from an institutional perspective. Global justice views events, actions and institutions "as effects of how our social world is structured—of our laws and conventions, practices and social institutions" (Pogge 2005). The moral analysis and diagnosis that follows from such an institutional perspective leads towards seeking explanations and counterfactuals in a very different way than that of such well reputed figures as Rawls or Giddens. Global justice does not mean all human beings ought to share the same values; one can conceive of many different notions of justice and espouse complementary ethical theories. As Pogge observes, they all would point in a particular direction, "distinct conceptions of global justice will differ in the specific criteria of global justice they propose. But such criteria will coincide in their emphasis on the question about how well is the global order doing, compared to its feasible alternatives, in regard to the fundamental human interests that matter from a moral point of view" (Pogge 2005: 7). In Pogge's account, the global system is such that it may be seen as one of the important reasons for the violation of human rights of the severely poor (Pogge 2002, 2005). I subscribe to Pogge's depiction of severe poverty as a violation of human rights not because of philosophical sophistication, neither because I think that human rights are the most appropriate model for global justice, nor because I believe that poverty should be illegal (although I may agree to some extent with some of these points). Rather, I defend and support such characterization of global poverty because it is a political tool and an ethically loaded idea difficult to distort and to dismiss. It points towards accountability and responsibility; it centers our attention on further investigation on structural conditions that produce and perpetuate poverty; it gives the poor a tool with which to fight for themselves while it forces all the non-poor to self-reflection: have we something to do with it? It makes painfully visible that the most cherished values of Western democracies are being violated every time someone dies of poverty-related causes (many every second).

I disagree with Pogge, however, in his, perhaps implicit, characterization of the "global." For him it seems to refer to the global forces that impinge on the production and perpetuation of poverty, yet it commits him to the same methodological territorialism of orthodox development research. I wish to argue that global poverty ought to refer to advanced economies as well, as it is very important to avoid making a radical distinction between poverty in the North and in the South. Again, I disagree not for mere academic reasons, and not because I think these poverties are similar; they are not, either in depth or in the ways in which people experience them. A malnourished child in the United States is as morally repulsive as one in Ghana, in the same way as a working mother unable to meet her children's basic needs is morally wrong no matter in which corner of the planet it takes place. Yet the issue here is to conceptualize and define poverty as a global and a moral problem affecting the North as well as the South as a way to force self-reflection on the West and to prevent the manipulation of development aid as a legitimizing tool for an unfair global system.

Pogge's more recent work centers on the elaboration of practical schemes and global reforms that may help solve several of the urgent problems associated with severe poverty, in unveiling some of the important flaws in the views and even on the data produced and used by orthodox development economics, and in offering arguments for the relative easiness and moral urgency of eradicating severe poverty, addressing health issues, etc. Pogge is also engaged in activism, by giving talks and interviews in popular media and thus helping raise a much needed moral awareness among the public of the serious moral problems posed by severe poverty, and by doing extensive editing work soliciting and compiling new scholarly work to further research on global justice (Barry and Pogge 2005; Føllesdal and Pogge 2005; see also Caney 2005; Wenar 2006).[10]

Various other senior philosophers are now following the path opened by Pogge and attempting to reframe their own ideas of justice to accommodate the increasingly perceived injustices associated with globalization. Nancy Fraser (2005), for example, argues that globalization forces thinkers to reframe their views of justice. To her own account of a dual notion of justice that concerns itself with both redistribution and recognition (Fraser and Honneth 2003), Fraser adds that struggles for socio-economic justice require a rethinking on the notion of political representation. But philosophers seem much removed from the problems of the world, and the dominant Anglo-American universities' curricula are mostly unconcerned with global problems.

Both Pogge and Fraser's arguments, as well as the theories and approaches developed by younger writers on global justice, however, would benefit from engaging more directly with the work of development ethicists. There is a risk that some of the new scholarship addressing global poverty, for example Caney (2006), ignores past work by ethicists, their achievements and their experiences of the constraints to having their views heard. For example, many global justice theorists would benefit from engagement with work on deliberative democracy as a tool for dealing with moral disagreements and their applications to poverty and development (Gutmann and Thomson 1998, 2004; Crocker 2008; Fung 2005; Fung and Wright 2003). For example, Archon Fung's (2005) excellent account of the synergies between activism and deliberative democracy in situations of material and political inequality and a lack of reciprocity complements calls for global rules by scholars working on global justice and critical globalization studies. Looking at the literature (and perhaps through personal knowledge) it seems that proponents of global justice within academia tend to disassociate themselves from development ethics, which remains too identified with the capabilities approach. At the same time, it is not that clear that the emerging body of research around capabilities identifies itself as a "development ethic."

---

10   Pogge has also edited an important volume for UNESCO debating the idea that poverty may best be seen as a violation of human rights. These essays were the result of a series of workshops organized by UNESCO's section for the social and the human sciences under the leadership of Pierre Sane, former Director General of Amnesty International (AI). The publication of the book, however, has been delayed for several years. Most of the texts of this volume are available at UNESCO website at: http://portal.unesco.org/shs/fr/ev.php-URL_ID¼4318andURL_DO¼DO_TOPICandURL_SECTION¼-277.html.

In my own work, I have argued that development ethics must also learn from global justice and critical globalization studies while engaging with the ways in which global development institutions use and abuse ethical ideas and morally legitimizing discourses such as human rights (St Clair 2007). In particular, I argue for a third stage development ethics enriched with a methodological pragmatism that centers on the interplay between facts, values, concepts and practices. Through a methodological pragmatism, it may be easier to unveil some of the limitations of the widespread acceptance of the capabilities and freedom approach, while respecting and promoting the depth and power of such an approach. In the hands of many donors and global institutions, capabilities and "ethics and development" in general lends itself to be reduced to provide moral grounds for relief and thus blind to questions of socio-economic justice, to the immense value conflicts and moral flaws posed by the contradictory values and goals of global justice and neoliberal economic globalization. For example, the narrow and superficial use of capabilities and freedom by the Inter American Development Bank's Initiative on Social Capital, Ethics and Development, coexists with development policies promoted by this institution that are very far from leading to a fair treatment of Latin America's poor. Ethics (or freedom) without qualification, outside its political, social, and cultural context, may be outright moralism, or worse, self-righteousness. Nevertheless, it is through careful and respectful engagement that such initiatives (in the same way as other multilateral agencies) could be challenged to improve, as they provide an arena for future debate on the role that ethics and justice may play for better and more effective development aid. The task may seem difficult but it is not pointless. Normative blindness is far more dangerous.

The merging of development ethics and global justice may be reinforced by attention and engagement with critical globalization studies. This may add new focus and a more explicit inclusion of analyses of power and acknowledgment of the challenges posed by the values promoted by neoliberal globalization, including the challenging of the unfairness produced and reproduced by the ethics of the market. The challenge is how to link ideal theory, normative analyses and proposals flowing from such work with other needed analytical tools so as to engage with questions of feasibility and actuality. How are proposals such as Pogge's going to find enough support? For activists and scholars working with social movements, the answer lies with massive mobilization and resistance that may lead to challenges to power structures and the inequalities that prevent people from exercising their agency. Pogge's perspective may be interpreted to suggest that neoliberal globalization is about people having mistaken ideas rather than people pursuing a project which serves their class interests. Development ethics may simply be seen as a justifying discourse for a system that permits the persistence of exploitation and subjugation. The proposals for a minimal conception of global justice offered by Caney (2006), and his evaluation of policy proposals, is in my view incomplete, although a useful and a needed normative analysis. I disagree, for example, with his suggestion that giving resources to the World Bank may be a way to meet requisites of global justice, as Caney seems to take for granted that all poverty reduction strategies are ways towards increased fairness. Many of the proposals coming from this global institution serve to justify an unfair global system. Caney's minimal justice therefore needs to be complemented and informed by actual political economy practices; by the often contradictory goals of these actors; and their organizational constraints. Under the leadership of Wolfowitz and the political and economic interests this represents, it is important to consider the extent to which this institution may become even more a tool for the justification of neoliberal restructuring as well as a machinery for collective charity.

The task of striving towards a world free of poverty is complex. It calls for engagement with the negative consequences of global socio-economic change; engagement with the Faustian value conflicts posed by global capitalism, its failures to deliver widely acknowledged values such as freedom and democracy at home and abroad, and the ways in which new forms of transnational practices have changed the landscape of development. It is amidst the new transnational practices where the moral worth of certain issues and people gets decided, where moral connectedness and disconnectedness is generated and sustained. The so-called "end of history," the triumph of liberalism and Western values as the victorious ideology, lacks a serious engagement with the different meanings of freedom and democracy or with possible negative consequences of promoting free markets and democracy. As Amy Chua claims, the twin results of increasing wealth for elites which often belong to minority ethnic groups and empowering masses through democratic ideas, may lead to ethnic hatred and violence (Chua 2003). In advanced economies, democratic institutions are no longer a sufficient mechanism to prevent the exploitation and exclusion of high percentages of the population. We are still blind in assessing the extent to which market relations are in themselves power relations that negatively affect democratic processes (Held 2004). The complexities call for a combined effort rather than discursive confrontation among the relevant areas of scholarship, and for more linkages with activism and social movements.

Concluding Remarks

I wish to conclude by arguing that research may be a form of activism and engagement. Although the rewards and incentive systems within academia prevent rather than encourage cross-disciplinary incursions and collaboration, the complexities posed by global forces require a combined effort. I have argued that the merging of development ethics and global justice may reinforce the arguments put forward by critical globalization studies and vice versa, as authors in these fields are driven by similar commitments to more fair and equal futures for all humanity. An enriched critical globalization studies could benefit from a long tradition in development ethics and the emergent work on global justice assessing the limitations of Western moral philosophy to provide answers to the conundrums posed by current transnational practices and building more appropriate political and ethical theories. A more focused critical globalization studies could join forces with global justice and development ethics authors to provide well founded work (normatively and empirically) that addresses the value assumptions and hidden values of the knowledge and policies for development of global institutions and the rhetoric of pro-neoliberal globalization. Global development agents are simultaneously building a system of global governance that needs to be made visible. Thus, envisioning alternative globalizations requires in-depth knowledge of development policies and ideologies and of the ways in which development bureaucracies work.

It is important to tackle head-on the ways in which the presumed accuracy and legitimacy of mainstream economics knowledge judgments co-opts or overshadows the space for "real" ethical reflection and prevents alternative values and envisioned social orders being considered. Not only are people surrounded with messages and practices that presume the current global distribution of wealth and power are optimal (fair) and the only channel for the eventual elimination of poverty and destitution, but such assumptions pervade what it is considered legitimate and authoritative knowledge for development and globalization. The problem is, then, not only a lack of ethical arguments for helping the poor, but an abundance of arguments for keeping power structures the way they are, for continuing business as usual; issues entangled with scientific knowledge that manipulate and politicize the moral worth of human beings.

Activists and researchers may add forces and focus on three issues that deserve our prima facie attention: the elimination of severe poverty and the reduction of radical inequalities in both advanced and developing countries and the striving towards equality; concerns for accountability and responsibility as social issues and ethical principles as well as legal and political tools, in particular, the elaboration of responsibilities to protect people from poverty; and studies about how to deepen and strengthen democratic processes and the voice of the poor to permit a space for ethical and political deliberation.

References

Aiken, W. and LaFollette, H. (1995), *World Hunger and Morality*. Chicago: Prentice Hall.
Appelbaun, R. and Robinson, W.I. (2005), *Critical Globalization Studies*. London: Routledge.
Barry, C. and Pogge, T. (2005), *Global Institutions and Responsibilities: Achieving Global Justice*. Oxford: Blackwell.
Bauman, Z. (2004), *Wasted Lives: Modernity and its Outcasts*. London: Polity Press.
Bhagwati, J. (2004), *In Defense of Globalization*. Oxford: Oxford University Press.
Boas, M. and McNeill, D. (eds) (2003), *Global Institutions and Development: Framing the World, RIPE Studies on Global Political Economy*. London: Routledge.
Broad, R. (2004), "The Washington Consensus Meets the Global Backlash," *Globalizations* 1(2), 129–54.
Bull, B, and Mcneill, D. (2006), *Market Multilateralism: Public Private Partnerships and Global Governance*. New York and London: Routledge.
Busch, L. (2000), *The Eclipse of Morality: Science, State and the Market*. New York: Aldine De Gruyter.

Caney, S. (2005), *Justice Beyond Borders: A Global Political Theory*. Oxford: Oxford University Press.

Caney, S. (2006), "Global Justice: From Theory to Practice," *Globalizations* 3(2), 121–37.

Castells, M. (1998), *End of Millennium: The Information Age*. Oxford: Blackwell.

Chatterjee, D. (2004), *The Ethics of Assistance: Morality and the Distant Needy*. Cambridge: Cambridge University Press.

Chua, A. (2003), *World on Fire: How Exporting Free-Market Democracy Breeds Ethnic Hatred and Global Instability*. London: Arrow.

Cowen, M.P. and Shenton, R.W. (1996), *Doctrines of Development*. New York and London: Routledge.

Crocker, D. (1991), "Toward Development Ethics," *World Development* 19(5), 458–61.

Crocker, D. (1995), "Functioning and Capability: The Foundations of Sen's and Nussbaum Development Ethic," in Nussbaum, M. and Glover, J. (eds) *Women, Culture and Development: A Study of Human Capabilities*. Oxford: Clarendon Press.

Crocker, D. (2005), "Development Ethics, Globalization, and Stiglitz," in Krausz, M. and Chatterjee, D. (eds) *Globalization, Development, and Democracy: Philosophical Perspectives*. Lanham, MD: Rowman and Littlefield.

Crocker, D. (2008), *Ethics of Global Development: Agency, Capability, and Deliberative Democracy*. Cambridge: Cambridge University Press.

Davis, M. (2000), *Late Victorian Holocausts: El Niñõ Famines and the Making of the Third World*. London: Verso.

Dower, N. (1988), "What is Development?—A Philosopher's Answer," *Centre for Development Studies Occasional Paper Series*, 3. Glasgow: University of Glasgow.

Dower, N. (1998), *World Ethics: The New Agenda*. Edinburgh: Edinburgh University Press.

Dower, N. (2003), *An Introduction to Global Citizenship*. Edinburgh: Edinburgh University Press.

Drydyk, J. (2005), "When is Development More Democratic?," *Journal of Human Development* 6(2), 247–67.

Duffield, M. (2002), "Social Reconstruction and the Radicalization of Development: Aid as a Relation of Global Liberal Governance," *Development and Change* 33(5), 1049–71.

Føllesdal, A. and Pogge, T. (2005), *Real World Justice: Grounds, Principles, Human Rights, and Social Institutions*. Berlin: Springer.

Fraser, N. (2005), "Reframing Justice in a Globalizing World," *New Left Review* 36 (November–December).

Fraser, N. and Honneth, A. (2003), *Redistribution or Recognition? A Political-Philosophical Exchange*. London: Verso Books.

Fung, A. (2005), "Deliberation Before the Revolution: Toward an Ethics of Deliberative Democracy in an Unjust World," *Political Theory*, 33(3).

Fung, A. and Wright, E.O. (2003), *Deepening Democracy—Institutional Innovations in Empowered Participatory Governance, Real Utopias Project S*. London: Verso.

Gallagher, K. (2005), *Putting Development First: The Importance of Policy Space in the WTO and IFIs*. London: Zed Books.

Gasper, D. (1999), "Development Aid: Charity and Obligation," *Forum for Development Studies* 1, 23–57.

Gasper, D. (2004), *The Ethics of Development: From Economism to Human Development*. Edinburgh: Edinburgh University Press.

Gasper, D. (2005), "Securing Humanity: Situating 'Human Security' as Concept and Discourse," *Journal of Human Development* 6(2), 221–45.

Gills, B. (2005), "Empire versus Cosmopolis: The Clash of Globalizations," *Globalizations* 2(1), 5–13.

Glennie, J. (2006), "The Myth of Charity: A 2005 Reality Check," *Globalizations* 3(2), 258–60.

Goulet, D. (1971), *The Cruel Choice: A New Concept in the Theory of Development*. New York: Anthenaeum.

Goulet, D. (1995), *Development Ethics: A Guide to Theory and Practice*. London: Apex PR.

Goulet, D. (2000), "The Evolving Nature of Development in the Light of Globalization," in *Proceedings of the Workshop on: The Social Dimensions of Globalization*, 21–22 February 2000. Vatican City: Pontifical Academy of Social Sciences, 27–46.

Goulet, D. (2005), "On Culture, Religion, and Development," in Mendell, M. (ed.) *Reclaiming Democracy: The Social Justice and Political Economy of Gregory Baum and Kari Polanyi Levitt*. Quebec: McGill-Queen's University Press.

Gutman, A. and Thompson, D. (1998), *Democracy and Disagreement*. Cambridge, MA: Harvard University Press.

Gutman, A. and Thompson, D. (2004), *Why Deliberative Democracy?* Princeton: Princeton University Press.

Held, D. (2004), *The Global Covenant: The Social Democratic Alternative to the Washington Consensus*. London: Polity Press.

Hickey, A. and Bracking, S. (2005), "Exploring the Politics of Poverty Reduction: From Representation to a Politics of Justice?," *World Development* 33(6).

Hickey, S. and Mohan, G. (2005), "Relocating Participation within a Radical Politics of Development: From Practice to Theory," *Development and Change* 36(2).

Hoogvelt, A. (1997), *Globalisation and the Postcolonial World*. London: Macmillan.

International Development Ethics Association (IDEA) Newsletter, http://www.development-ethics.org.

Kiely, R. (2005), "Globalization and Poverty, and the Poverty of Globalization Theory," *Current Sociology* 53(6), 895–914.

Krugman, P. (2002), "For Richer," *New York Times*, 10 November.

McNeill, D. and St Clair, A.L. (2006), "Development Ethics and Human Rights as the Basis for Poverty Reduction: The Case of the World Bank," in Stone, D. and Wright, C. (eds) *The World Bank and Governance: A Decade of Reform and Reaction*. London: Routledge, 29–47.

Milanovic, B. (2005), *Worlds Apart: Measuring International and Global Inequality*. Princeton: Princeton University Press.

Newman, K. (1999), *Falling From Grace: Downward Mobility in the Age of Affluence*. Berkeley and Los Angeles: University of California Press.

Nilsen, A. (2005), "Social Movements from Above and from Below at the Dawn of the New Millennium," Working Paper, Department of Sociology, University of Bergen.

Nussbaum, M. (2001), *Women and Human Development: The Capabilities Approach*. Cambridge: Cambridge University Press.

O'Neill, O. (1986), *Faces of Hunger: Essay on Poverty, Justice and Development*. New York: HarperCollins.

Oosthoek, J. and Gills, B.K. (eds) (2005), *Globalizations* 2(3), December, Special Issue "The Globalization of Environmental Crisis."

Pantazis, C., Gordon, D., and Levitas, R. (eds) (2006), *Poverty and Social Exclusion in Britain: The Millennium Survey*. London: Policy Press.

Patomäki, H. (2006), "Global Justice: A Democratic Perspective," *Globalizations* 3(2), 99–120.

Patomäki, H. and Teivanen, T. (2004), *A Possible World: Democratic Transformations of Global Institutions*. London: Zed Books.

Pogge, T. (2002), *Poverty and Human Rights*. London: Polity Press.

Pogge, T. (2004a), "Can the Capability Approach be Justified?," *Philosophical Topics* 30(2), 167–228.

Pogge, T. (2004b), "'Assisting' the Global Poor," in Chatterjee, D. (ed.) *The Ethics of Assistance: Morality and the Distant Needy*. Cambridge: Cambridge University Press, 260–88.

Pogge, T. (2005), "What is Global Justice?," in Follesdal, A. and Pogge, T. (eds) *Real World Justice*. Berlin: Springer, 2–11.

Rawls, J. (1993), "The Law of Peoples," in Shute, S. and Hurley, S. (eds) *On Human Rights*. New York: Basic Books.

Rawls, J. (1999), *The Law of Peoples*. Cambridge, MA: Harvard University Press.

Robinson, W.I. (2002), "Remapping Development in Light of Globalization: From a Territorial to a Social Cartography," *Third World Quarterly* 23(6).

Scholte, J.A. (2000), *Globalization: A Critical Introduction*. London: Palgrave.

Sen, A.K. (1985), "Well-being, Agency and Freedom: The Dewey Lectures 1984," *Journal of Philosophy* 82, 169–221.

Sen, A.K. (1999), *Development as Freedom*. New York: Knopf.

Shipler, D.K. (2004), *The Working Poor: Invisible in America*. New York: Alfred Knopf.

Shue, H. (1980), *Basic Rights: Subsistence, Affluence and US Foreign Policy*. Princeton: Princeton University Press.

Singer, P. (1972), "Famine, Affluence, and Morality," *Philosophy and Public Affairs* 1(1), 229–43.

Sklair, L. (2002), *Globalization: Capitalism and Its Alternatives*. Oxford: Oxford University Press.

St Clair, A.L. (2006a), "Global Poverty: The Co-production of Knowledge and Politics," *Global Social Policy* 6(1).

St Clair, A.L. (2006b), "The World Bank as a transnational expertised institution," *Global Governance* 12(1).

St Clair, A.L. (2006c), "How Can Human Rights Work for Poverty Reduction: An Assessment of the Human Development Report 2000," in Williams, L. (ed.) *International Poverty Law: An Emerging Discourse*. London: Zed Books.

St Clair, A.L. (2007), "A Methodologically Pragmatist Approach to Development Ethics," *Journal of Global Ethics* 3(2), 141–62.

Townsend, P. (2002), "Poverty, Social Exclusion and Social Polarization: The Need to Construct an International Welfare State," in Townsend, P. and Gordon, D. (eds) *World Poverty: New Policies an Old Enemy*. London: The Policy Press.

UNICEF (2006), *The State of the World's Children 2006: Excluded and Invisible*. Geneva: UNICEF, available at http://www.unicef.org/sowc06/index.php (accessed 2 February 2006).

Wenar, L. (2006), "Accountability in International Development Aid," *Ethics and International Affairs* 20(1), 1–20.

Wood, G. (2000), "Desperately Seeking Security," available at http://staff.bath.ac.uk/hssgdw/g-research.htm#reports.

Wolf, E. (1982), *Europe and the People without History*. Los Angeles/Berkeley: University of California Press.

Young, I. (2004), "Responsibility and Global Labor Justice," *Journal of Political Philosophy* 12(4), 365–88.

Chapter 10

Reflections on Global Responsibilities and the Nature of Morality

Thomas Mertens

In this chapter, I want to contribute to our understanding of why arguments for global justice, such as those formulated by Peter Singer and Thomas Pogge, seem to be failing in attracting sufficient motivational support. I will briefly introduce their arguments and point at their possible flaws. In doing so, I rely heavily on insights provided by John Rawls. I will conclude that Rawls's "duty to assist" is not a bad point of departure when thinking about global justice and trying to change the present situation of world poverty.

Introduction: Singer's Utilitarian Approach

In 1972, Peter Singer published a seminal article entitled "Famine, Affluence and Morality," in which he argued that the inhabitants of affluent industrialized societies have the duty of morality to help the millions of poor in undeveloped societies; the concept of charity does not apply here.[1] His argument was based on a number of simple and convincing premises: severe poverty and what this entails in terms of suffering are bad; it is in the power of the affluent part of this globe to prevent this from happening without sacrificing something morally significant; the rich ought to do that. While being well-dressed is morally insignificant in comparison with being dressed at all, it is morally compulsory to give up superfluous goods like a Hugo Boss suit in order to make way for what is morally significant, namely being able to live beyond the level of sheer poverty and distress. The situation in which the rich inhabitants of this "one world" (Singer 2002) find themselves vis-à-vis the global poor is therefore not much different from the situation in which one is confronted with a drowning child in a nearby pond. In the latter situation, it is evident that one ought to help even at the cost of ruining one's suit. In the former situation, an equal duty to help exists and one ought to give away a substantial portion of one's income to do so. If one can prevent bad from happening without making great sacrifices, one ought to do it. It is irrelevant whether the suffering takes place within our close vicinity so that

---

1   In *Philosophy and Public Affairs* 1 (1972); I refer to a reprint of that text (Singer 1990).

we are physically confronted with it, as in the case of a drowning child, or not, as in the case of the global poor.

Many people found this argument and the resulting moral appeal highly persuasive and this article therefore marked the beginning of a large and ongoing debate on global distributive justice. Indeed, one cannot study carefully the figures on the worldwide distribution of wealth and poverty without a sense of embarrassment and shame. While Singer's article did indeed bring a new approach to "global ethics," in the philosophical tradition, it has never been denied that people have duties towards others across ethnic, national or political borders, irrespective of distance or proximity. While the most demanding duties were often said to apply to those to whom we have close emotional or political ties, it has always been recognized that general duties towards all others exist, to both foreign individuals and foreign communities. These general duties are often conceived of in terms of restraint, such as the duty to refrain from interference in someone else's basic interests, like the duty not to kill or to harm. However, negative obligations are not all that is required. The positive duty of hospitality i.e. to accept the stranger as a guest within our community or to help him if he is in distress, has a long tradition ranging from the biblical command to remember that "we" all have been strangers in the house of Egypt to Kant's cosmopolitan article according to which foreigners and foreign communities must be treated with respect (Kant 1970a: 105). General duties towards foreigners have also found their way into the domain of international relations. Part of the duty to behave justly towards foreign communities is the duty not to inflict a war upon them unless there is a just cause to do so. The tradition of the *justum bellum* formulates when and how wars should be conducted. Obviously, these efforts to limit the violence of war have often been abused, but they can still be understood as a way to formulate "global obligations" that bind us with all foreigners even if we are at war with them. The *ius ad bellum* tries to restrict the resort to war and the *ius in bello* aims to uphold a minimal form of respect during warfare.

What is new, however, in Singer's approach is that it aims at deepening the reach of global ethics so that it includes distributive justice. He argues in favor of redistribution between the rich and poor communities of this world and thereby shifts the emphasis from negative duties towards positive duties. Whereas duties of redistributive duties are usually thought to apply only to domestic communities, in which schemes of cooperation exist, and not to the realm of the international, where giving is a matter of charity, Singer argues in favor of a transfer from what is superfluous in the world of the rich to the world of the poor in order to comply with our duties. Singer argues that the concept of a charitable act does not apply to famine relief (Singer 1990: 253). Charitable acts apply only to situations in which the beneficiaries become relatively better off in comparison to their present situation, as when I buy my daughter hiking boots in order to accommodate her planned hiking holiday. Not buying her boots is not a violation of a moral duty, but just a matter of being simply less charitable. Charity does not apply to situations in which assistance will likely result in rescuing the other person from sheer misery. These are situations in which the concept of moral duty applies, according to Singer, since it is our duty to "increase the balance of happiness over misery." The basis of this duty to augment the overall wellbeing in the world is utilitarianism, which Singer applies as a global rather than a communitarian principle (Singer 1990: 256). As a principle of impartiality, universalisability or equality, the utilitarian principle is so strong that it overrules all prejudiced considerations based on proximity or on emotional ties. In matters of (utilitarian) morality it does not really make a difference whose welfare is being furthered as long as the total sum of utility increases.

Back in 1972, many readers were impressed by this forceful and seemingly convincing argument in favor of radically changing our views on our duties to the global poor. But the hope that it would bring about a changing attitude was disappointed. Many readers were struck by the radical implications of Singer's view and by the apparently counterintuitive assertion that our obligations to the near and dear do not have priority. Not all his readers were convinced. In his later works, Singer tried to address the variety of objections raised to his approach. Some of these objections concerned important, yet primarily practical matters. What if I give my share but other wealthy people do not? Do I then have to raise my contribution? How do I know if my donation will have a beneficial effect; will it not just be "a drop in the bucket"? Who should be the addressee of this duty to help: individual citizens of the affluent nations or their governments?[2] Another objection to Singer's view concerns the nature of morality: is it really true that distance from the preventable evil or proximity to its victims (Singer 1990: 252) is as irrelevant as he thinks? Is buying hiking boots for my daughter instead of donating the same amount of money to Oxfam really a matter of me, selfishly and wrongly, giving priority to charity instead of to moral duty? Or has Singer simply given us a wrong account of what morality demands?

Rawls's *A Theory of Justice*

Around the moment when Singer published his famous article, the book which is widely considered to be the most important contribution to the problem of public morality in our era was published too. In his *A Theory of Justice*, Rawls (1971) argued that the virtue of distributive justice applies to relatively closed communities only. In an "omission" that Singer has labeled as astonishing in a book of nearly 600 pages, Rawls paid little attention to the question of international justice.[3] Despite this lack, the book can be read, or so I will argue, as an explanation of where Singer's account of what morality demands might be flawed. In order to demonstrate this, I will focus on the underlying reason why Rawls lines up with the classic tradition and attributes issues of distributive justice to limited, "relatively closed," political communities and not to humanity as a

---

2   An excellent summary of these objections, as well as of the "moral" one, is Lichtenberg 2005.

3   Later, in his *The Law of Peoples* (1999), Rawls addresses the problem of global inequality in terms of a "duty to assist," which is not sufficient according to Singer and many others. See Singer 2005.

whole. This reason is found in Rawls's rejection of the principle of utilitarianism from which Singer seeks his support. Although this is a well-known point, it is worth considering it in more detail.

According to Rawls, parties in the original position, if duly modeled, would give preference to "his" two principles of justice over classical utilitarianism, although at first the latter seems an appealing idea for structuring a just society. Utilitarianism aims at enhancing the welfare of society as a whole and therefore takes the wellbeing of each and every individual into account. Thus Singer argues for enhancing the wellbeing of humanity as a whole by the rich giving up what is only marginally significant for them in order to free the poor from poverty and distress.

Rawls's classic objection to the application of the principle of utilitarianism in a domestic society is that it does not take seriously the question of how utility is distributed over the members of that society, and thus the parties in the original position will not accept it. This objection, however, is based on a deeper level of criticism which should not be overlooked. According to Rawls, utilitarianism starts from a deficient view of how human beings are morally constituted. These two levels of criticism are obviously related: since utilitarianism only focuses on the overall welfare of society and not on the question of its distribution over its participants, it extrapolates a principle for individuals—to weigh up benefits and burdens when deciding on how to act—to society as a whole. Persons behind the veil of ignorance would not accept this as the structuring principle of justice for their society, because they would not accept that "the greater gains of some should [not] compensate for the lesser losses of others," nor agree that "the violation of the liberty of a few might [not] be made right by the greater good shared by many" (Rawls 1971: 26). The persons in the original position would not accept this because it presupposes that they further more than only their own rational interest (Rawls 2001: 6–7, 81–2). Instead of arguing that human beings are mutually interested, Rawls holds that persons in the original position are mutually disinterested.

For Rawls, the problems with the utilitarian point of view are obvious. On the practical level: can we really defend the possibility of an impartial view on the overall welfare of society, be it domestic or – even more complicated – worldwide? Are individual interests homogeneous in terms of pleasure and pain and thus comparable? How far should redistribution go, and does the duty to improve the overall welfare have a clear target or cut-off point? On the moral level, accepting the utilitarian conception of justice would require people to identify with the interests of others to a much larger extent than can fairly be expected of them. Holding that people should identify with each other's wellbeing when structuring their society with an eye to the division of wealth and poverty is highly implausible, according to Rawls. It would namely imply the acceptance of one singular standpoint, symbolized by the impartial spectator, in whose imagination the interests of all separate individuals merge in order to determine whether or not a particular institution or a particular distribution is justified (Rawls 1971: 30, 2001: 127). In addition, utilitarianism not only requires such an ideal point of reference, but indeed supposes the willingness of ordinary individuals to identity with the wellbeing of others, as well as their readiness to give up utilities which are insignificant from that ideal point of view for the purpose of what is significant for others. In short, utilitarianism postulates within individuals a general tendency towards benevolence, and is thus the ethics of perfect altruists.[4] Rawls criticizes utilitarianism for holding sympathy to be much stronger then it in fact is. Sympathy is, he argues, "not a strong feeling" (Rawls 1971: 186), and the desire to establish just principles for a stable society cannot be met by a moral theory which relies on such implausible capacities for sympathetic identification among its participants. As long as the "circumstances of justice" such as scarcity and conflicting conceptions of the good exist, a reasonably just society can only be based on principles which rely on reciprocity, not on benevolence.

Utilitarianism's tendency to subordinate the superfluous needs of the few to the basic interests of the many will only work if we take human nature to be moved by altruism and sympathy. But this is false utopianism. I might feel sympathy and compassion when confronted with the misery that befall the people of developing countries, but I will not necessarily feel the need to take action as long as I do not consider myself responsible for their misery. My sympathy will remain primarily with the needs of those with whom I find myself connected by strong emotional ties or by the system of mutual cooperation in a domestic society. While the need for hiking boots may seem superfluous or insignificant from an impartial perspective, they are not for my daughter. Wrongly then, utilitarianism takes impartiality to mean impersonality (Rawls 1971: 190). Yet, a meaningful account of the impartiality of justice must take the distinction between persons seriously. This means that principles of justice must solve in a fair way conflicting claims over the benefits and burdens that result from schemes of mutual cooperation. When schemes of cooperation, as well as fair modes of solving conflicts of interests, develop, feelings of mutual disinterestedness might give way to feelings of civic friendship and mutual responsibility. Rawls does thus not deny that feelings of common sympathies might arise, but rather contends that they normally only do so within the framework of institutional political ties (Rawls 1999: 23).

Rawls therefore concludes that the principle of utilitarianism will not be sufficient to hold a domestic society together, and that it certainly cannot be applied to the global one. The fact that principles of distributive justice do not apply at the global level does not imply that no moral principles apply. On the contrary, Rawls confirms that "natural duties" exist independently of any institutional affiliation, such as the duty not to harm or the duty to help others when they are in distress, but these "general" duties do not replace the more specific duties generated by the acceptance of the principles of justice in a situation of the original position towards co-nationals.

Singer does not agree. In a recent reconsideration of his 1972 article he repeats that "it makes no difference whether the person I help is a neighbor's child ten yards away from me or a Bengali whose name I shall never know, ten thousand

---

4   An ethical system of perfect altruism is impossible because in order for me to act altruistically someone else must have first order desires to which I can then apply my second order desire (Rawls 1971: 189).

miles away" (Singer 2005: 11). Singer dismisses all claims of the sort that we have special obligations only to those who are close to us and that distance makes a moral difference as straightforward violations of the impartiality principle. He is only prepared to accept that we have special obligations, e.g. to our children or our co-nationals, if these obligations are based on the principle of impartiality itself. Children are best off if taken care of by their own parents; special obligations towards co-nationals might be the most efficient way to divide universal moral labor. However, the fact that specific moral attachments seem deeply rooted in our human nature independently or even in violation of the utilitarian principle of universality does not count as an argument. Moral duties based on specific human feelings and attachments have given rise to forms of racism that led to the worst crimes of the twentieth century (Singer 2005: 12).[5] As regards to the objection that many do not act according to their utilitarian moral duty, Singer answers that no contradiction exists between the proposition that "everyone ought to do x" and the proposition that "it is certain that most people will not do x."

However, true as this may be, the discrepancy between what is morally required and how people act remains a major problem. Singer's approach faces a serious motivational problem. What else should be concluded from the fact that despite many arguments in favor of poverty relief the position of the global poor has barely improved since the 1970s?[6] Why do large sections of the population in the West refuse to act in accordance with what morality requires? Faced with this problem, others have stepped in to the debate, focusing on what might be the reason why many in the developed world refuse to "comply" with what morality, at least according to Singer, requires. One reason why many still hold that helping the global poor is a matter of benevolence only rather than of moral duty is that they do not consider their wealth as causally related to the poverty of the poor. Without a sense of responsibility, people will not act. And here Singer is not of much help. His argument is based on the principle of utilitarianism, not on considerations of causality or responsibility. He does not argue that the situation of the poor is caused by the rich. Is this, then, the weak spot in his argument?

The principle according to which I should not harm another and have the duty to compensate for the harm I have caused is arguably much stronger than utilitarianism. To help someone in distress is a supererogatory act and as such is considered praiseworthy unless his distress is causally linked to my wrongdoing. Where no harm is caused no responsibility exists, but if the case can be made that the global poor suffer from "our" wrongdoing, the argument becomes much stronger. Singer deviates from common moral sense in that he does not rely on any causal claim about how the suffering of the global poor is related to the well being of the rich. Singer only emphasizes that the rich must help the poor if they can, irrespective of relations of proximity or causality. The analogy with the

---

5   In this regard, highly respected philosophers such as Sidgwick and strongly despised "politicians" such as Himmler can be put on a continuum.

6   I leave aside that this is contested. Some defend that a decent interpretation of the data leads indeed to another conclusion and that the global poor are better off now in comparison to say 30 years ago. For an overview of the discussion, see Robeyns (2005).

drowning child is thus well chosen, as here too no causal relation exists between the child and the bystander who is obliged to help. Morality tells us that it is our duty to help and to relief suffering wherever one can.

The original strength of the argument comes thus at the price of being at odds with ordinary moral discourse. This discourse is replete with concepts such as the prohibition to cause harm and the responsibility to compensate for one's wrong doing. The distress of the global poor is indeed a situation of severe misery for them, but maybe their poverty is their own fault and in any case not related to how we live our lives. I admit that I have to act when confronted with a drowning child despite not being responsible for that situation, but the motivational gap is closed here by proximity, or perhaps even by reciprocity: the hope that others will act the same way when confronted with my child. Singer's problem can be solved when making plausible that a causal relation exists between the poverty of the many and the wealth of the few. The duty to help the global poor need then no longer be understood as a specification of the general principle of utilitarianism, but could be derived from the *prima facie* stronger duty to compensate for past injustices or to inflict no harm on others. If a causal relation between the well-being of affluent societies on the one hand and the poverty of the burdened societies exists, the burden is no longer on utilitarianism. The reason why we have to rescue the "drowning child" is because "we" have thrown her in.

Pogge's Argument in Favor of Cosmopolitan Justice

Pogge's work on the global poor is related to that of Singer by its comparable sense of moral urgency, but it receives its, perhaps more compelling, character from the fact that it stresses the causal relation between the wellbeing of the affluent part of the world and the suffering of the poor. The present situation is not primarily seen as a violation of the utility principle, but of the much less contested harm principle. No-one should cause harm to others, either directly or by upholding unjust institutions that cause harm. If harm occurs, it needs to be compensated; if institutions cause harm they need reform. This principle is at work in domestic private law when one is liable for tort, or in domestic public law that holds that public institutions should be organized so that they do not systematically violate justified interests of parts of the population. Pogge thus invokes a central element of the morality which is prevalent in the West (Pogge 2002: 25) in order to argue for its application to the global realm. Since the prevailing rules and institutions that structure the legal and economic relations on this globe have a devastating effect on the global poor, these rules and institutions need to be reformed. Contrary to what he calls "explanatory nationalism," according to which world poverty is to be explained in terms of national and local factors (Pogge 2002: 15), the truth is that the hardships the poor have to endure are the consequences of the global institutional order from which the rich are both the beneficiaries and supporters (Pogge 2002: 116–17).

In making these claims, Pogge draws heavily on concepts derived from Rawls's *A Theory of Justice*. Like Singer, he is astonished by the fact that Rawls's theory restricts the question of distributive justice to a domestic society, but unlike Singer he appreciates Rawls's emphasis on the basic structure of a society and of basic human rights as the main issues of justice. Together with others, Pogge aims at liberating Rawls's approach from its bias toward a closed political community and at redirecting it into a truly cosmopolitan direction. Under the heading of "taking Rawls seriously," he argues that Rawls's principles for domestic institutions would indeed be adequate and just if it were true that modern societies are relatively closed. But since they are not, since they form part of a more determining global basic structure, the principles that the representatives would choose in the original position should be valid for structuring the world at large. Formulated differently, in the original position representatives of persons will reach an agreement on the principles not for a domestic society but for a global society. They will compare a variety of principles on the basis of which the global basic structure can be ordered. If this comparison is decided according to how these different principles affect those who are globally least well-off, as Rawls proposes, the representatives will opt for the combination of equal basic rights, equal rights of opportunity and the difference principle. To choose otherwise would be grossly unjust, being greatly advantageous to some and severely harming many, just as the principles on which the prevailing global order are in fact. Thus, for Pogge, Rawls is right in holding that the life prospect of many inhabitants of this world is determined to a large extent by elements which are morally arbitrary, but he is wrong in holding that these elements consist mainly of domestics factors, while they in fact depend on where and in what region of this world one is born, i.e. the global basic structure.

This means that Rawls's conception of international justice in *The Law of Peoples* by means of a two-level bottom-up approach is no longer tenable. Falsely, Rawls defends that the two principles of justice are determined on the domestic level, first, by means of social contract procedure between representatives of persons, and secondly, that principles of international justice are to be decided by means of an analogous procedure between representatives of peoples. Since these representatives represent peoples rather than persons, they aim at defending the best interest of their societies, rather then of individual persons wherever they are. The process of negotiation will thus lead to international principles that will primarily serve peoples and not individual persons. Pogge and others, like e.g. Beitz (1990), opt for a cosmopolitan rather than for an international approach and reject Rawls's two-level procedure (Pogge 1994). The life prospects of individuals in the contemporary world are determined not so much by their position within their societies, but by the position of their society within the global basic structure. The question of domestic justice thus no longer has priority; the structure of any domestic society nowadays depends on the overarching global basic structure. Yet, the prevailing global structure "with its rules of governance, trade and diplomacy" would never be the outcome of a consensus within an original position. As the benefits and burdens are divided extremely unevenly, the system is in moral need of substantial reform.

Such a plea for reforming international institutions goes much further than what Singer thought necessary. Instead of transferring resources from the rich to the poor—resulting from our positive duty to help—the global basic structure has to be transformed in order to do justice to the interests of all human beings that are affected by it—resulting from our negative duty not to harm or to comply with fundamentally unjust structures. What this means in more concrete terms and how such reforms can be implemented—at relatively little cost to the ones who now benefit from the prevailing scheme, so it is said—forms a important part of Pogge's work. These proposals include the establishment of redistributive arrangements such as a Global Resources Dividend or a Tobin Tax, and the redesigning of some key principles of international economic life. In particular, Pogge argues in favor of the abolition of the International Borrowing Principle and the International Resources Privilege (Pogge 2002: 113–15). According to these principles, any internationally recognized government of a state, whether it is internally legitimate or not and irrespective of the means by which it established its predominant position, has the right to borrow money in the name of "its" people or to sell the natural resources available from the territory concerned. As these privileges provide powerful incentives to gain access to state power, they should be made conditional on whether the government is indeed representative and can be held accountable as such. Governments should only be permitted to borrow money on the international market or to sell the country's natural resources if this is done with the democratic consent of the people and in its interest. Whether this is the case should be determined by an independent international body, such as a "Democratic Panel" that should monitor and assess the democratic accountability of states. By so doing, it can prevent efforts to gain access to political power for private reasons only (Pogge 2002: 156–8).

Rawls's Arguments against Cosmopolitan Justice

I do not intend to discuss in detail Pogge's well-elaborated proposals to restructure the global basic structure so as to prevent the infliction of harm and to reach a situation of a more fair distribution of basic goods worldwide. I want to focus instead—like in the case of the argument made by Singer—on why so little seems to be happening in terms of implementing institutional reforms. We continue to be confronted with the gap between what is morally required and what is actually done. Why does the acknowledgment of the plight of the global poor not result in the willingness to take institutional global measures? Why is it that even the establishment of causal structural relations between extreme poverty and the global economic system does not lead to serious efforts to transform the international global structure?

Pogge gives some explanations. In part, the gap between the "ought" and the "is" can be explained by a series of common excuses which downplay the possibility of doing something about it. Some say that fighting poverty by the transfer of resources would just make the problem worse by destroying the poor's initiative to solve their own problems. Others say that the problem is too immense to be solved anyway. Pogge answers that these excuses are not valid: restructuring the global basic structure is no more than giving people the fair chance they now lack; further, that it is not true that the problem is immense in terms of resources (Pogge 2002: 7–8). For the other part, he attributes the gap to the continuing strong tendency to explain poverty by reference to domestic factors. This he calls "explanatory nationalism:" the view that world poverty can be fully explained in terms of national and local factors (Pogge 2005: 262–5). Pogge accuses Rawls's *The Law of Peoples* of holding such a myopic view of the problem. By emphasizing the substantial differences between how different underdeveloped nations fare, one underestimates the effects of the global structure. This is unfair. The underlying global structure can be shown to be the overall determining factor. The causal link between the suffering of the poor nations and the wellbeing of the affluent ones should, he argues, not be—deliberately or not—overlooked. When it also stresses the moral point that national communities are solely responsible for the wellbeing of its members, "nationalism" is no longer "explanatory" but becomes "common:" the claim that the nation state is the primary unit for distributive justice and that "citizens and governments should show more concern for the survival and the flourishing of their own state, culture and compatriots than for the survival and flourishing of foreign states, cultures and persons" (Pogge 2002: 119). There would be nothing wrong with the idea, Pogge answers, that citizens and governments should give priority to their compatriots if all citizens and governments had had an equally fair global starting position. As long as this is not the case and a just global basic structure is not in place, nationalism, be it "explanatory" or "common," is solely a mechanism by which the present injustice is perpetuated.

There are explanations to add to this list, however, and these will bring us back to Rawls. On the empirical level, the existence of the transnational bonds between and across domestic societies via trade agreements and multi-national corporations should be acknowledged, but this need not imply the existence of a global basic structure as the overall determining factor for how nations fare. The national state is certainly not obsolete, not even in contexts in which certain degrees of stable institutional transnational cooperation between states exist, as in the context of the European Union. Recent experience seems to confirm that its participating states do better or worse in economic terms due to the domestic policies they adopt. If this is true within a set of affluent nations, why would "explanatory nationalism" not be true for developing countries, such as Zimbabwe, at least to a significant extent? Rawls therefore argues that we ought to start with the world as it is here and now, and that entails the acknowledgment of the *Faktum* of the plurality of peoples. A realistic *Law of Peoples* should primarily aim at regulating their peaceful coexistence. This would imply the "duty of assistance" as a principle of law and not as a matter of benevolence (Rawls 1999: 37), because the society of liberal and decent societies can only reach stability by aiming to include all peoples; it should enable burdened societies to establish a decent society by providing assistance. The problem of the distribution of primary social goods should, however, be primarily regulated within the political institutions of the peoples according to their domestic standards, and these standards do not necessarily coincide with the egalitarian standards as formulated in e.g. *A Theory of Justice*. While liberalism sees society as a cooperative enterprise of free and equal citizens, some liberal societies accept Rawls's principles of justice while others do not (Rawls 1993: 51). Non liberal, decent societies have other understandings of what a just distribution is, and, given reasonable pluralism, they are entitled to think this way.

On the conceptual level: is it really true that the proposals to eradicate poverty by means of global institutional reforms are merely modest adjustments and not the means to establish world government? These proposals are said to aim only at a global dispersal of sovereignty (Pogge 2002: 178), but it is difficult to imagine how these proposals for global redistributive arrangements can function without some form of world government. Imagine the introduction of an international tax system or the reform of the two mentioned privileges in the light of democratic accountability to be decided by a Democracy Panel. The implementation of such proposals will inevitably lead to a centralization of political power on a global level. While this might be a much needed development from a moral perspective, it seems not a realistic option from a political perspective. The cosmopolitan reply to this objection is surely in part correct. Certain institutions with global adjudicatory powers such as the World Bank, the IMF and WTO are already in place and the question is not whether we want global institutions but rather whether we want these institutions or rather different institutions based on principles of global justice. Cosmopolitan proposals aim at replacing an unjust global structure by a morally more defensible one. Even though this is true, it is not to be expected that these changes will take place easily. The present global structure functions precisely because it is not perceived as a form of world government. An interesting parallel is found in the present European Union; as long as this institution was perceived as intergovernmental and as a means to economic prosperity only, the problem of its legitimacy was not raised. At the moment however when the peoples of Europe started to realize that this project might result in political integration, the "democracy deficit" was widely reported and the reaffirmation of national self-determination began (Weiler 1999). Tendencies towards unity always seem to be counterbalanced by centrifugal powers.[7]

However, the most serious problems for cosmopolitan approaches such as Pogge's concern the nature of morality. In order to understand this, let us take for granted that the existence of an unjust global basic structure is to a large extent responsible for the existence of world poverty. This should make the plea for global justice stronger because it is now based on the harm principle rather than on the much weaker utilitarian principle. Yet, the motivational problem continues to exist. The proposals for replacing these unjust structures are met with skepticism. Arguing that a causality relation exists and thus relying on the harm principle seems to be insufficient to motivate people to do what morality requires. The problem then is the following: how is it possible that people in the affluent world accept the validity of universal moral principles such as the harm principle, and yet seem to be hesitant to change the global institutions accordingly?

In order to answer this question, it is necessary to look again at Rawls's *The Law of Peoples*. As Singer and Pogge do, Rawls accepts the validity of universal moral principles, but his approach is very different. Rawls's work testifies to a

---

7   Kant calls this man's "social unsociability" (Kant 1970b: 44).

much greater awareness of the importance of the worldwide pluralism of human communities[8] and of the importance of strong local ties. While Singer and Pogge present human beings primarily as bearers of basic needs or of basis rights, they recognize the psychological difference between helping a person that I know or with whose need I am personally confronted and an unknown person, like Singer's Bengali woman, but they do not acknowledge that this difference has moral implications. From their perspective, if one attributes higher moral value to helping one's neighbors or one compatriots than to helping an unknown stranger, one then values the life of the former higher than that of the latter. Utilitarianism stresses that this is immoral: each and every individual counts as one; a rights-based approach refers to the set of common and universal basic rights to enable comparison across cultural and national boundaries (Pogge 2002: 37–9). Rawls takes a different approach. He takes the diversity between peoples with regard to culture and tradition and the resulting differences in moral commitment for granted, provided however that all human communities have the absolute minimum of resources at their disposal to establish a decent society and that basic, non-politically parochial human rights are guaranteed (Rawls 1999: 65, 79). Just societies exist on the basis of reciprocity and relations of reciprocity might gradually result in shared traditions. When these traditions take shape in the form of language, religion, or history, they account for the gradual existence of what Rawls, with Mill, calls "common sympathies" (Rawls 1999: 23). These sympathies explain that some people are more willing to cooperate with each other than with other people and that they put a higher emphasis on their common life than on the interests of individuals irrespective of where they live.

When establishing international law, Rawls holds that this "fact" must be taken into account. According to Rawls, there is no contradiction between the acceptance of universal moral principles and the acknowledgment of local commitments and attachments. Obviously, the latter does not mean that the actual separation of peoples is an unchangeable historic law or that federations of peoples are impossible. On the contrary, Rawls argues for the establishment of an all-inclusive League of Peoples, but it does mean that efforts to reach such a league should not overstretch the bounds of affinity between peoples, e.g. by arguing in favor of a global "difference principle." The problem of global poverty should be solved by means of the introduction of a legal duty of assistance. By means of this duty, all peoples will be enabled to build up just or decent basic institutions. If the members of the League of Peoples comply with the natural duty to establish and uphold just institutions, they will assist all other peoples in the setting up of such institutions and thereby make their League into a stable institution.

According to the cosmopolitan approach, this is too modest a line to tackle the problem of global injustice. Rawls, however, has another fear, namely that even this modest goal and thus the necessary acceptance of the duty of assistance might overestimate the degree of affinity between peoples (Rawls 1999: 18, 112). Like feelings of sympathy, affinity as a source of cohesion and closeness is

---

8   The extent to which Rawls is aware of its importance grew from *A Theory* via *Political Liberalism* to *The Law of Peoples*, see Sadurski (2003).

not a particularly strong force, and it is not something that can be relied upon but something to be brought about by having peoples entering into schemes of cooperation and by appealing to their self-interest. The law of peoples can therefore not aim at institutions that distribute global primary goods over all the inhabitants of this "one world" in accordance with the two principles of justice, but only at institutions that establish peaceful relations between the existing political communities. Because of their *amour-propre*, these communities primarily seek international recognition and respect for its common life (Rawls 1999: 11, 18, 23, 34). As a matter of moral fact, people care primarily about what is common and close to them and not about humanity as a whole.[9] Rawls does not see this as the denial of moral universalism, but as a warning, namely that moral duty must take serious note of the facts of life: it should focus on the "modest" but nonetheless extremely important goal (Rawls 1999: 124–8)[10] of a League of Peoples by means of the global acceptance of a universal set of principles of which the acceptance of a limited set of truly universal human rights and of a duty to assist burdened societies forms an essential part.

Would it be possible to argue that Rawls's understanding of global obligations is not simply an alternative to Singer's and Pogge's cosmopolitan approaches, but in fact a better understanding of what morality requires? I think that one can. Pogge suggests an analogy between the situation of ordinary citizens of rich countries with regard to starvation and world hunger and the situation of ordinary Germans in Nazi Germany with regard to the Holocaust. Similarly, Singer suggests a sliding scale between those in favor of special obligations on the basis of proximity and those in favor of outright racism (Pogge 2002: 135–6, 145; Singer 2005: 12–13).[11] These are morally delicate analogies and comparisons. On the one hand these analogies make sense as they indicate that as a matter of fact, morality is indeed connected with proximity and that the absence of proximity seems to lead to indifference and immorality (Bauman 1989). When evil acts take place in far away places, people tend not to think about them. Maybe the concept of "thoughtlessness" (Pogge 2002: 145)[12] captures nicely both the attitude of ordinary German citizens during the Nazi era and that of the citizens of rich and privileged countries now. In cases in which the miserable lives of the poor take place far away from us, in terms of physical as well as social space, so that it is almost impossible to imagine ourselves in their position, the voice of morality is not very strong. Most rich people live in extreme isolation from severe poverty and are not familiar with

---

9   Rawls (1999: 39n) quotes Walzer's famous remark that to tear down the walls of the state is not to create a world without walls but rather to create a thousand petty fortresses.

10   The establishing of just institutions worldwide is needed in order to reconcile ourselves with the social world; see also Rawls (2001: 3, 38).

11   On whether or not giving enough to poverty relief could be understood as being equal to murder, see Abelson (2005).

12   Arendt uses this concept to describe Eichmann's personality, in Arendt (1992: 116, 287).

people that are extremely poor. "If we had such people as friends or neighbors," we might feel compelled to help eradicate this problem (Pogge 2002: 4).

But in another sense these analogies and comparison do not make any sense. Accepting the existence of special obligations to our nearest and dearest does not imply the denial of any obligation to the distant and the unrelated. The morality of patriotism advocated by MacIntyre is different from the racist murderous ideology of Himmler; the way in which we, the rich in the West, supposedly support the present unjust global basic structure differs from the way in which ordinary Germans supported the Nazi regime. Analogies and comparisons like these tend to conceal important specific differences: in the night all cats are black. And thus they are not very helpful in generating motivational support for institutional reform. The problem therefore still remains: why is it possible for people to hold universalistic moral values and nonetheless to refuse to combat world hunger in the way in which Pogge and Singer deem appropriate. In an interesting essay, Bittner argued that no contradiction exists between people holding universal moral values and acknowledging the importance of proximity. Cosmopolitanism with regard to the principles of moral action is not the same as cosmopolitanism with regard to moral action itself. That "moral agents should act on principles that could receive approval of all human beings" does not mean that all human being have the obligation to similar kinds of conduct to all other human beings. Impartiality is not equivalent to the impersonality of universal equal treatment (Bittner 2001). This comes close to the point Rawls makes against utilitarianism: impartiality does not mean impersonality (Rawls 1971: 190). Universal moral principles do not exclude a variety of relations between human beings which result in a variety of moral commitments, some stronger and some weaker. Closeness and proximity play an important role in defining what our moral responsibilities are, but not primarily in the sense of space, but in the sense of responsibility or "imputability." I am responsible for the well-being of my daughter; I can be held accountable for my acts and their consequences. Morality is thus primarily concerned with those states and events that can be ascribed to a specific agent or a specific group of agents. I find myself born into a world in which specific individuals take responsibility for me; later I accept my responsibility for them and for some others. I am also responsible for my own acts and can be held accountable.

While this picture of morality clearly differs from Singer, it does not appear at first glance to counter Pogge's argument. He defends the same view. However, Pogge's argument does differ from the perspective sketched above in the following respect. While morality does indeed urge me to take responsibility for my actions, it is often far from clear what this means. In the case of complex events where many actors are involved it is often very difficult to identify those who are responsible or at fault, or to whom and to what extent the duty to compensate can be attributed.[13] Ample evidence for this exists in complex liability lawsuits or complex criminal cases. In the case of world hunger, it is only possible to ascribe or

---

13   For this reason Jaspers distinguished between several kinds of guilt (Jaspers 1946).

impute the misery to "the rich" in very broad terms such as a global basic structure or of certain privileges of international law. It is, however, very difficult, if not impossible, to impute world hunger to any identifiable agent or group of agents. World hunger results from a long series of actions, interactions and institutions and we do not know exactly who is responsible and to what extent (Bittner 2001: 31). The situation might be very different if we had a clear idea of how to define the crime of world hunger, of whom its perpetrators were and how these criminals were linked to their crimes. In such a case, the moral imperative to blame the perpetrators and to do something would not face the problem of motivational support. This is clear from cases in which relatively clearly "imputable" instances of global injustice exist, such as the case of the Nazi genocide or of more recent cases of international criminality. Yet, we have also recently seen how difficult it is to institutionalize "criminal global justice" despite the element of imputability. It is not surprising then that most people see themselves not as perpetrators but as bystanders when the issue of global poverty is raised.

Conclusion

What would follow from the above analysis, that all efforts to do something about global economic injustice are in vein, if it were true? That global ethics do not exist? Hardly. Rather global ethics should capitalize on the fact that moral obligations towards foreigners, i.e. cosmopolitan duties have always been acknowledged. The important question is how to implement them in our world. Rawls's plea for embedding the duty of assistance within the *Law of Peoples* is then not such a bad idea. As with Singer's argument, the duty of assistance does not require the establishment of causal connections between the suffering of burdened societies and the prosperity of the affluent. The need to do something about their plight is not dependent on such causality. As with Pogge's argument, the duty of assistance draws it support from considerations of justice and reciprocity and focuses on the establishment of an international framework, yet it does not implausibly overstretch the forces of sympathy and affinity. In the *Law of Peoples*, Rawls's proposal relies on reciprocity, namely on the common interest of all peoples that the League of Peoples united by a common international law will gradually embrace all the peoples of the earth. Rawls held that the "great evils of human history follow from political injustice and that eliminating them would make those great evils eventually disappear" (Rawls 1999: 7). To this end, efforts must be made to establish a more just "law of peoples" in which the duty of assistance is a fully recognized and established legal duty. There is little doubt that the affluent world as it is today does not meet the standards set by that duty. But since Rawls's *The Law of Peoples* sets realistic demands that are feasible within international law as it is today and utopian enough to enable us to reconcile with the world we live in (Rawls 2001: 3), it is a valuable alternative to the discussed cosmopolitan approaches. Incorporating the duty of assistance into international law would improve the lives of the global poor significantly, even if this duty stands in need of being specified as Rawls is most ready to admit.

References

Abelson, R. (2005), "Moral Distance: What Do We Owe to Unknown Strangers," *The Philosophical Forum* 36, 31–9.

Arendt, H. (1992) (orig. 1963), *Eichmann in Jerusalem. A Report on the Banality of Evil.* Harmondsworth: Penguin Books.

Bauman, Z. (1989), *Modernity and the Holocaust.* Cambridge: Cambridge University Press.

Beitz, C.R. (1990), "Justice and International Relations," in Beitz, C. (ed.) *International Ethics, A Philosophy and Public Affairs Reader.* Princeton: Princeton University Press, 282–311.

Bittner, R. (2001), "Morality and World Hunger," *Metaphilosophy* 32, 25–33.

Jaspers, K. (1946), *Die Schuldfrage,* Heidelberg.

Kant, I. (1970a), "Toward Perpetual Peace," in Reiss, H. (ed.) *Kant's Political Writings.* Cambridge: Cambridge University Press.

Kant, I. (1970b), "Idea for a Universal History with a Cosmopolitan Purpose," in Reiss, H. (ed.) *Kant's Political Writings.* Cambridge: Cambridge University Press.

Lichtenberg, J. (2005), "Absence and the Unfound Heart: Why People are less Giving than They Might Be," in Chatterjee, D.K. (ed.) *The Ethics of Assistance. Morality and the Distant Needy.* Cambridge: Cambridge University Press, 75–97.

Pogge, T. (1994), "An Egalitarian Law of Peoples," *Philosophy and Public Affairs,* 23, 195–224.

Pogge, T. (2002), *World Poverty and Human Rights.* Cambridge: Polity Press.

Pogge, T. (2005), "'Assisting' the Global Poor," in Chatterjee, D.K. (ed.) *The Ethics of Assistance. Morality and the Distant Needy.* Cambridge: Cambridge University Press.

Rawls, J. (1971), *A Theory of Justice.* Cambridge, MA: Harvard University Press.

Rawls, J. (1993), "The Law of Peoples," in Shute, S. and Hurley, S. (eds) *On Human Rights.* New York: Basic Books.

Rawls, J. (1999), *The Law of Peoples.* Cambridge, MA: Harvard University Press.

Rawls, J. (2001), *Justice as Fairness, A Restatement.* Cambridge, MA: Harvard University Press.

Robeyns, I. (2005), "Assessing Global Poverty and Inequality: Income, Resources, and Capabilities," *Metaphilosophy* 36, 30–49.

Sadurski, W. (2003), "The Last Thing He Wanted. Realism and Utopia in *The Law of Peoples* by John Rawls," *European University Working Papers,* Law 2003/16.

Singer, P. (1990), "Famine, Affluence and Morality," in Beitz, C. (ed.) *International Ethics, A Philosophy and Public Affairs Reader.* Princeton: Princeton University Press, 247–61.

Singer, P. (2002), *One World, The Ethics of Globalisation.* New Haven: Yale University Press.

Singer, P. (2005), "Outsiders: Our Obligations to Those Beyond our Borders," in Chatterjee, D.K. (ed.) *The Ethics of Assistance. Morality and the Distant Needy.* Cambridge: Cambridge University Press.

Weiler, J.H.H. (1999), *The Constitution of Europe.* Cambridge: Cambridge University Press.

Chapter 11

Global Ethics as Dialogism

An Verlinden

Several political and social events of the last half of the twentieth century have brought into relief a number of important moral issues in international affairs. Real-world events, like the Vietnam War, the Six Days War, the Chernobyl disaster, the collapse of the Berlin Wall and the process of globalization, all increasingly confront us with the following kind of questions: should we care about the poverty of people living in other countries? Is it justifiable for a state to use the force of arms in the name of human rights? Should nation-states be protected against intervention from other states or entities? What should we do against the destruction of the global environment? How to treat people arriving at our borders as refugees or economic migrants? Should minorities enjoy any special rights or protection?[1]

The Chequered Road to Global Ethics

These normative questions—questions about what *ought* to be done—arise frequently in day-to-day international practice. They not only urgently press in on political leaders and international elites, but are also important issues for individuals, either as ordinary citizens or in association with others. How we decide on these questions has remarkable ramifications on the life and prospects of large numbers of people and shapes the future pathways of human society. In order to deal rationally with these challenging questions, we have to engage in normative theory. As opposed to empirical theory[2]—which is descriptive, explanatory and predictive—normative international theory is concerned with "the ethical nature of the relations between communities and/or states and with

---

1   Frost (1996: 76–7) identifies at least 12 "pressing normative issues" in the sphere of international affairs: the causes and conduct of war, nuclear armaments, the use of force against other states or political groupings, terrorism, intervention in the domestic affairs of other states, national liberation wars, the treatment of refugees, secession, the distribution of the natural resources of the world, global ecological issues, international organizations and human rights protection.

2   The orthodox ethics and international relations literature is based on a sharp distinction between "normative" concerns and "empirical" theory (Campbell and Shapiro 1999: viii). As will become clear in the discussion of a renewed conception of global ethics, this chapter explicitly argues against this opposition.

wider questions regarding meaning and interpretation generated by the discipline" (Brown 1992: 2–3). Normative theory attempts to show the importance of moral questions on the working of international relations. Thus, with normative theory, ethics explicitly enters the realm of international relations.

Despite the centrality of the above-mentioned normative questions in today's international society and the "naturalness of ethical statements about world affairs" (Dower 1998: 1–2), political theory has long neglected the idea and significance of moral considerations and ethical reasoning in international relations (Beitz 1979: 3–5). Neither were moral and political philosophy, due to the analytical and linguistic "turn," any more interested in incorporating international relations in their intellectual and theoretical frameworks (Brown 1992: 84–9). It was not before the second half of the twentieth century that both moral and political philosophy and international political theory have gradually converged and provided the context for the revival of normative international relations theory.[3]

Normative approaches to international relations are inspired by a variety of ethical traditions and different classifications have been proposed to set out the terms of the debate. Three major classifications can be discerned:[4] the first is the classic distinction between realism and idealism/utopianism, as defined by Carr (1939). This distinction refers to the so-called "first of the Great Debates" in the new academic discipline of international relations (IR) that developed in the 1930s and 1940s.[5] The realist paradigm—internally very diverse, but always placing power and national interest at the centre of analysis, emphasizing anarchy and conflict in the international realm and thus raising serious doubts about the validity or applicability of ethical norms in international relations—would dominate the field until the 1970s. Idealists, starting from a belief in progress and arguing for more universal or cosmopolitan values in international relations, were labelled by realists as "utopians" or "revolutionists."

A second, more elaborate classification is Wight's distinction between "Machiavellian," "Grotian" and "Kantian" international theory (Wight and Porter 1992). This threefold classification, originally developed as an addition to Carr's dichotomy, has inspired other authors (Beitz 1979; Bull 1985) who assume a similar triple division, but identify the different positions by very diverse labels and slightly different interpretations. Dower (1998: 17–20) has characterized and assessed the manifold variants of each of these three normative approaches to international relations and has come to the following classification:

1) sceptical realism/international scepticism/Machiavellianism:
   • focus on power, competition ("war" in Hobbes's terms) and national interest in the international realm.

---

3   For an elaborated overview of the intellectual context of contemporary international political philosophy, see Brown 1992: 82–106.

4   Other, more extended classifications are to be found in Mapel and Nardin 1992, 1998; Donelan 1990; Burchill et al. 1996.

5   For an in-depth analysis of the realism versus idealism dichotomy within IR, see Harbour 1999.

- International norms are maxims of prudence, which eventually override agreements.

2) Internationalism/"morality of states"/rationalism/Grotianism:[6]
   - Although nationals interests dominate the international realm, there is to some degree a "society of states" in which an established ethical framework operates.
   - This "morality of states" is a set of established norms[7] that must be respected.

3) Cosmopolitanism/universalism/idealism/utopianism/Kantianism:
   - Despite the dominance of the international order, there is a worldwide community of all human beings, sharing a set of common values.
   - As world citizens, human beings have some global responsibilities that can go beyond or even conflict with their obligations as citizens of their own state.

Because both classifications—the realist/idealist dichotomy and the Machiavellian/Grotian/Kantian triad—are still very much influenced by the academic discipline of international relations, which is mainly concerned with inter-*state* relations, a third classification is proposed by authors as Brown (1992) and Thompson (1992). This classification focuses on general types of thought with regard to the source (social life or individual rationality) and the nature (universal or particular) of values and norms in modern political life, rather than on the narrow issue of (causes of) conflict which is characteristic of the two former classifications (Brown 1992: 25; Dower 1998: 102–3). Thus, instead of defining international relations as primarily inter-state relations, this broader account focuses on the position of (groups of) individuals and their relations with each other worldwide. A distinction is made between cosmopolitanism and communitarianism. For cosmopolitanism—in accordance with the third "Kantian" strand of the former classification—human beings as such are the bearers of value: it are persons, not families, tribes or communities that are "the ultimate unit of moral concern" (Pogge 1994: 89). Since this special status applies to all members of the human community equally, the duties that stem from it are global in scope. Particularist loyalties, from this perspective, are ultimately irrational. Communitarianism, on the other hand, starts from the primacy of the relationships between human beings, rather than from the independent character of individual human beings. People's identities, as well as the nature and scope of ethical norms and values are "rooted" or socially embedded in particular

---

6   Gasper (2005: 9–13), in his analysis of Dower's classification, adds communitarianism to this category. Dower himself does not include communitarianism in the Grotian tradition, although he refers to it as one of the possible arguments for a "morality of states." I prefer to leave out communitarianism from this classification, as will become clear when we move forward to a third possible classification of normative approaches to international relations.

7   These norms concern respect for sovereignty, principles of just war, rules of diplomacy and the principle of respecting agreements.

practices, customs and traditions. Therefore, the domain of (at least primary) duties is limited to those to whom one stands in some meaningful relation (Dower 1998: 22–4). Strong forms of communitarianism end up in ethical relativism, simply denying any universal values or global responsibilities. Weaker forms of communitarianism emphasize diverse forms of communal and social solidarity without denying that some universal values and global obligations may exist.

This twofold classification has the advantage of focusing on broad philosophical accounts of "how things hang together" (Brown 1992: 76). Both cosmopolitanism and communitarianism can be seen as more or less comprehensive frameworks within which a range of more specific theories can be situated: they are background theories which provide a justification for a certain set of most fundamental, basic assumptions about the essentials of human existence. They provide a coherent, overarching conception of the ultimate source of value in life—"the most central question of any normative international relations theory" (Brown 1992: 12).[8] Different theories about international relations can be situated within those frameworks, although mainstream IR theory has tried to discount or silence these background theories (Brown 1992: 77).

Nevertheless, since the fall of the Berlin Wall, the concern for ethics in international relations has enormously expanded. The collapse of the Soviet empire and the bipolar system of international politics opened new dimensions of international ethics, because ethical concerns could now be expressed without being constrained by ideological discord. Furthermore, the end of the Cold War facilitated the process of globalization, which enlarged the range and impact of ethical issues. A number of new issues has come to the fore and has instigated a range of new ethical theories (Seckinelgin and Shinoda 2001: 1). In the 1990s different approaches to global or international ethics start to flourish, working from various perspectives and disciplines,[9] ending up in a "cacophony of voices" about globalization and its ethical challenges (Peters 2004: 3–15). A whole series of concepts is used to describe these new theoretical outlooks, varying from

---

8   Brown indicates three philosophical sources of cosmopolitan thought: Kantianism, Benthamite utilitarianism and Marxism, all giving an account of a presocial individual and a ahistorical rationality and morality. Communitarianism is traced back to the intellectual heritage of German Romanticism and Hegelian accounts of politics, which see the individual as "encumbered" in meaning-generating communities.

9   Within the academic discipline of IR, new theories have developed, such as constructivism (Barnett 1997; Finnemore 1996; Wendt 1992), critical theory (Cox 1987; Linklater 1990) and postmodernism (Der Derrian 1995; Der Derrian and Shapiro 1989). But also outside IR theory, different new fields of research have analysed and questioned the perplexities of globalization, e.g. studies in intercultural and interreligious dialogue (Küng 1991; Swidler 1994; UNESCO 1998), studies in international development ethics (Aiken and LaFolette 1994; Gasper 1994) and global justice studies (Beitz 2000; Miller 1998; Pogge 2002; Pogge and Follesdal 2005). Outside the academy, incentives for a more global approach towards the great political, socio-economic and cultural challenges of the current era have been given by the World Commission on Culture and Development (Pérez de Cuéllar et al. 1995), the Commission on Global Governance (1995) and the InterAction Council (1997).

"ethics in international relations" and "international ethics," to "global ethics," "the globalization of ethics" and "world ethics" or "universal ethics." What is precisely meant by these different labels, is not always obvious. But the mere fact that the phrase "global ethics" has gained currency in recent years indicates that it is perceived as some kind of new phenomenon.

Global Ethics: A Pluriform Definition

But is global ethics really representing a "new agenda?" Is it true that the end of the Cold War demarcates a significant turning point in world politics? After all, the idea that all human beings belong to one universal moral community goes as far back as the Stoics (Heater 1966), while considerations of just war date from as long ago as the writings of Aristotle, Cicero and Augustine (Howard 1994). In this sense, the history of ethical thinking about international relations is a very old one.

On the other hand, what makes "global ethics" a significantly new agenda is the profound transformation of the structure of the post-Cold War world. After 1989, there was a breakthrough in global material integration: new technologies in the fields of transport, communication, production and information technology created a truly *global* or *world* society, in which a range of actors besides the state[10] started to take part. As a consequence of the intensification of global interdependencies, the issues around which political activity takes place and public concerns are raised have changed drastically: the all-pervasive ideological struggle between liberal democracy and communism/socialism has made room for considerations of a global scope such as terrorist threats, the widening gap between rich and poor, environmental degradation, rising ethnic conflicts, nuclear proliferation, the exploitation of labor by global corporations, the lack of transparency and democratic accountability, the erosion of traditional values and rights of local self-determination, the consequences of assisted reproductive technology, increased migration flows, the search for a "New World Order," etc (White et al. 2005: 3–5).

Although it can be argued that a lot of these "new" issues have arisen gradually out of previous developments, e.g. decolonization or the post-war period of globalization (Hogan 1992: 22), it cannot be denied that they now have a salience they did not have in the past and that explorations of them in different

---

10 The debate on the future of, and alternatives to, the nation-state has been a central issue in political science and sociology in the post-Cold War period. Some proclaim the end or the decline of the nation-state (Ohmae 1995; Strange 1996), others think the picture is mixed (Held 2000; Mann 1997), while still others see globalization merely as a "myth," defending the continued existence of the international system of nation-states (Hall 2000). What is clear, however, is that the end of the Cold War has brought a novel redistribution of power because of the increasing role of non-state actors like multinational corporations, networks of private organizations, the media and civic organizations in international politics (Mathews 2003).

fields of academic research are increasingly formulated in an ethical terminology (Widdows 1995: 75–7). It is precisely the dismantling of barriers and the cross-fertilization between ethics and other disciplines (e.g. international relations, political theory, social and cultural studies, management research, migration research and development studies) that can be labelled the "new agenda" of global ethics. Because of the complexity and multi-faceted character of these new dilemmas, our traditional moral frameworks—in terms of the communitarian/cosmopolitan dichotomy or similar classifications[11]—are no longer capable of addressing them adequately (Taylor 1989: 16). The new global constellation has created a widespread moral unease, a "moral vacuum" in which there are no norms to regulate our encounters and behavior or to determine our mutual claims or duties (Parekh 2005: 15). It seems as if contemporary ethics has reached its limits in dealing with the new, complex and pressing issues of today's world. As MacIntyre (1981: 2) has stated: "we have—very largely, if not entirely—lost our comprehension, both theoretically and practically, of morality." The challenge, then, in a time of intensified material integration, is to look for some new kind of normative integration, to rethink and re-establish the grounding of our moral frameworks as to make them adequate for the twenty-first century.

Now that we have argued why global ethics is a new approach toward international relations, the next question is: How to define it exactly? One possibility is to draw a very strict distinction between the institutional and the interactional level of international conduct (Caney 2005: 2; Pogge and Follesdal 2005: 1–3; Tan 2004: 21–9). The interactional level of analysis refers to the actions of individual and collective agents as members of the whole of humanity and focuses on their moral obligations without presupposing an underlying institutional context. Duties on the interactional level are formulated in terms of humanitarian assistance. Institutional moral analysis, on the other hand, focuses primarily on the global institutional arrangements that form the background for individual interactions. Social institutions, established rules, laws, practices and conventions are explored in terms of global distributive justice (a fair distribution of benefits and burdens). This framework of analysis draws a sharp distinction between global *ethics* (interactional analysis of international relations) and global *justice* (*institutional* analysis of international relations).

I think this view reflects a very narrow view on both what ethics and justice in the international domain stand for, or at least, should stand for. The domain of justice, so it seems to me, is not restricted to the institutional context, since it could be argued that a proper account of justice not only refers to the rights or goods to be enjoyed by all human beings, as set forth in social practices, laws, conventions and institutions, but also to the obligations that will realize and secure those rights

---

11　　In IR theory, feminist, poststructuralist, critical and postmodern theory have been developed as an alternative to "theorising in the old [modern] way about new problems" (Brown 1992: 195). These approaches have proposed new modes of thought that transcend the cosmopolitan/communitarian antinomy.

and goods and thus on the specific, identifiable agents and agencies[12] on which the burdens of justice fall (O'Neill 2001): "If we are to maintain that international relations is not an amoral realm, and that ethical guidelines can govern actions, it is essential to correctly identify the agents that are capable of responding to these guidelines" (O'Neill 1986: 63). Therefore, accounts of justice should also include the interactional realm of individual and collective moral agency. Moreover, since it can be argued that moral agency is not the prerogative of (groups of) individuals, but is instead also applicable to (supranational) institutions,[13] e.g. the EU or the UN, an account of global ethics as individual and collective moral agency seems just as inappropriate in the current global constellation as the limited account of justice as a mere institutional matter. As O'Neill asserts, "If ethical reasoning is accessible only to individuals, its meagre help with global problems should not surprise" (O'Neill 1986: 53).

The position that is defended here, seeks to move beyond the dichotomized thinking between ethics and justice, and tries to develop a normative framework which takes into consideration a broad account of global justice, while at the same time being able to guide individual and collective actions. A broad account of global justice refers to an acknowledgment and incorporation of the different aspects that have to do with it. Global justice is more than only egalitarian or distributive justice—a proper distribution of benefits and burdens. The concept is tied with a range of concrete topics (e.g. international migration, global poverty, exploitation, cultural misrecognition, status subordination) and theoretical accounts (ranging from particularism to universalism), that encompass not only distributive justice but also political justice (the protection of political and civil rights), cultural justice and linguistic justice (the recognition of differences and the promotion of cultural freedoms). From this perspective, justice is no longer perceived as a distributive duty which is opposed to the duty of benevolence or humanitarian assistance, but a duty that covers a continuum ranging from humanitarianism on the one hand to distributive justice on the other.[14]

---

12   O'Neill argues against "statist" approaches to global justice, which see a plurality of bounded states as the primary agents of justice and all other agents and agencies as secondary. Instead, she sees a multiplicity of primary and secondary agents, ranging from individuals (e.g. statesmen), over non-state actors like international nongovernmental organizations and transnational corporations, to a system of states.

13   The discussion about moral agency in international relations has—strangely enough—not commanded much attention among theorists of international relations. Generally human individuals are considered the paradigmatic moral agents. But when it comes to international relations a paradox arises: though states are assumed to be actors in international relations (by the persons-state analogy—Beitz 1979: 52–4), they are often thought to be not or only partially capable of specifically moral action (this is the dominating realist approach to international relations). Against this position, Erskine (2001: 69–74) argues that states, as well as supra-national political institutions can be accounted for as institutional moral agents if they meet certain criteria (compare O'Neill 2001).

14   For proposals of a broad conception of justice, see Carens (2000: 8–14), Fraser (2003: 7–109), and Young (1990).

The proposed normative framework requires a renewed, broadened vision on what ethics stands for in the current era. Characteristic for such an enriched conception of global ethics—and therefore the term world ethics seems more appropriate[15]—is that it is directed both at the level of individuals and collectivities (like civil society organizations) and at the institutional level of inter- and supra-state relations. Because the ultimate goal of such a global ethics is to realize global justice as much as possible, we could say that global ethics is simultaneously oriented on persons, institutions and results (Riklin 1998: 37–8). To this degree, global ethics does not just focus on the vague notion of collective responsibilities, "as if only the "conditions," "history" and the "system" were to blame for specific abuses" (Küng 2002: 11), but also on the global dimension of the responsibility of individuals (especially political leaders) and informal groups.

Global ethics in this renewed, broad definition does not only distinguish itself by its dual focus on both the interactional and the institutional level. Its area of research is also twofold. First of all, global ethics deals with the moral questions that arise from the process of globalization. As we have seen, a range of "new" pressing issues has raised public and political awareness. Consequently, a number of new multidisciplinary research areas, such as environmental ethics, business ethics, development ethics and bio-medical ethics, has been developed in order to analyse these political, economical, social and cultural issues from a perspective in which the impact of globalization figures predominantly. This is what we could call global ethics as *ethics of globalization*. On the other hand, the above paragraphs also referred to the need of rethinking or reconsidering ethics: globalization has restructured our ways of life in a profound way. Intensified global human interdependency deeply affects our worldview and disrupts our traditional conceptions of ethics and moral reasoning. It seems as if our established intellectual frameworks are no longer able to give adequate guidance. Therefore, "as globalization increases, ethics must itself become globalized" (Kymlicka 2007: 1). Global ethics as *globalized ethics* or *ethics under globalization* implies the critical study of ethics and morality under the conditions of globalization and the attempt to discover ways of moral guidance in an interdependent, multi-polar, multi-cultural and multi-faith world.[16]

---

15   Dower (1998: 4–5) prefers the term "world ethics," because it better captures the emphasis on both the level of individuals and non-state bodies and the state-level, whereas "global ethics" is often used as opposed to (inter-state) "international ethics," referring to individuals or informal groupings or movements rather than states. However, since the overwhelming prevalence of the term "global ethics" as well in recent literature, as in the naming of new research centers, study programs and other initiatives, I will keep to this terminology. Moreover, the term "global" better captures the collective and increasingly integrated and interdependent nature of our moral life under conditions of globalization and the far-reaching effects that stem from it (Parekh 2005: 20).

16   The conception of global ethics as both ethics under globalization and ethics of globalization, as developed by the Center for Ethics and Value Inquiry (CEVI), is discussed more extensively in the introductory chapter of this volume.

Global Ethics as a "Third Way:" The Need for a Contextual Turn

A two-track conception of global ethics as both an ethics *of* globalization and an ethics *under* globalization is able to avoid the standoff between an oversimplified moral universalism on the one hand and a fatalist relativism on the other. Instead of the old either/or framework—which is typical for the communitarianism/ cosmopolitanism dichotomy as well as for the two older classifications exposited above—global ethics tries to discover a "third way" that is "sensitive to the particularities and complexities of actual moral reasoning but does not succumb to the temptations of relativism" (Bader and Engelen 2003: 375). Let me explain. First, as the world transforms towards an increasingly interdependent and diverse "global village," the context as well as the content of the traditional discourse on moral universals or "moral absolutes"—present throughout much of the history of Western ethics—is radically altered. Today, universal or cosmopolitan sources of moral authority, however "thin" and procedural they might be formulated, are no longer sustainable as shared sources of moral value if they do not take into account the normative relevance of cultural diversity and plurality and of contingent moral practices in concrete social and communal settings (Esposito and Murphy 2005: 46–50). Insofar the normative role of particular communities and cultures—with common habits, shared practices and specific notions of virtues—are negated, we end up in an abstract universalism, that has no longer any practical relevance. Second, it is equally important to recognize that a strong commitment towards communitarian particularism runs the risk of ignoring the exclusionary effects that might be embedded in communal and cultural practices. Insofar these excesses are not acknowledged, we head towards an extremely relativistic position that takes practices of exploitation, oppression, discrimination and ethnocentrism as "just the way we do things around here" (Carens 2000: 4). Therefore,

> [a]ll productive moral reasoning has to tackle the *tension* between the *universalizing* trend of *moral principles* on the one hand, the *particularizing* trend of normative *institutions, cultures and practices* on the other. There has to be some "critical, *reflexive* equilibrium," some back and forth connecting "our" moral intuitions which are always intuitions of a historically and socially situated moral community to more universally shared moral principles. Otherwise two dangers are imminent: (i) the danger of abstract, merely stipulated universalism; an imaginary moral view from nowhere would not have any plausibility, let alone binding force; (ii) the dangers of unreflected particularism or of an uncritical acceptance of "our" particular institutions and practices as morally right or at least as defensible "first approximations". (Bader 1997a: 51–2n, emphasis in original)

In striving for an appropriate middle way between both positions, global ethics is not directed at "harmonizing" or transcending them (cf. Habermas 1994), since such a "go beyond" strategy rather continues the dichotomous either/or approach that has proven to block much of Western thinking about ethics in international relations (Seckinelgin and Shinoda 2001: 4). Global ethics as a "third way" does not want to create just another dichotomy. Instead, it aims at *balancing* the conflicting interests by taking a contextualized, politically, historically and culturally sensitive and nuanced view (Bader 1997b: 790–99). The contextual approach has only recently gained currency in moral and political philosophy[17] and is up till now used in an unsystematic and rather tentative way (Bader and Engelen 2007: 377). Nevertheless, it seems to be a very promising perspective to conceive of global ethics.

As far back as the early 1930s, American pragmatist philosopher John Dewey, working within the tradition of Charles Sanders Peirce and William James, observed that neither traditional morality nor traditional philosophical ethics was able to cope with the problems raised by the transformations which characterized American society in the period between the second half of the nineteenth century and the beginning of the Cold War (e.g. mass migration, class conflict, the Great Depression, see Commers 2007 and Commers's chapter in this volume). According to Dewey, traditional ethics offered no longer practical service to ordinary people, since it sought to discover and justify fixed moral goals and principles by dogmatic, abstract methods of deductive reasoning. Instead of a search for universal certainty and enduring stability, Dewey argued for a reconstruction of moral philosophy in view of rescuing a genuine moral practice in the service of people (Dewey 1948: 1–15). This reconstruction, which starts from an anti-foundationalist stance asserting the absence of any firm grounds for human knowledge and values, should aim at discovering a working method for morality, directed at improving the practical value judgments that guide our conduct.[18] In order to realize such an "edifying philosophy" of value clarification (Rorty 1980: 365ff), Dewey preferred a contextual, action-oriented method instead of a procedural or systematic approach based on universals or essentials. This method starts from the intricate connection between theory and practice: theory is an abstraction from direct experience that must be tested again and again in concrete, practical settings in order "not to practicalize intelligence, but to intellectualize practice" (Dewey cited in Eldridge 1998: 5). Moral value, for

---

17   In political philosophy, participants in the multiculturalism debate have frequently adopted a contextual approach. This applies as well to communitarian-oriented authors like Kymlicka (1995), MacIntyre (1981), Parekh (2000), Tamir (1993) and Walzer (1983), as to liberal egalitarians like Bader (1997a) and Carens (2000) and to feminist writers such as Benhabib (2002). Within moral philosophy, contextualism has a longer, albeit often neglected history and was defended by pragmatists like Peirce (1905) and Dewey (1939). Contemporary pragmatists are Putnam (1994) and Shapiro (1999).

18   Unlike his contemporary analytical colleagues, Dewey was not concerned with the nature of values, but with the *process* of valuation, which is for him essentially a method of *inquiry*. For Dewey, value judgments are practical judgments composed of descriptive and action-guiding components. The constitutive point of making value judgments is to alter or guide our "prizings" or pre-critical impulses and habits through the use of reflective intelligence (Dewey 1939: 5 and 28–34). Therefore, value judgments are practical *tools* for (re)directing future human conduct – they can be evaluated instrumentally by putting them into practice and seeing whether their consequences are acceptable or satisfying to us. Moral progress is achieved by this enduring experimental and reflective process of valuation.

Dewey, is thus always contextual: value is meant to offer a solution to a problem encountered in a *specific* situation (Dewey 1922: 199 and 208). Therefore, values never exist outside practice: value judgment is always relative to the particular context that gives meaning and sense to these judgments (Dewey 1939: 230).

I think Dewey's insights are of great relevance for today's globalized world. Indeed, the analysis that Dewey has made about late-nineteenth- and early-twentieth-century American society is a forerunner of the "moral crisis" that affects the world in the twenty-first century on a global scale—"We stand today at a place very much like that occupied by Dewey in 1938" (Putnam and Conant 1994: 221–2). Therefore, Dewey's pragmatic approach could be a way out of the paralysing deadlock between universalist and particularist perspectives as described above. If ethics is to take seriously "the pluralism of our moral universe, the multi-layeredness of our social reality, the indeterminacy of our normative principles and the complexity of our practical reasoning" (Bader and Engelen 2003: 375–82; Bader and Saharso 2004: 107–9),[19] it is in need of a pragmatic, contextual turn.

Global ethics, then, conceived as a contextual "third way," starts from the intricate structure of theoretical and practical outlooks, of abstract principles and local, context-sensitive considerations, acknowledging that morality is fundamentally context-dependent and embedded in the ways of life it is practiced in. Giving up the illusion of an ultimate, comprehensive theory that could serve as a standard guide for action, global ethics focuses on an appropriate *method* for practical moral reasoning—a method that moves forth and back between the abstract and the concrete, between theory and practice, connecting theoretical formulations to actual practises and intuitive judgments and "engaging in an ongoing dialectic that involves mutual challenging of theory by practice and of practice by theory" (Carens 2004: 123). The advantages of a contextual global

---

19   (1) Moral pluralism: While some authors accept ethical and cultural pluralism, though reject moral pluralism (e.g. Habermas's critical theory of communicative interaction, 1984), a contextual approach argues that the multiplicity of (incompatible) conceptions of the good life is necessarily accompanied by the impossibility of an overarching hierarchical order of moral principles. (2) Multi-layeredness: Social reality consists of different intertwined institutions (e.g. markets, liberal constitution) that are all based on specific interpretations and implementations of general principles and supported by specific cultural practices. As a consequence, just as different cultural practices allow for some actions but not for others, so do different institutions allow for different practices. (3) Indeterminacy: Normative principles are multi-interpretable, depending upon the specificities of the situation and the institutional or cultural context in which they are applied. Therefore, our practical judgment is in- or at least under-determined. Practical judgment is contingent, diverse and specific and misses a sound or definite ground. (4) Complexity: Practical reasoning encompasses a complex and rich set of arguments. Besides moral oughts (imposing the equal treatment of human beings), human reason is also determined by prudential arguments (considerations of well-informed, rational, long-term interest), realist arguments (determining what is feasible given the different political, institutional and behavioral constraints at hand) and ethical-political arguments (imposing respect for particular, culturally determined notions of the good life).

ethics are twofold. First, as a method, it is likely to yield greater normative insights compared with standard deductive moral reasoning because of its focus on arbitration and mutual adjustment rather than on adjudication (Verhaar and Saharso 2004: 180 and 193). Arbitration is aimed at clarifying standpoints and at resolving disputes through reconciliation of the contending parties. Yet, this is not to say that global ethics will always end up in agreement. In a world of constant change, no answer can ever be definite or final. Therefore, the process of interpretation and arbitration is an ongoing endeavor: global ethics is the difficult art of sensitively balancing without ever coming to fixed solutions or closure. As Marcus Singer (1961: 340) rightly remarked, it is "in the reasonable disagreements of reasonable men that we may find, so far as we are reasonable, both hope and enlightenment." Second, as a theoretical orientation,[20] the surplus value of a contextual global ethics is to be found in its recognition and appreciation of diversity and difference. Defending an explicitly anti-foundational stance, global ethics is sensitive to the richness of a deeper understanding of differences and alterity. It welcomes the complex diversity and plurality of social reality as a source of value and considers the varied, multi-layered empirical context as an important precondition for a broadened en deepened practical morality (Verhaar and Saharso 2004: 179–80). Instead of neglecting differences, global ethics actively engages in it: it carefully compares, balances and dialogues, so that cross-fertilization can occur and reasonable moral trade-offs can be attained. In this way, global ethics gives voice and contributes to the never ending conversation of mankind.

However, while the advantages of a contextual global ethics may be manifold, we should be wary of some possible traps. First of all, an unqualified openness to context and difference runs the risk of losing itself in the details of particularities. Engaging in the situational, the historically contingent and the non-ideal may be inevitable from a contextual point of view, it cannot be overriding or decisively authoritative. If we limit the moral domain to the local—if "every substantive account of [distributive] justice is a local account" (Walzer 1983: 314–5)—we lose sight of the wider, global context of our common humanity and the structural injustices and power inequalities that are part and parcel of it. Therefore, it is important that our particular, context-sensitive considerations and judgments be tested against the critical threshold of more abstract "considered convictions of justice" with regard to the world as a whole[21] (Carens 2000: 6–12). This is not to say that we should abstract from all particularity. On the contrary, we should embrace it as an essential part of all normative thinking, but always in such a

---

20   I use the term "theoretical orientation" as opposed to a full-fledged theory that would present global ethics as a (foundationalist) global *ethic* in the singular, which is not the position defended here.

21   As was mentioned earlier, "considered convictions of justice" are open to conflicting interpretations. While some authors, e.g. Barry (1995), defend a thin, universalistic conception of justice, others argue for a fuller understanding of justice, e.g. "justice as redistribution and recognition" (Fraser 2003: 7–109) or "justice as even-handedness" (Carens 2000: 8–14).

way that it is fair to all the different particularities. Otherwise, contextual global ethics slips into a radical relativism that is incapable of drawing the line between morally tolerable "ethnicism" and intolerable "ethnocentrism" or between "noble patriotism" and "nasty nationalism." Secondly, and related to the first possible trap, the emphasis of a contextual global ethics on openness to cultural diversity and differences challenges our idea of human solidarity. Insofar our norms and values and our conceptions of the good are deeply embedded in our particular ways of life, the question arises whether we can genuinely care for the particular needs and interests of other (groups of) people. Are we justified in taking up responsibility in only a limited sense—that is towards those we call our "own"—or is there nevertheless a wider "sense of belonging" to the community of mankind? An unqualified acceptation of human diversity and moral plurality runs the risk of rendering any notion of global moral concern meaningless. The challenge, then is, whether global ethics, properly conceived, is not only capable of arriving at "reasonable trade-offs" between parties under a common social reality, but also between people who do not share a specific context or common practice. If we do accept that people can have responsibilities towards the "distant other," then global ethics, while being a non-foundational, context-sensitive enterprise, cannot go beyond some notion of global human connectedness. Again, this points to the critical vulnerability of contextual global ethics to (implicit) forms of relativism.

Global Ethics and Dialogism

A deliberate defence of global ethics as a "third way," thus, especially needs to deal with the traps of ethical and moral relativism, while recognizing the importance of diversity and difference. This concern is shared by a broad range of academic disciplines.[22] Common to all these approaches is the refusal to use the established frameworks of cosmopolitanism and communitarianism as a starting point. For them, these modern frameworks fail to contribute to a real understanding of the late-modern ethical subject. Instead, they seek to explore new forms of identity and community which overcome the traps of both abstract universalist "imperialism" and unqualified particularistic "provincialism" (Robinson 2001: 64–7). The intended results are accounts in which differences can co-exist with some form of universal inclusion, without ending up in a "clash" or "standoff" between inside/outside, self/other, universal/particular, public/private.

A "third way" normative approach must abandon the traditional quest for epistemological certainty with regard to the question of moral conduct,

---

22   "Third way" theories that focus on the meaning of difference, are feminist ones like those of Friedman (1993), Held (2006) and Robinson (1999). Similar positions, although not from a care-perspective, can be found in poststructuralist theories (e.g. Jabri 2001) and Critical Theory (e.g. Shapiro 2001). Other "third way" approaches start from a universalistic perspective, emphasizing the possibility of overlapping consensus, rather than differences (e.g. Charvet 2001).

conceived of as a dualism between the Cartesian autonomous, self-interested subject on the one hand and the situated, "embedded" self on the other. Instead, it should apply a non-foundationalist approach that acknowledges the uncertainty, ambiguity, spontaneity and complexity of late-modern moral conduct (Bauman 1994: 32–4). The subject of late-modern ethics, engaged in a variety of relationships on both the local and the global level, can be described as having a hybrid identity: a complex, multi-layered identity that is the (ever provisory) result of profound interactions and mutual adjustments out of the interplay with other agents and cultures (Hannerz 1992: 266). The hybrid de-centred subject is always "becoming," constituted within and through diverse contexts of interaction and capable of redefining herself and reformulating the social spaces that surround her (Jabri 2001: 165–80). This conception of the late-modern subject has far-reaching consequences for a contextualized global ethics: instead of focussing on "boundaries" and fixed identities—as is common to essentialist approaches—a recognition of hybrid identities engenders an enriched normative vocabulary for moral agency, focussing on the notions of dialogue, conversation and communication. This vocabulary defines social space as a rich moral "laboratory" in which differences are no longer interpreted as threatening or hostile, but instead as constitutive to a deeper understanding of our changing moral horizons (Colpaert 2005: 135–6). For global ethics, moral pluralism is a "global common good" (Parekh 2005: 30): it opens the possibility of meaningful dialogue, of conversation within and across cultures and of mutual learning and understanding. Global ethics, then, comes down to a practical, relational rationality, an engagement in dialogue which moves beyond merely understanding or "respecting" differences towards a "third space," in which a principled openness to the other results in a mutual process of transformative "giving" and "taking," combining elements of each of the participant's original cultures and offering common, cross-cultural, dialogical grounds for new moral values and principles.

Global ethics as dialogism or "relational" ethics is defended in various ways.[23] Nevertheless, the concept is often used in a very generalized or unspecified way. Feminist ethics, although internally very diverse,[24] has given the most convincing proposal so far of a relational conception of global ethics. With its emphasis on contextual morality and the values of care, empathy and responsiveness, feminist ethics has offered a promising alternative to the leading traditions in international relations (e.g., Bubeck 1995; Held 2006; Robinson 1999). However, I will turn

---

23   Theologian Küng (1991) argues for a conception of a "global ethic" based on "interreligious dialogue;" feminist philosopher Robinson (1999) defends a "critical ethics of care," based on a "relational ontology;" political theorist Parekh (2005) asserts that a "global ethic" can only be arrived at by means of a "cross-cultural dialogue;" liberation philosopher Serrano-Caldera (1993) maintains that global ethics must be derived from an "intercultural dialogue" aimed at "unity within diversity;" cultural philosopher Colpaert (2005) is a proponent of "intercultural dialogue" and "relational ethics."

24   For an overview of different feminist perspectives on global ethics, see Hutchings (2007).

to an older and a less usual source of dialogical or relational ethics, that is the dialogical philosophy of Martin Buber.[25] Martin Buber (1878–1965)[26] can be considered as the founding father of dialogism, falling in between the modern and the postmodern, together with such thinkers as Mikhail Bakhtin (1895–1975) and Emmanuel Levinas (1905–1995) (Friedman 2002: xx). Both Bakhtin's literary theories (Bakhtin 1930s) and Levinas's phenomenology of the face-to-face (Levinas 1961) were deeply influenced by Buber's conception of the *I-Thou* relationship. Although Levinas has gained much popularity among philosophers in recent years, I focus on the philosophical foundations of dialogism set out by Buber, since Levinas himself wrote:

> That valuation of the dia-logical relation and its phenomenological irreducibility, its fitness to constitute a meaningful order that is autonomous and as legitimate as the traditional and privileged subject-object correlation in the operation of knowledge—that will remain the unforgettable contribution of Martin Buber's philosophical labours. ... Nothing could limit the homage to him. Any reflection of the alterity of the others in his or her irreducibility to the objectivity of objects and the being of beings must recognize the new perspective Buber opened—and find encouragement in it. (Levinas, cited in Friedman 2002: 338)

Insofar the majority of literature on global or international ethics is situated within the Anglo-American tradition, Buber's dialogical philosophy offers a welcome hermeneutical enrichment. His insights are not argumentatively demonstrated or proven, but instead offer an experiential description and articulation of the world: "I have no doctrine. [...] I am no philosopher, prophet, or theologian, but a man who has seen something and who goes to the window and points to what he has seen" (Buber 2002: 39). The starting point for Buber's philosophy is his rejection of any one-sided prizing of knowledge. Traditional philosophy, either in its idealist or realist form, leads to an overemphasis of objective, impersonal knowledge and the theoretical concepts that derive from it. In both cases, there is a problematic relation between the general maxim that addresses everyone and no one and the concrete situation that addresses the person in his or her uniqueness (Schilpp and Friedman 1969: 88–100). "True norms," Buber says, never become a maxim: they do not command our obedience to authority but they command our-*selves*: they address us *directly* in the situation where we are and leave us to respond with our whole being (Buber 2002: 69). Therefore, "Reason [...] may not sacrifice to consistency anything of that reality itself which the experience that has happened commands it to point to. If the thought remains true to its task, a system will not come out of it, but certainly a connected body of thought more resolved in itself, more transmittable" (Schilpp and Friedman 1969: 689–90). This clearly anti-foundationalist stance is the basis of Buber's dialogical philosophy, which is especially considered with the very *nature* of moral relations.

In his magnum opus *Ich und Du*, dating from 1923, Buber describes two radically different kinds of relationships that constitute human existence (Buber 2004). Both relations categorize the modes of consciousness, interaction and being through which individuals engage with each other and with reality. The first mode of being is the monological I-It relation (*Ich-Es Verhältnis*): the everyday relation of a human being towards the world surrounding him. In the I-It relation, the I qualifies and conceptualizes things and people in mental representations. The other is not seen as an independent person, nor as a partner, but as an object. Therefore, this relation can be described as a subject-object relation—a monological relation with oneself, using other objects to serve one's own interests. The I-It relation is the relation of "the self-willed" man, who does not know real connection, but only the outside world and his desire to use and "appropriate" it unto itself. The I of the I-It relation is called "individuality" by Buber: the I that becomes conscious of itself as the subject of experiencing and using, detached and differentiated from other individualities and only concerned with its "My:" my kind, my race, my creation, my genius (Buber 2004: 51–53). In the world of It, there is a sharp dividing line between the public life of institutions (state and economy—*It*) and the private life of feelings (*I*). While both institutions and feelings are necessary for man, neither of them, if simply put together, have access to real *mutual* life (Buber 2004: 39–43).

Opposed to the self-differentiating and appropriating individual of the world of I-It, stands the *person* of the I-Thou relationship (*Ich-Du Beziehung*). This kind of relationship—which is the foundation underlying and giving meaning to the world of It[27]—is described by Buber as a direct one—a relation of immediacy

---

27   In emphasizing the prior reality of the I-Thou relationship, Buber does not direct to a dualism between I-It and I-Thou. On the contrary, for Buber, both the I-Thou and the I-It relation are necessary for human existence. It is impossible to avoid all reification of other human beings, since we encounter them not only in close, intimate relationships, but also interact with them in many other "instrumental" ways. The I-Thou encounter will, and indeed must, inevitably collapse into the world of It, whereby Thou will become a He or She—an object for consciousness. At the same time, however, man is capable of continually leaving the world of It for the world of relation, in which I and Thou freely

between two beings, not bounded or mediated by any external elements (e.g. prejudices, assumptions, reservedness) or frameworks of reference. Human beings enter into this relation with their innermost and whole being—they reveal themselves to each other as they are, as persons, as ends in themselves, so that real encounter or meeting in full authenticity and uniqueness can happen. The other does not appear as an It, or a He or She—a loose bundle of named qualities—but is immediately tied to the I (Buber 2004: 15–17). The I-Thou relationship is the relationship of "the free man:" a two-sided event in which each participant experiences mutual presence, a vital reciprocity, an elementary togetherness emerging from genuine listening and responsible responding (Kramer 2003: 19–20). Through the dialogue between I and Thou, which is an interplay of engaging and being engaged, of fully affirming, accepting and confirming the otherness of the other, a new third dimension is created—a "real, filled present" of intensity and wholeness, which cannot be appropriated but only be shared (Buber 2004: 18 and 52).

This new dimension, which Bubers calls the "Interhuman" or the interactive sphere of the "between" (*das Zwischen, das Zwischenmenschliche*), is essential to his dialogical philosophy. The realm of the Interhuman refers to the sphere that is generated when authentic, unreserved human relationship spontaneously occurs between a conscious self (*I*) and a conscious other (*Thou*), when one turns to the other (*Umkehr*) and enters into an undivided relationship. The between is a deep bonding (*Verbundenheit*), a relational space that is ever and again re-constituted in accordance with men's genuine meetings with one another (Buber 2002: 241). It is a new, third reality unfolding out of the turning of the I to the other as a real self in his/her particularity, in order to communicate with him/her in a sphere which is common to both but which reaches out beyond the special sphere of each. The "between," Buber says, is the elusive sphere where the genuine middle way between subjectivity and objectivity must begin: unlike the subject-object relation of I-It, the I-Thou relation takes place neither in the "subjective" (the realm of emotions) nor the "objective" (the realm of rationality), but in the reciprocal lived relationships of whole and active beings (Friedman 2002, 69).

Being a whole or a real person, then, is nothing more and nothing less than being a dialogical person, a person that believes in the real solidarity of I and Thou and that is continually open to the "signs of address" that rise out of the genuine dialogue (Buber 2002: 12–15). These signs are unique and urge us to "imagine the real" or "experience the other side" in order to respond to the unique and irreducible situation one faces. "Imagining the real" is the silent command to feel an event from the side of the person one meets, while remaining on one's own side of the relationship—being aware of the otherness of the other, imagining quite concretely what another person is wishing, feeling, perceiving and

---

confront each other in mutual effect and (re)direct the drive of the I to reify the other. The alternation of I-It and I-Thou, the interpenetration of I-Thou in the world of It, allows every It to be taken again into the meeting with Thou and thereby prevent the world of It from overtaking us by introducing ultimate meaning and intrinsic value into life (Buber 2004: 21 and 44–5).

thinking without imposing one's truth on the other or assimilating its otherness into "another I" (Schilpp and Friedman 1967: 723).[28] The address revealed in entering the Interhuman involves a responsiveness, a readiness of each of the participants to be openly attentive to all voices, to respond with ones whole life to the claims made by the other(s), to understand, acknowledge and honor them and to endeavor to reconcile them with one's own claims. (Buber 2002: 135) Because of the directness and irreducibility of the I-Thou relationship, responsibility[29] cannot be captured in general categories or in an abstract moral code or universal idea. Responsibility presupposes the "ever anew" address of the concrete other in the realm of the Interhuman. Therefore, "the idea of responsibility is to be brought back from the province of specialized ethics, of an ought that swings free in the air, into that of lived life. Genuine responsibility exists only where there is real responding to the events of everyday life" (Buber 2002: 18).

Contextual Global Ethics as the Space of the Interhuman

Buber's conception of the human condition as a continuous, healthy alternation between I-It and I-Thou and his explication of the Interhuman as the fragile moral space that is "in between" offer important insights for a contextual global ethics. He himself described his existentialist philosophy as the "narrow ridge:" "a narrow rocky ridge between the gulfs where there is no sureness of expressible knowledge but the certainty of meeting what remains undisclosed" (Buber 2002: 218). There is indeed perhaps no better phrase to characterize the significance of Buber's thought than that of the narrow ridge, which offers a genuine third alternative to "the insistent either-or's of our age" (Friedman 2002: 3). Instead of the dichotomous thinking in terms of irreconcilable alternatives, that is so characteristic for our traditional philosophical frameworks, Buber's account of the Interhuman and the dia-*logical* relation that is essential for it, offers a middle way that tries to arrive at a paradoxical unity of what is usually understand only as alternatives: objectivism versus subjectivism, universalism versus particularism, knowledge versus will, reason versus emotion, collectivism versus individualism, good versus evil. It is precisely on the narrow ridge, "on the far side of the subjective, on this

---

28   The inter-subjective I-Thou relation is not parcelled into different realms like the I-It relation, but is nevertheless characterized by the twofold basis out of which each human being is constituted: relation (an openness to otherness) and distance (separateness of the other) (Buber 1951: 105–13). Therefore, the mutuality of the dialogical relation is not equal to simple unity or empathy: each of the members of the relation really remains him/herself, remains different from the other.

29   Responsibility is described by Buber in terms of *Wort, Antwort, antworten, verantworten*, etc. Responsibility is thus not an abstraction, but is part of a closely interrelated situation in which address and response, answering for and being responsible for are intimately connected. Responsibility, for Buber, carries in itself the root sense of being *answerable* in the lived life.

side of the objective," in the lived life of the meeting between I and Thou (Buber 2002: 243), that a renewed contextual global ethics must operate.

For Buber, morality is neither self-created and autonomous, nor externally imposed.[30] Morality consists of the narrow ridge between both the "address" from without and free "response" from within. On that narrow ridge, in the space of the lived live, of the genuine meeting with the other as a Thou, moral values and meaning are discovered or revealed (Buber 1998: 93 and 129–30). Thinking through the different normative challenges of our current globalized era, Buber's conception of the narrow ridge suggests a radical breach with our traditional ethical frameworks. The dominant moral-philosophical discourse of modernity is deeply permeated by the Cartesian dualism of subject versus object (*I* versus *It*), which results in an either-or logic of absolutism versus relativism, objectivism versus subjectivism.[31] Whether the subjective *I* or the objective *It* prevails, this dichotomous way of thinking fails to consider normative problems in terms of the inter-subjectivity of ethics—the relation of I and Thou, which has been so aptly explained by Buber. The dismissal of the dialogical relation, Buber says, ultimately ends up in the submission of the I to the world of It, whereby the true dialogical person is reduced to the empty I of individuality (Buber 2004: 35). Such a world is the world of ontological fundamentalism which sets itself up as the final reality and thereby reduces the other to the same (Friedman 2002: 194 and 238). Instead of a foundational ethics, starting from the autonomous moral agent, Buber's dialogism suggests a radically new point of departure for ethical reflection in the global world: since moral values are not invented or chosen (neither from the outside, nor from the inside), but are discovered in the "between"—in the process of "becoming aware"—ethical investigation into the normative issues of our time should start from the relationships between people instead of from fixed identities. Starting from the relational or the inter-subjective "illuminates" otherness and differences and makes it possible to think of it in a non-instrumental way. Global ethics, thus, should disclose the lived "inter" of the international realm, the concurrent operation of difference inhabiting human existence that prevents any identity or meaning from ever becoming fully stabilized. Incorporating otherness in ethical consideration therefore implies accepting the radical instability of meaning and value and the ever provisory character of ethics.

Global ethics as a dialogical contextual ethics is no longer an ethics of ultimate ends. On the contrary, while abstract values can be useful and suggestive, we

---

30   Pure moral autonomy, according to Buber is only a negative "freedom from" without any "freedom for." Pure moral heteronomy, on the other hand, is an imposed responsibility without any genuine freedom or spontaneity (Buber 1998: 129).

31   Objectivist ethical theories want to rescue ethics from the identification of the "ought" with the "is" and posit absolute moral values that command the autonomous moral agent through abstract impartial reason. Subjectivist theories, on the other hand, tend to make the "is" equal to the "ought" and reduce all value to the interests of individuals and groups. Modern moral philosophy, according to Buber, is dominated by the objectivist perspective of the autonomous, impartial moral agent (the Cartesian ego).

should not take them as the starting point of our ethical deliberation. Ethics cannot be cut off from the lived life. Therefore, we should work the other way around: starting form the concrete situation, we move towards those values and norms that point to the right direction in that specific context, recognizing that no definite truth can be established (Friedman 2004: 123). However, while the moral oughts that derive from the ethical reflection in the Interhuman are always "for the time being," they are not purely subjectivist. Since Buber insisted on the proper alternation between I-Thou and I-It and on the twofold movement within the I-Thou relation of relating (turning towards the other) and distancing (remaining different from the other, "hold your ground when you meet the other"—Buber 2004: 31), the space of the Interhuman takes both sameness and difference into account: the Interhuman is not the uncritical realm of preferences, but instead the lively interface between the factual world of intelligibility (I-It) and the ethical world of responsibility (I-Thou)—the moral laboratory in which both the abstract and the concrete, both theory and practice meet each other in the confrontation with difference.

Focussing on the relations between people, Buber's dialogism also offers very concrete methodological suggestions to deal with the normative challenges of globalization. Buber's situational ethics is a thoroughly horizontal, communicational ethics, which situates the address of "true norms" on the level where human being stand over against each other, so that "each of them knows and means, recognizes and acknowledges, accepts and confirms the other, even in the severest conflict, as this particular person" (Schilpp and Friedman 1967: 723). Ethics springs from the basic reality and value of the meeting between man and man and the unmediated response to what addresses them in this meeting. This basic reality takes place not only on the individual level (I-Thou), but also on the community-level. Everyone, Buber argues, has from a very young age a natural relation of immediacy towards persons and things around him—an "inborn Thou," an openness or readiness towards the world out of which follows and grows the "essential Thou" of the direct I-Thou relation. Exactly the same happens on the level of community (*Gemeinschaft*): the "essential We" occurs when independent people come together in direct relationship to one another, willing to truly say *Thou* to one another. Through the "essential We," man escapes from the impersonal, nameless and faceless "collectivity" of institutionalized social relations (the "crowd," the "people," the "citizens") (Kramer 2003: 76–78). True community, Buber says, is not just a collection of individuals pursuing common interests, needs or appetites, but is instead the "vital interaction" between complete and thoroughly responsive persons, arising in *das Zwischenmenschliche*—in the elemental social-psychological *togetherness* of men in its dialogical forms and actions (Buber 1988: 109–11).

It is precisely here that Buber's dialogism offers a forceful tool for global ethics: if the basic reality and value is not the organic group, but the concrete dialogical relations between men, then "there is a vital necessity for a restructuring of society that will enable the relations between men to be of a more genuinely dialogical nature" (Friedman 2002: 247). The vertical, hierarchical structure of late-modern society, which is especially dominant in international relations, makes true dialogue very difficult. Global ethics as a contextual, practical discipline should try—through its very practice—to address the "essential We," to facilitate truly lived communal relations of fellowship and association as a counterweight to the well-ordered and static realm of social and political institutions (the world of *It*). This means opening up or broadening the moral scope of traditional normative international theories, which take the nation-state and the institutional level of abstract, anonymous laws and principles of inter-national conduct, as the ultimate point of departure. Broadening our moral scope makes real the third space of "de-territorialized" experienced responsibility where (groups of) people stand over against each other in dialogical relations. The very challenge, then, in order to create such a "third space" in our ethical considerations of (issues in) international relations, is the full and respectful incorporation of the "inter"—the endless variety of all kinds of bottom-up initiatives, i.e. spontaneous grass-roots movements that cut across international borders and that form trans-national spaces of lived, shared practices out of which grows an elementary sense of togetherness, meaning and value. Global ethics as a dialogical, practical discipline should disclose these "horizontal" ethical horizons as an enriching complement of our abstract thinking about what responsibility means in today's globalized world. In continually disclosing this fragile, temporary "inter," global ethics not only avoids the objectivism of moral universalism, but also the subjectivism of moral relativism.

The "Third Way" in Practice

There are numerous possible research areas in which such a "third way" dialogical approach would be fruitful. For instance, discussions about international migration[32] would strike out on a whole new course if the horizontal dimension of the "Interhuman" were included. Today, debates on cross-border movements of people merely focus on the institutional level of state-policies and the pros and cons that migratory movements have on political and societal structure. (Potential) migrants and refugees are approached from an I-It perspective defining them as abstract categories—as impersonal, nameless and faceless objects of thought and deliberation in order to serve states's interests and concerns about "their" citizens, "their" nation, "their" security and "their" welfare. But migrants are more than an organic group of "non-citizens" or "outsiders" that can be reified and decided upon. They are first and foremost human subjects, cherishing their own values, interests and practices and striving for their own aims and ideals. Coping with the challenge of international migration from the contextual global ethics perspective that is defended here, requires an openness to these "others," a recognition of and commitment to their *subject*-ivity and inter-relatedness with "us," a readiness to be attentive and responsive to their voices. Buber's sphere of the "Interhuman" shows the ethical importance of incorporating a genuine I-Thou

---

32   Other possible examples include poverty reduction strategies, climate change action plans, foreign "humanitarian" intervention.

dialogue into "our" relations with migrants and refugees. Creating such trans-national dialogical spaces, in which communities of origin and host communities encounter each other on an equal footing, makes it possible to break through the vertical, hierarchical logic which dominates migration debates today and opens up a new, pioneering way of thinking about migration in a global era.

One promising way of implementing a truly *lived* dialogue within migration debates, is the system of town twinning which exists worldwide in various forms.[33] Town twinning developed in post-war Europe with the aim of bringing about a lasting peace by reordering international politics on the basis of municipal institutions (Vion 2002). The underlying idea was that war could be prevented if people of different nations got to know and understand each other on a grass roots level by meeting in their normal environments. Whereas town twinning originally was a political initiative, inspired by an organic conception of the municipality and aiming at cultural exchange and economic cooperation, it broadened its scope towards partnerships with communities in developing countries and countries in transition (Weyreter 2003: 42). This shift resulted in town twinning becoming an important factor of global awareness raising about worldwide problems such as desertification, poverty and migration. It is precisely in this most recent form that town twinning offers a possibility to implement trans-national dialogical spaces within the migration debate. As opposed to existing international agreements and "partnerships" between countries of origin and countries of destination, town twinning initiatives are community-based, horizontal projects that start from voluntary initiatives within civil society and that work towards a better mutual understanding and towards proper, sustainable solutions that are acceptable to all parties involved. Instead of unilaterally imposing certain measures or policies upon the "other," town twinning seeks to implement commonly agreed projects and aims that empower the communities involved. By incorporating the perspective of migrants and migrant communities, town twinning can make a difference to the thinking and actions of individuals about migration. It are the central values of communication, mutual respect and cooperation, that makes town twinning a truly dialogical event that can function as a valuable complement to current state-based migration policies. For while town twinning does exist within the wider context of national government and foreign policy strategies, it is not and cannot be fully controlled by national governments or by any other large international institution. Town twinning, as a means to shared, dialogical spaces at grass roots level, succeeds in making concrete the adagio "think global, act local," thereby uniting and balancing the interactional and the institutional level which are both important from a global ethics perspective. In today's world, in

---

33 Town twinning is a formal partnership between two municipalities aimed at encouraging cooperation and mutual understanding between their citizens in order to foster human contacts and cultural exchange, to exchange experiences, to promote peaceful coexistence and to raise awareness about the daily lives and concerns of people living in other countries. It relies upon the voluntary commitment and participation of citizens, in collaboration with their local authorities and local associations. The cornerstone of town twinning is real, mutual interaction and concrete problem-solving.

which all kinds of security concerns threaten to split the world in different camps, there is probably no more urgent and important task than that of (re)establishing some kind of interactional dialogue. The most suitable level to achieve this, is probably that of the "narrow ridge"—the lived life of meeting and of sharing ideas and practices between different (groups of) people.

Concluding Remarks

This chapter started with a critical evaluation of traditional normative theories of international relations. Whether they work from the realist/idealist dichotomy, the Machiavellian/Grotian/ Kantian triad or the communitarian/cosmopolitan divide, they are no longer capable of dealing adequately with the pressing normative issues of today's late-modern globalized world. Global poverty, environmental degradation, rising ethnicism, etc. have instigated a new field of academic research, operating on the intersection between ethics and other human sciences, in order to challenge this "moral vacuum." Global ethics as this "new agenda" is often used as a container concept, referring to "the ethical issues that arise in the context of globalization."

In order to clarify the research domain of global ethics, this chapter has tried to develop a pluriform definition of global ethics as simultaneously oriented on persons (individuals and collectivities) and institutions and directed at realizing global justice in all its distributive, social, political and cultural aspects. Global ethics, therefore, is not restricted to the analysis of multiple issues and problems from a perspective in which the impact of globalization figures predominantly, but also aims at a critical re-evaluation of what ethics itself can and should be in an era of globalization. The two-track conception of global ethics as both an ethics *of* globalization and an ethics *under* globalization leaves the either-or logic of mainstream modern moral philosophy and tries to offer moral guidance by discovering a "third way" between the extremes of objectivist universalism and subjectivist relativism.

Global ethics as a "third way" aims at tackling the tension between the universalizing trend of moral principles and the particularizing trend of institutions, cultures and practices through a contextual, action-oriented method of "moving back and forward" between those two opposites. Global ethics, therefore, should be focussed on an appropriate working method rather than on a foundationalist system of thought. In developing this working method, global ethics can find inspiration in the insights of American pragmatism, with its emphasis on moral practice, context-sensitive, embodied reasoning and the continuous interplay between theory and practice, between facts and values, between the abstract and the concrete. The advantage of such a pragmatical/ contextual turn is twofold. First, it offers adequate, concrete moral guidance because of its focus on arbitration and mutual adjustment rather than on adjudication by means of deductive reasoning. Second, it recognizes diversity and difference as an enriching source of moral value and an important precondition for practical morality.

A contextual global ethics as a practical, action-oriented discipline leads to an enriched moral vocabulary by which the "moral space" is defined in terms of hybrid identities, multi-layeredness, dialogue, conversation, communication. By focussing on the "founding father" of such a renewed "third way" ethics, we have been able to reformulate global ethics as a radical hermeneutico-phenomenological practice of the "between." Martin Buber's dialogism, most essentially captured in his conception of the "Interhuman" and the "narrow ridge," is therefore a radical breach with the traditional literature of ethics and international affairs. It leaves the unsustainable distinction between the realm of the normative on the one hand and that of the empirical on the other. It also gives up the foundationalist ambition to arrive at universal truths in favor of a hospitable openness towards the contingencies and complexities of the ethical. Buber's ontology of the "between" is not the totality of being that has dominated Western philosophy throughout history, but it is what he calls the "really real:" the *meeting* of I and Thou which is the touchstone of reality. Dialogism is the permanent disengagement of the temptation to abstract, to conceptualize, to theorize. Instead it sees the world fundamentally in terms of relation, meeting, dialogue and encounter, ending up in an ethics of responsibility in the sense of *answerability* out of the confrontation with difference and otherness.

Buber's phenomenological account of the ethical life, then, is of major importance for the recognition of the sociality or inter-subjectivity of human existence and the moral relevance of otherness and difference. Morality, as a fact of human interdependency, is fundamentally a relational matter, characterized by the inappropriable otherness of the other. Interdependency as the essential feature of the human condition, plays as much between as within societies. Therefore, dialogism insists on the global connectedness of people apart from territorial boundaries. The I-Thou relation is just as well the face to face relation between I and the other, as the ethical relation between I and the third person (the stranger, the foreigner with whom there may be no actual, but certainly an inborn potential personal bond). This does not mean that our ethical responsibility is "endless" in the sense of requiring far-reaching self-sacrifice. Rather it is "borderless" in the sense that it breaks into the world of It, into the world of social and political institutions, where it voices the particularity of lived relations—the fragile "here I am" of the other—and thereby tempers the totalizing tendency of the institutional realm. If global ethics has one thing to do in order to face up to the "moral crisis" of our time, where moral certainties are lost and postmodern attitudes cast doubts on any claims of truth, it certainly is this "breaking through" on the narrow ridge of *experienced* responsibility.

References

Aiken, W. and LaFolette, H. (eds) (1996), *World Hunger and Morality.* Engelwood Cliffs, NJ: Prentice Hall.

Bader, V. (ed.) (1997a), *Citizenship and Exclusion*. London: Macmillan Press.

Bader, V. (1997b), "Transnational Citizenship," *Political Theory* 25(6), 771–813.

Bader, V. and Engelen, E. (2003), "Taking Pluralism Seriously. Arguing for an Institutional Turn in Political Philosophy," *Philosophy and Social Criticism* 29(4), 375–406.

Bader, V. and Saharso, S. (2004), "Contextualized Morality and Ethno-religious Diversity. Introduction," *Ethical Theory and Moral Practice* 7(2), 107–15.

Bakhtin, M. [1930s] (1981), *The Dialogical Imagination*, ed. M. Holquist, transl. C. Emerson and M. Holquist. Austin/London: University of Texas Press.

Barnett, M. (1997), "Bringing in the New World Order," *World Politics* 49, 526–51.

Barry, B. (1995), *Justice as Impartiality*. Oxford: Clarendon Press.

Bauman, Z. (1994), *Postmodern Ethics*. Oxford: Blackwell.

Beitz, C. (1979), *Political Theory and International Relations*. Princeton: Princeton University Press.

Beitz, C. (2000), "Rawls's Law of Peoples," *Ethics* 110(4), 669–97.

Benhabib, S. (2002), *The Claims of Culture: Equality and Diversity in the Global Era*. Princeton/Oxford: Princeton University Press.

Brown, C. (1992), *International Relations Theory. New Normative Approaches*. New York: Columbia University Press.

Bubeck, D. (1995), *Care, Gender and Justice*. Oxford: Clarendon Press.

Buber, M. (1951), "Distance and Relation," transl. R.G. Smith, *The Hibbert Journal* XLIX, 105–13.

Buber, M. (1988), *The Knowledge of Man. Selected Essays*, transl. M. Friedman and R.G. Smith. New York: Prometheus Books.

Buber, M. (1998), *Eclipse of God: Studies in the Relation between Religion and Philosophy*, transl. M.S. Friedman et al. New York: Humanity Books.

Buber, M. (2002), *Between Man and Man*, transl. R.G. Smith. London/New York: Routledge.

Buber, M. (2004), *I and Thou* (2nd edn), transl. R.G. Smith. London/New York: Continuum.

Burggrave, R. (1999), "Violence and the Vulnerable Face of the Other: The Vision of Emmanuel Levinas on Moral Evil and Our Responsibility," *Journal of Social Philosophy* 30(1), 29–45.

Campbell, D. and Shapiro, M.J. (eds) (1996), *Moral Spaces. Rethinking Ethics and World Politics*. Minneapolis/London: University of Minnesota Press.

Caney, S. (2005), *Justice Beyond Borders: A Global Political Theory*. Oxford: Oxford University Press.

Carens, J. (2000), *Culture, Citizenship and Community. A Contextual Exploration of Justice as Evenhandedness*. Oxford: Oxford University Press.

Carens, J. (2004), "A Contextual Approach to Political Theory," *Ethical Theory and Moral Practice* 7, 117–32.

Carr, E.H. [1993] (1939), *The Twenty Years's Crisis 1919–1939. An Introduction to the Study of International Relations*. London: Macmillan.

Charvet, J. (2001), "The Possibility of a Cosmopolitan Ethical Order Based on the Idea of Universal Human Rights," in Seckinelgin, H. and Shinoda, H. (eds) *Ethics and International Relations*. Houndmills: Palgrave.

Colpaert, M. (2005), "Culture, Hospitality and Relational Ethics: Some Philosophical Reflections," *Diversity in Health and Social Care* 2, 135–42.

Commers, M.S.R. (2007). *Wijsgerige Ethiek: Methodiek*. Leuven/Ghent: Acco.

Commission on Global Governance (1995), *Our Global Neighbourhood*. Oxford: Oxford University Press.

Cox, R. (1987), *Production, Power and World Order: Social Forces in the Making of History*. New York: Columbia University Press.

Cuéllar, J.P. de, et al. (1995), *Our Creative Diversity. Report of the World Commission on Culture and Development.* Paris: UNESCO Publishing.

Der Derian, J. (ed.) (1995), *International Theory: Critical Investigations.* New York University Press.

Der Derian, J. and Shapiro, M. (eds) (1989), *International/Intertextual Relations: Postmodern Readings of World Politics.* Lexington, MA: Lexington Books.

Dewey, J. (1922), "Human Nature and Conduct," in Boydston, J.A. (ed.) (1976), *Dewey. The Middle Works, 1899–1924.* Carbondale: Southern Illinois University Press.

Dewey, J. (1939), "Theory of Valuation," *International Encyclopedia of Unified Science,* Vol. II (4). Chicago: University of Chicago Press.

Dewey, J. (1948), *Reconstruction in Philosophy.* Boston: Beacon Press.

Donelan, M. (1990), *Elements of International Political Theory.* Oxford: Clarendon Press.

Dower, N. (1998), *World Ethics: The New Agenda.* Edinburgh: Edinburgh University Press.

Eldridge, M. (1998), *Transforming Experience: John Dewey's Cultural Instrumentalism.* Nashville: Vanderbilt University Press.

Erskine, T. (2001), "Assigning Responsibilities to Institutional Moral Agents: The Case of States and Quasi-States," *Ethics and International Affairs* 15(2), 67–85.

Esposito, L. and Murphy, J.W. (2005), "Towards an Embodied Global Ethics," in Eade, J. and O'Byrne, D. (eds) *Global Ethics and Civil Society.* Aldershot: Ashgate.

Finnemore, M. (1996), "Norms, Culture and World Politics," *International Organization* 50(2), 325–47.

Fraser, N. (2003), "Social Justice in the Age of Identity Politics: Redistribution, Recognition, and Participation," in Fraser, N. and Honneth, A. (eds) *Redistribution or Recognition? A Political Philosophical Exchange.* London: Verso / Frankfurt: Suhrkamp.

Friedman, M.S. (1993), *What are Friends for? Feminist Perspectives on Personal Relationships and Moral Theory.* Ithaca/London: Cornell University Press.

Friedman, M.S. (2002), *Martin Buber: The Life of Dialogue.* London/New York: Routledge.

Friedman, M.S. (2004), "Buber and Levinas: An Ethical Query," in Atterton et al., P. (eds) *Levinas and Buber. Dialogue and Difference.* Pittsburgh: Duquesne University Press.

Frost, M. (1996), *Ethics in International Relations: A Constitutive Theory.* Cambridge: Cambridge University Press.

Gasper, D. (1994), "Development Ethics: An Emergent Field?," in Prendergast, R. and Stewart, F. (eds) *Market Forces and World Development.* London: Macmillan/New York: St Martin's Press.

Gasper, D. (2005), "Beyond the International Relations Framework: an Essay in Descriptive Global Ethics," *Journal of Global Ethics* 1(1), 5–23.

Goodman, L.E. (1998), "Jewish Philosophy," in Craig, E. (ed.) *Routledge Encyclopedia of Philosophy.* London: Routledge.

Gutmann, A. and Thompson, D. (1994), *Democracy and Disagreement.* Harvard: Harvard University Press.

Habermas, J. (1984), *The Theory of Communicative Action,* Vols I and II. Cambridge: Polity Press.

Habermas, J. (1994), "Struggles for Recognition in the Democratic Constitutional State," in Gutmann, A. (ed.) *Democratic Education.* Princeton: Princeton University Press.

Hall, J.A. (2000), "Globalisation and Nationalism," *Thesis Eleven* 63, 63–79.

Hannerz, U. (1992), *Cultural Complexity. Studies in the Social Organisation of Meaning.* New York: Columbia Press.

Held, D. (2000), "Regulating Globalisation? The Reinvention of Politics," *International Sociology* 15, 394–408.

Heater, D. (1966), *World Citizenship and Government: Cosmopolitan Ideas in the History of Western Thought*. London: Macmillan.

Held, V. (2006), *The Ethics of Care. Personal, Political and Global*. Oxford: Oxford University Press.

Howard, M. et al. (eds) (1994), *The Laws of War: Constraints on Warfare in the Western World*. New Haven and London: Yale University Press.

Hutchings, K. (2007), "Feminist Perspectives on a Planetary Ethic," in Sullivan, W.M. and Kymlicka, W. (eds) *The Globalization of Ethics. Religious and Secular Perspectives*. Cambridge: Cambridge University Press.

Interaction Council (1997), *A Universal Declaration of Human Responsibilities*. http://www.interactioncouncil.org/meetings/report/m972.doc.

Jabri, V. (2001), "Restyling the Subject of Responsibility in International Relations," in Seckinelgin, H. and Shinoda, H. (eds) *Ethics and International Relations*. Houndmills: Palgrave.

Kramer, K.P. (2003), *Martin Buber's I and Thou. Practicing Living Dialogue*. New York/Mahwah: Paulist Press.

Küng, H. (1991), "Toward a Universal Declaration of Global Ethos," *Journal of Ecumenical Studies* 28(1), 123–5.

Küng, H. (2002), "Global Politics and Global Ethics. Status Quo and Perspectives," *Seton Hall Journal of Diplomacy and International Relations* 3(1), 8–20.

Kymlicka, W. (1995), *Multicultural Citizenship*. Oxford: Oxford University Press.

Kymlicka, W. (2007), "Introduction: The Globalization of Ethics," in Sullivan, W.M. and Kymlicka, W. (eds) *The Globalization of Ethics. Religious and Secular Perspectives*. Cambridge. Cambridge University Press.

Levinas, E. (1961), *Totalité et Infini. Essai sur l'exteriorité*. La Haye: Nijhoff.

Linklater, A. (1990), *Men and Citizens in the Theory of International Relations*. London: Macmillan.

Macintyre, A. (1981), *After Virtue*. London: Duckworth.

Mann, M. (1997), "Has Globalization Ended the Rise and Rise of the Nation-State?," *Review of International Political Economy* 4, 472–96.

Mathews, J. (2003), "Power Shift," in Held, D. and Mcgrew, A. (eds) *The Global Transformations Reader. An Introduction into the Globalization Debate*. Cambridge: Blackwell.

Miller, D. (1998), "The Limits of Cosmopolitan Justice," in Mapel, D. and Nardin, T. (eds) *The Constitution of International Society*, Princeton: Princeton University Press.

Ohmae, K. (1995), *The End of the Nation State: The Rise of Regional Economies*. New York: The Free Press.

O'Neill, O. (1986), "Who Can Endeavour Peace?," *Canadian Journal of Philosophy* 12 (suppl.), 41–73.

O'Neill, O. (2001), "Agents of Justice," *Metaphilosophy* 32(1/2), 180–95.

Parekh, B. (2000), *Rethinking Multiculturalism*. Houndsmill: Macmillan.

Parekh, B. (2005), "Principles of a Global Ethic," in Eade, J. and O'Byrne, D. (eds) *Global Ethics and Civil Society*. Aldershot: Ashgate.

Peirce, C. (1905), "What Pragmatism is," *The Monist* 15(2), 161–81.

Peters, R.T. (2004), *In Search of the Good Life: The Ethics of Globalization*. New York : Continuum.

Pogge, T. (1994), "Cosmopolitanism and Sovereignty," in Brown, E. (ed.) *Political restructuring in Europe. Ethical Perspectives*. London/New York: Routledge, 89–122.

Pogge, T. (2002), *World Poverty and Human Rights*. Cambridge: Polity Press.

Pogge, T. and Follesdal, A. (eds) (2005), *Real World Justice. Grounds, Principles, Human Rights, and Social Institutions*. Dordrecht: Springer.

Putnam, H. and Conant, J. (1994), *Words and Life*. Harvard: Harvard University Press.

Riklin, A. (1998), "Politische Ethik, Ein Grundriss aus der Sicht der westlichen Zivilisation," in Küng, H. and Kuschel, K.-J. (eds) *Wissenschaft und Weltethos*. München/Zürich: Piper.

Robinson, F. (1999), *Globalizing Care. Ethics, Feminist Theory, and International Relations*. Boulder: Westview Press.

Robinson, F. (2001), "Exploring Social Relations, Understanding Power, and Valuing Care: The Role of Critical Feminist Ethics in International Relations Theory," in Seckinelgin, H. and Shinoda, H. (eds) *Ethics and International Relations*. Houndmills: Palgrave.

Rorty, R. (1980), *Philosophy and the Mirror of Nature*. Oxford: Oxford University Press.

Schilpp, P.A. and Friedman, M.S. (eds) (1967), *The Philosophy of Martin Buber*. La Salle: Open Court.

Seckinelgin, H. and Shinoda, H. (2001), "Introduction: Beyond Dichotomies," in Seckinelgin, H. and Shinoda, H. (eds) *Ethics and International Relations*. Houndmills: Palgrave.

Serrano-Caldera, A. (1993), *La Unidad en la Diversidad*. Managua: Editorial San Rafael.

Shapiro, I. (1999), *Democratic Justice*. New Haven: Yale University Press.

Shapiro, M.J. (2001), "The Events of Discourse and the Ethics of Global Hospitality," in Seckinelgin, H. and Shinoda, H. (eds) *Ethics and International Relations*. Houndmills: Palgrave.

Strange, S. (1996), *The Retreat of the State: The Diffusion of Power in the World Economy*. Cambridge: Cambridge University Press.

Swidler, L. (1994), "Toward a Universal Declaration of a Global Ethic," *Dialogue and Humanism* IV(4), 51–64.

Tamir, Y. (1993), *Liberal Nationalism*. Princeton: Princeton University Press.

Tan, K. (2004), *Justice Without Borders. Cosmopolitanism, Nationalism, Patriotism*. Cambridge: Cambridge University Press.

Taylor, C. (1989), *Sources of the Self. The Making of the Modern Identity*. Harvard: Harvard University Press.

Thompson, J. (1992), *Justice and World Order. A Philosophical Inquiry*. London: Routledge.

Todd-Peters, R. (2004), *In Search of the Good Life: the Ethics of Globalization*. New York: Continuum.

UNESCO (1998), *The Universal Ethics Project. Preliminary Report*. Paris: UNESCO. http://unesdoc.unesco.org/images/0011/001126/112681eb.pdf.

Verhaar, O. and Saharso, S. (2004), "The Weight of Context: Headscarves in Holland," *Ethical Theory and Moral Practice* 7, 179–95.

Vion, A. (2002), "Europe from the Bottom Up: Town Twinning in France during the Cold War," *Contemporary European History* 11(1), 623–40.

Walzer, M. (1983), *Spheres of Justice. A Defense of Pluralism and Equality*. Oxford: Blackwell.

Wendt, A. (1992), "Anarchy is What States Make of It: The Social Construction of power Politics," *International Organization* 46(2).

Weyreter, M. (2003), "Germany and the Town Twinning Movement," *Contemporary Review* 281(1644), 37–44.

White, B. et al. (2005), "Issues in World Politics," in White, B. et al. (eds) *Issues in World Politics*. New York: Palgrave Macmillan.

Widdows, H. (2005), "Global Ethics: Foundations and Methodologies," in Eade, J. and O'Byrne, D. (eds) *Global Ethics and Civil Society*. Aldershot: Ashgate.

Wight, G. and Porter, G. (1992), *International Theory. The Three Traditions: Martin Wight*. Leicester/London: Leicester University Press.

Young, I.M. (1990), *Justice and the Politics of Difference*. Princeton: Princeton University Press.

Chapter 12

Redistributing Global Inequality: A Thought Experiment[1]

József Böröcz[2]

Homage to Karl Polányi

At its 96th plenary meeting of 20 December 1995, the General Assembly of the United Nations proclaimed the period of 1997 to 2006 as the "First United Nations Decade for the Eradication of Poverty" (henceforth: "the Decade"). The first part of the Resolution took a state-centric, modernizationist view, suggesting that key sites for the reduction of global inequality were inside the worst-affected societies (UN 1995: 4, §5.c): It

> *recommends* [emphasis in original] that all States [… f]ormulate or strengthen, as a matter of urgency, national policies and strategies geared to substantially reducing overall poverty in the shortest possible time, reducing inequalities and eradicating absolute poverty by a target date to be specified by each country in its national context.

The second part of the Resolution *"calls upon"* [emphasis in original] not only "States," but also

> the United Nations system, relevant international organizations and all other actors concerned with the Decade to participate actively in the financial and technical support of the Decade, in particular with a view to translating all measures and recommendations into operational and concrete poverty eradication programmes and activities. (UN 1995: 7, §23)

In setting tasks to actors "beyond" states, the document seems tacitly to recognize the origins of global inequalities—largely exogenous to individual states—and the general contribution of state-by-state differences to the gross amount of social inequalities in the world. At this point the Resolution

---

1   An earlier version of this chapter has been published, in English original, in the *Economic and Political Weekly* (Mumbai, India), 26 February 2005: 886–92 and in Magyar as "Gondolatkisérlet a globális újraelosztásról," *Eszmélet*, 66 (2005): 61–70.
2   The author is deeply grateful for Mahua Sarkar's indispensable encouragement, comments, suggestions and criticisms.

touches upon—of course without ever mentioning them explicitly—some deep controversies within the sociological literature on the relative magnitudes and the proportion between the within-state and state-to-state components of global inequality.[3]

This remarkably complex document proceeds, then, to address the world's affluent and poor states separately, and assigns different tasks to them: It

> [*r*]*ecommends* that donor countries give greater priority to the eradication of poverty in their assistance programmes and budgets, on either a bilateral or multilateral basis; [and ... *e*]*ncourages* developing countries to mobilize domestic and external resources for poverty eradication programmes and activities, and to facilitate their full and effective implementation. (UN 1995: 7, §26–7, emphasis in original)

By setting diverse tasks for the wealthy and the poor states, the Resolution depicts the world as a binary structure and, hence, again, shifts the global official discussion from an isolated focus on the reduction of poverty *per se* to a statement concerning the tasks of states depending on their position in the world economy. Since a discussion of poverty without any reference to the underlying system of inequality that produces and maintains it has no option but to remain silent also about what specific actors, which institutions, and occupants of what global locations have the potential to alleviate this particular feature of the global system, the closing section of the Resolution makes a conceptually very significant policy step. Here we have a reference to global *inequality* rather than "just" poverty in isolation.

The Resolution is also burdened by its silence about the historicity of global inequality—historicity in two senses. First, the document does not acknowledge that, until quite recently, global inequality used not to be of the magnitude humankind is enduring today. As economic historian Angus Maddison's historical estimates (Maddison 2001, 2003)—made under contract with the OECD, an organization typically not associated with militant anti-capitalism—suggest, at the beginning of global capitalism, global differences in per capita regional income were negligible, and certainly incomparable to today's figures. Second, the United Nations' General Assembly also chose to ignore the specific, rationally organized, *longue-durée* historic contribution to the creation, maintenance and defence of today's global structure of inequalities by the three most powerful types of global organizations in the contemporary world: the states forming the core of the world economy, the transnational corporations substantively rooted in those states, and the supra- or meta-state organizations of public authority, formal and informal networks of collusion, coordination, governance, agenda-

---

3   See, e.g.: Korzeniewicz and Moran 1997 vs. Firebaugh 1999.0 For an excellent recent overview of the debate and a conceptual history of the measurement of national income, see Korzeniewicz et al. 2004; see also Bata and Bergesen 2002, and the studies included in the special double issue of the *Journal for World-System Research* devoted to global inequality (Bergesen and Bata 2002–2003).

and policy-setting mechanisms and other tools of "remote-control" that have recently mushroomed around the word.

In this chapter, I will not revisit those valid and important arguments. Instead, I focus merely on the fiscal feasibility of a plan for global inequality reduction, a project that can be defined as a large-scale, historic social process of social change aiming to diminish "oligarchic wealth"[4] (Arrighi 1991) in favor of a less extremely unbalanced structure of distribution, something akin to what Arrighi (1991) has called "democratic wealth."

In the first four years of the Decade—the period for which global state-by-state comparative economic performance data (IBRD 2002) are available at the time of writing this essay—global inequality has not been reduced perceptibly. The measures of global inequality summarized in Table 12.1 show only minuscule movement, and in both directions.

Table 12.1 Global state-to-state income inequality: coefficient of variation (standard deviation/mean) for mean per capita income measures, 1997–2000

Method of measurement	1997	1998	1999	2000
GNI/cap, Atlas	1.829	1.817	1.792	1.773
GNI/cap, PPP	1.225	1.229	1.220	1.219
GDP/cap, FX	1.840	1.862	1.885	1.899
GDP/cap, PPP	1.198	1.206	1.224	1.242

Source: IBRD 2002.

Below I examine some of the contours and implications of a scheme of an as yet non-existent project of global collective action that would seriously and boldly seek to reduce global interstate inequality in per capita economic performance. This is an emphatically speculative exercise that serves only one purpose: It provides an empirical assessment of the magnitude of the resources that would need to be redistributed for a perceptible reduction in global inequalities, and the possible numerical impact of a project that would establish a *global, redistributive* (see Polányi 1957) counterpart to an already existing, *global market* system of capitalist accumulation, much in the same way as the redistributive welfare state partly complements, and corrects, the process of the accumulation of capital within its own territory. In search for the simple numerical connections, I do not concern myself with any of the myriad possible and even probable, positive as well as negative, nonlinear effects of global redistribution—something that would

---

4   Defined recently by Beverly Silver and Giovanni Arrighi (Silver and Arrighi 2001) as: a kind of long-term income that bears no relation to the intensity and efficiency of the efforts of its recipients and is never available to all no matter how intense and efficient their efforts are.

of course be eminently reasonable to expect, were such an endeavor implemented in practice.

In this exercise, I shall not consider the political feasibility of such a redistributive system, at least not in liberal terms, hence it might be justified to call my approach and method—in this form, and in the present global political context—utopian. A modicum of controlled utopianism is necessary, however, in order to be able to think beyond the constraints of the current institutional system. The fact that the history of world capitalism has organized global structures in a particular manner is important; it certainly does not mean, however, that the existing organizational setup is the only one that is *possible*. My thought experiment examines one aspect of the possibility of a system of global distribution that can be conceived as more equitable than that of today.

Table 12.2 summarizes some aspects of the distribution of global income among the 173 states that have published relevant data for the year 2000, according to the same four measures of income as in the previous table. As citizens of the states around the mean (some of the most well-to-do states of Latin America and eastern Europe) could testify, the average income of the world's states affords, by and large, quite reasonable living conditions. The contemporary world economy produces enough to provide material means to the entirety of humankind on levels that match those of Belarus, Botswana, Brazil, the Czech Republic, Hungary, Lithuania, Mexico or Uruguay. This is a respectable and, as far as much of humankind today is concerned, much-desired, level of livelihood.

Also to be noted is the fact that the states near the mean of per capita income tend to show quality of life conditions better than the world average of those measures: According to the 2003 edition of the *Human Development Report,* world mean life expectancy at birth stood at 66.7 years, and adult literacy rates for the states in the "middle income" range was at 86.6 per cent in 2001. With the exception of Botswana, all seven of the remaining states near the global income mean show higher results than the world mean in the quality of life.

As for those at the very top and the bottom of the global average per capita income scale, these income disparities are truly staggering. The most affluent state (according to all four of the measures listed here: Luxembourg) has per capita income figures 6.14[5] to 10.01[6] times higher than the global mean, while the world's poorest states' average per capita income is 14.52[7] to 51.7[8] times less than the world average. When computed in GNI/cap with the Atlas method (I shall explain both of them briefly below), citizens of the world's most affluent state have an *average* level of income that is *420 times higher* than those of the poorest state. This disparity is absurd and well nigh incomprehensible.

I am therefore moved to ask what it would take, and what kind of a global rearrangement it would produce, if some kind of a global redistributive mechanism were to bring all the world's states markedly closer to the world mean. To be noted

---

5   GNI/cap at PPP.
6   GDP/cap, FX.
7   GDP/cap, PPP.
8   GNI/cap, Atlas.

Table 12.2   Global mean per capita incomes and states that occupy top, near-mean and bottom positions,* 2000, life expectancy at birth and adult literacy rate in those states, 2001[†]

Method of measurement	Estimate of mean per capita income, US$	States at the top, the mean, and the bottom of the global distribution of per capita income	Life expectancy at birth	Adult literacy rate
GNI/cap, Atlas	5170	**Top:**		
		Luxembourg: 42060	78.1	99.0
		Switzerland: 38140	79. 0	99.0
		Japan: 35620	81.3	99.0
		Mean:		
		Czech Republic: 5250	75.1	99.0
		Mexico: 5070	73.1	93.4
		Bottom:		
		Ethiopia: 100	45.4	40.3
		Burundi: 110	40.4	49.2
		Sierra Leone: 130	34.5	36. 0
GNI/cap, PPP	7410	**Top:**		
		Luxembourg: 45470	78.1	99.0
		United States: 34100	76.9	99.0
		Switzerland: 30450	79. 0	99.0
		Mean:		
		Belarus: 7550	69.6	99.07
		Brazil: 7300	67.8	87.3
		Bottom:		
		Sierra Leone: 480	34.5	36.0
		Tanzania: 520	44.0	76.0
		Rep. of Congo: 570	40.6	62.7
GDP/cap, FX	5634	**Top:**		
		Luxembourg: 56372	78.1	99.0
		Switzerland: 46737	79.0	99.0
		Japan: 44830	81.3	99.0
		Mean:		
		Uruguay: 6114	75.0	97.6
		Hungary: 5425	71.5	99.03
		Bottom:		
		Ethiopia: 116	45.4	40.3
		Burundi: 141	40.4	49.2
		Sierra Leone: 147	34.5	36. 0
GDP/cap, PPP	7115	**Top:**		
		Luxembourg: 50061	78.1	99.0
		United States: 34142	76.9	99.0
		Norway: 29948	78.7	99.0
		Mean:		
		Botswana: 7184	44.7	82.7
		Lithuania: 7106	72.3	99.06
		Bottom:		
		Sierra Leone: 490	34.5	36.0
		Tanzania: 523	44.0	76.0
		Burundi: 591	40.4	49.2

Sources: * IBRD 2002; [†] UNDP 2003: 237–40.

is that this would not create full equality, only a less extreme system of global inequalities. Instead of expecting the whole world to converge exactly on the world mean, I explore the possibility of a less ambitious step, and consider what the world would look like if all states were to "move" toward the global mean by reducing their distance to it *by 50 per cent*. This is quite a moderate first step: if implemented, it would still leave the poor strikingly poorer than the rich—only half as much as today. The 50 per cent I use is an arbitrary figure: of course one could set any other percentage.

Implementing a redistributive scheme across the board would be equivalent, in the language of statistics, to cutting the standard deviation in global state-to-state income distribution by half, while leaving the world mean at the reasonably comfortable current levels. If this were to be done in a systematic, organized and globally equitable way, it would be of course the wealthiest states—those farthest away from the mean in the positive direction—that would have to foot the bulk of the bill, proportionate to the degree to which their per capita income is higher than the mean. Conversely, citizens of the poorest states of the world would benefit most, proportionate to how low their per capita income is today.

For the computations that follow, I used the per capita Gross National Income figures, computed by the Atlas method, as included in a CD-ROM dataset published by the Word Bank. GNI has the advantage over GDP that the former is a more precise measure of a society's economic performance as it excludes value added realized by foreign-owned corporations in the host country, while including the foreign revenues of transnationals rooted in the given country. The Atlas method takes the GNI estimate as it is provided by the state in its national currency unit and converts it into US dollar figures at the last three years' average exchange rates between the national currency and the US$. For the purpose of my calculations, the Atlas technique is more useful than its alternative, the Purchasing Power Parity (PPP) method, since the exchange-rate calculation reflects more accurately the purchasing power of actors who are in possession of domestic currencies, when they participate in world trade. Put simply, when actors from the poor states engage with the world economy, the terms under which they can do so are revealed much more exactly in the exchange-rate measures than in purchasing power parity.[9] Table 12.3 summarizes some of the results of this exercise.

Table 12.3   Gross national income per capita (GNI/cap) and modified GNI/cap, 2000 (US$)

Country name	GNI/cap 2000	Modified GNI/cap 2000
Luxembourg	42060	23615
Switzerland	38140	21655
Japan	35620	20395

---

9   PPP is useful for other purposes: Its advantage lies in serving better the purpose of another comparison across state borders: that of comparing the domestic purchasing power of actors.

Table 12.3 cont'd

Country name	GNI/cap 2000	Modified GNI/cap 2000
Norway	34530	19850
United States	34100	19635
Denmark	32280	18725
Iceland	30390	17780
Sweden	27140	16155
Hong Kong, China	25920	15545
Austria	25220	15195
Finland	25130	15150
Germany	25120	15145
Netherlands	24970	15070
Singapore	24740	14955
Belgium	24540	14855
United Kingdom	24430	14800
France	24090	14630
Ireland	22660	13915
Canada	21130	13150
Australia	20240	12705
Italy	20160	12665
Kuwait	18030	11600
French Polynesia	17290	11230
Israel	16710	10940
Spain	15080	10125
New Caledonia	15060	10115
Bahamas, The	14960	10065
Macao, China	14580	9875
New Zealand	12990	9080
Cyprus	12370	8770
Greece	11960	8565
Portugal	11120	8145
Slovenia	10050	7610
Antigua and Barbuda	9440	7305
Barbados	9250	7210
Malta	9120	7145
Korea, Rep.	8910	7040
Argentina	7460	6315

Table 12.3 cont'd

Country name	GNI/cap 2000	Modified GNI/cap 2000
Saudi Arabia	7230	6200
Seychelles	7050	6110
St Kitts and Nevis	6570	5870
Uruguay	6000	5585
Czech Republic	5250	5210
Mexico	5070	5120
Trinidad and Tobago	4930	5050
Hungary	4710	4940
Croatia	4620	4895
Chile	4590	4880
Venezuela, RB	4310	4740
Poland	4190	4680
St Lucia	4120	4645
Lebanon	4010	4590
Costa Rica	3810	4490
Grenada	3770	4470
Mauritius	3750	4460
Slovak Republic	3700	4435
Brazil	3580	4375
Estonia	3580	4375
Malaysia	3380	4275
Botswana	3300	4235
Panama	3260	4215
Gabon	3190	4180
Belize	3110	4140
Turkey	3100	4135
South Africa	3020	4095
Lithuania	2930	4050
Latvia	2920	4045
Belarus	2870	4020
St Vincent and the Grenadines	2720	3945
Jamaica	2610	3890
Dominican Republic	2130	3650
Micronesia, Fed. Sts.	2110	3640

Table 12.3 cont'd

Country name	GNI/cap 2000	Modified GNI/cap 2000
Tunisia	2100	3635
Peru	2080	3625
Namibia	2030	3600
Colombia	2020	3595
El Salvador	2000	3585
Thailand	2000	3585
Marshall Islands	1970	3570
Maldives	1960	3565
Suriname	1890	3530
Fiji	1820	3495
Macedonia, FYR	1820	3495
Jordan	1710	3440
Guatemala	1680	3425
Iran, Islamic Rep.	1680	3425
Romania	1670	3420
Russian Federation	1660	3415
Tonga	1660	3415
West Bank and Gaza	1660	3415
Algeria	1580	3375
Bulgaria	1520	3345
Egypt, Arab Rep.	1490	3330
Samoa	1450	3310
Paraguay	1440	3305
Swaziland	1390	3280
Cape Verde	1330	3250
Kazakhstan	1260	3215
Bosnia and Herzegovina	1230	3200
Ecuador	1210	3190
Morocco	1180	3175
Vanuatu	1150	3160
Albania	1120	3145
Philippines	1040	3105
Bolivia	990	3080
Kiribati	950	3060
Syrian Arab Republic	940	3055

Table 12.3 cont'd

Country name	GNI/cap 2000	Modified GNI/cap 2000
Yugoslavia, Fed. Rep.	940	3055
Djibouti	880	3025
Guyana	860	3015
Honduras	860	3015
Sri Lanka	850	3010
China	840	3005
Equatorial Guinea	800	2985
Turkmenistan	750	2960
Papua New Guinea	700	2935
Ukraine	700	2935
Georgia	630	2900
Solomon Islands	620	2895
Azerbaijan	600	2885
Cote d'Ivoire	600	2885
Bhutan	590	2880
Cameroon	580	2875
Lesotho	580	2875
Congo, Rep.	570	2870
Indonesia	570	2870
Armenia	520	2845
Haiti	510	2840
Senegal	490	2830
Zimbabwe	460	2815
Guinea	450	2810
India	450	2810
Pakistan	440	2805
Moldova	400	2785
Nicaragua	400	2785
Mongolia	390	2780
Vietnam	390	2780
Comoros	380	2775
Bangladesh	370	2770
Benin	370	2770
Mauritania	370	2770
Yemen, Rep.	370	2770

Table 12.3 cont'd

Country name	GNI/cap 2000	Modified GNI/cap 2000
Uzbekistan	360	2765
Kenya	350	2760
Gambia, The	340	2755
Ghana	340	2755
Sudan	310	2740
Uganda	300	2735
Zambia	300	2735
Angola	290	2730
Lao PDR	290	2730
Sao Tome and Principe	290	2730
Togo	290	2730
Central African Republic	280	2725
Kyrgyz Republic	270	2720
Tanzania	270	2720
Cambodia	260	2715
Nigeria	260	2715
Madagascar	250	2710
Mali	240	2705
Nepal	240	2705
Rwanda	230	2700
Burkina Faso	210	2690
Mozambique	210	2690
Chad	200	2685
Guinea-Bissau	180	2675
Niger	180	2675
Tajikistan	180	2675
Eritrea	170	2670
Malawi	170	2670
Sierra Leone	130	2650
Burundi	110	2640
Ethiopia	100	2635

Sources: IBRD. 2002 and author's calculations.

Table 12.3 ought to be read as a simple heuristic device answering one basic question: "Where would each of the world's states be, were a twice more equitable system of redistribution—one that would create 50 per cent less inequality than the one we have in place today—implemented?" The rank order of the states of the world would of course remain the same: today's wealthiest would still be at the top, the poorest at the bottom. The per capita income of top-ranked Luxembourg would be reduced the most; there would be a bit less reduction for second-ranked Switzerland, etc. As we proceed down the list, the reduction in per capita income becomes smaller and smaller—to the point of reaching the Czech Republic (with a nearly unnoticeable reduction from US$ 5250 to US$ 5,210). Below the Czech Republic, the redistributive feature of the system "kicks in:" Mexico's per capita income increases by a minuscule amount (from US$ 5,070 to US$ 5,120). As we proceed further down the list, the increases in per capita income become more and more noticeable. The per capita income of states from Jordan to Paraguay would be doubled; those between Swaziland and Turkmenistan more than tripled, and so on until, finally, we reach Ethiopia that would see a per capita income increase by 2,500 per cent.

This project of global redistribution would indeed sharply reduce the income of the most affluent societies in the world. Luxembourg would have to make it on an average income that is equivalent to somewhere between today's France and Ireland; Switzerland would be similar in income to today's Ireland and Canada; Japan would fall between Canada and Australia. These are very significant reductions in income indeed. In terms of the above measures of the quality of life, however, they are almost imperceptible: Luxembourg's life expectancy at birth today (78.1) is already exactly between that of France and Ireland (78.7 and 76.7, respectively) (UNDP 2006: 237), with no difference in the adult literacy rates; the situation with respect to Switzerland and the Ireland-Canada pair is identical; only Japan's life expectancy is noticeably higher than that of Australia and Canada. Substantively, differences in the average living conditions among the wealthier group of states are so minuscule, and in all likelihood the institutional system that provides for it is so firmly in place, that the reduction in income would not exert any adverse effect of unmanageable proportions on their societies' quality of life.

Meanwhile, this redistributive project would make an impact on the bottom part of the list—a majority of humankind—that is no less than spectacular. At the bottom of the scale, we would have states like Ethiopia, Burundi, Sierra Leone, Malawi, Eritrea—altogether *19* states (currently with average incomes between US$ 100 and US$ 270)—that would rise to somewhere between Jamaica and St Vincent/the Grenadines (i.e., between US$ 2,610 and US$ 2,720). Meanwhile, of course, Jamaica and St Vincent/the Grenadines would "move" to somewhere between today's Costa Rica and Lebanon; the latter two would move on par with Chile and Venezuela, which would become similar to Hungary and Trinidad/Tobago. Occupying positions near the world mean, Hungary and Trinidad/Tobago would essentially remain "in place." Looking at the largest states on the list, China's estimate would match that of Turkey's, and India's per capita income would fall between St Vincent/the Grenadines and Belarus. Belarus would find itself near today's Lebanon and St Lucia, Turkey between St Lucia and Poland. Meanwhile, St Lucia and Poland would be between present Croatia and Hungary, and Croatia would catch up with today's Hungary.

Table 12.4 Examples of upward movement in terms of quality of life

	Life expectancy	Adult literacy rate
Ethiopia	45.7	40.3
Burundi	40.4	49.2
Sierra Leone	34.5	36.0
Malawi	38.5	61. 0
Eritrea	52.5	56.7
India	63.3	58. 0
P.R. China	70.6	85.5
Jamaica	75.5	87.3
St Vincent/the Grenadines	73.8	88.9
Belarus	69.6	99.07
Costa Rica	77.9	95.7
Lebanon	73.3	86.5
Turkey	70.1	85.5
Chile	75.8	95.9
Venezuela	73.5	92.8
St Lucia	72.2	98.2
Poland	73.6	99.07
Hungary	71.5	99.03
Trinidad/Tobago	71.5	98.4

All this would have tremendous implications for the quality of life of humankind as a whole by creating the possibility of elevating the tangible living standards in the peripheries of the world economy. Table 12.4 contains some of the relevant information. Life expectancy at the bottom of the income scale could go from between 34.5 and 52.5 years to well over 70—an improvement of 20 to 200 per cent, depending on the choice of states to be included in the comparison. In terms of literacy, the increases would be 40 per cent to twice the current rates.

Would this be feasible, then? In purely monetary terms, the system could almost finance itself: Although the balance of out- and inflows would be negative, the magnitude of the deficit is equivalent to 0.93 per cent of the total world GNI, a serious but not necessarily insurmountable problem. In terms of gross sums, the greatest outflows would have to come from the United States, Japan, Germany, the United Kingdom, France, Italy, Canada, Spain, the Netherlands and Australia; the greatest recipients would be China, India, Indonesia, Pakistan, Bangladesh, Nigeria, the Russian Federation, Vietnam, Ethiopia and the Philippines. Of the top ten would-be contributors, eight are members of NATO; this might suggest a possible peace dividend, as long as there is a will to achieve such results.

Because of the differences in population size among both the most affluent and the poorest societies, the list of biggest contributors and recipients is different when considered in terms of what proportion of their total income they would have to devote to this project. Table 12.5 contains the results of the latter calculation: Positive numbers signify outflows and negative numbers stand for inflows.

Table 12.5   Out- and inflows as percentages of gross national income

State	% of GNI out- or inflows
Luxembourg	43.85
Switzerland	43.22
Japan	42.74
Norway	42.51
United States	42.42
Denmark	41.99
Iceland	41.49
Sweden	40.48
Hong Kong, China	40.03
Austria	39.75
Finland	39.71
Germany	39.71
Netherlands	39.65
Singapore	39.55
Belgium	39.47
United Kingdom	39.42
France	39.27
Ireland	38.59
Canada	37.77
Australia	37.23
Italy	37.18
Kuwait	35.66
French Polynesia	35.05
Israel	34.53
Spain	32.86
New Caledonia	32.84
Bahamas, The	32.72
Macao, China	32.27
New Zealand	30.10
Cyprus	29.10
Greece	28.39
Portugal	26.75
Slovenia	24.28
Antigua and Barbuda	22.62
Barbados	22.05
Malta	21.66

Table 12.5 cont'd

State	% of GNI out- or inflows
Korea, Rep.	20.99
Argentina	15.35
Saudi Arabia	14.25
Seychelles	13.33
St Kitts and Nevis	10.65
Uruguay	6.92
Czech Republic	0.76
Mexico	−0.99
Trinidad and Tobago	−2.43
Hungary	−4.88
Croatia	−5.95
Chile	−6.32
Venezuela, RB	−9.98
Poland	−11.69
St Lucia	−12.74
Lebanon	−14.46
Costa Rica	−17.85
Grenada	−18.57
Mauritius	−18.93
Slovak Republic	−19.86
Estonia	−22.21
Brazil	−22.21
Malaysia	−26.48
Botswana	−28.33
Panama	−29.29
Gabon	−31.03
Belize	−33.12
Turkey	−33.39
South Africa	−35.60
Lithuania	−38.23
Latvia	−38.53
Belarus	−40.07
St Vincent and the Grenadines	−45.04
Jamaica	−49.04
Dominican Republic	−71.36
Micronesia, Fed. Sts.	−72.51
Tunisia	−73.10
Peru	−74.28
Namibia	−77.34
Colombia	−77.97

Table 12.5 cont'd

State	% of GNI out- or inflows
El Salvador	−79.25
Thailand	−79.25
Marshall Islands	−81.22
Maldives	−81.89
Suriname	−86.77
Fiji	−92.03
Macedonia, FYR	−92.03
Jordan	−101.17
Guatemala	−103.87
Iran, Islamic Rep.	−103.87
Romania	−104.79
West Bank and Gaza	−105.72
Russian Federation	−105.72
Tonga	−105.72
Algeria	−113.61
Bulgaria	−120.07
Egypt, Arab Rep.	−123.49
Samoa	−128.28
Paraguay	−129.51
Swaziland	−135.97
Cape Verde	−144.36
Kazakhstan	−155.16
Bosnia and Herzegovina	−160.16
Ecuador	−163.64
Morocco	−169.07
Vanuatu	−174.78
Albania	−180.80
Philippines	−198.56
Bolivia	−211.11
Kiribati	−222.11
Syrian Arab Republic	−225.00
Yugoslavia, Fed. Rep.	−225.00
Djibouti	−243.75
Guyana	−250.58
Honduras	−250.58
Sri Lanka	−254.12
China	−257.74
Equatorial Guinea	−273.13
Turkmenistan	−294.67
Papua New Guinea	−319.29

Table 12.5 cont'd

State	% of GNI out- or inflows
Ukraine	−319.29
Georgia	−360.32
Solomon Islands	−366.94
Cote d'Ivoire	−380.83
Azerbaijan	−380.83
Bhutan	−388.14
Cameroon	−395.69
Lesotho	−395.69
Congo, Rep.	−403.51
Indonesia	−403.51
Armenia	−447.12
Haiti	−456.86
Senegal	−477.55
Zimbabwe	−511.96
India	−524.44
Guinea	−524.44
Pakistan	−537.50
Moldova	−596.25
Nicaragua	−596.25
Mongolia	−612.82
Vietnam	−612.82
Comoros	−630.26
Bangladesh	−648.65
Benin	−648.65
Mauritania	−648.65
Yemen, Rep.	−648.65
Uzbekistan	−668.06
Kenya	−688.57
Ghana	−710.29
Gambia, The	−710.29
Sudan	−783.87
Uganda	−811.67
Zambia	−811.67
Angola	−841.38
Lao PDR	−841.38
Sao Tome and Principe	−841.38
Togo	−841.38
Central African Republic	−873.21
Kyrgyz Republic	−907.41
Tanzania	−907.41

Table 12.5 cont'd

State	% of GNI out- or inflows
Cambodia	−944.23
Nigeria	−944.23
Madagascar	−984.00
Mali	−1027.08
Nepal	−1027.08
Rwanda	−1073.91
Burkina Faso	−1180.95
Mozambique	−1180.95
Chad	−1242.50
Guinea-Bissau	−1386.11
Niger	−1386.11
Tajikistan	−1386.11
Eritrea	−1470.59
Malawi	−1470.59
Sierra Leone	−1938.46
Burundi	−2300.00
Ethiopia	−2535.00

Source: Author's calculations from IBRD. 2002.

The burden of financing this project would have to be shouldered, of course, by the wealthiest states, reducing top-ranked Luxembourg's GNI by 43.9 per cent. Even the South Korea, ranked 37th, would have to contribute the equivalent of over 20 per cent of its GNI. Due to the unevenness of the global distribution of incomes, outflows suddenly drop to below 10 per cent at 42nd-ranked Uruguay (with 6.92 per cent to be required), eventually to fizzle out with the next state on the list, the Czech Republic (0.76 per cent), and turns into inflows with 44th-ranked Mexico. The highest contributor in terms of a gross sum—the United States—is the fifth on the list in terms of the proportion of its GNI to be siphoned off; four of the top ten, and 11 of the top 20, states with the highest proportional outflows are members of the European Union. Nineteen of the 25 current members of the recently-enlarged European Union would register outflows, and if we consider the European Union a single unit, it becomes the entity with the second largest outflow, approximately 80 per cent of the figure for the United States.

Whether this is a reasonable burden, what exact economic mechanisms would be capable of ascertaining the accurate execution of a redistributive project of this magnitude, and what the appropriate, corruption-proof techniques, socially and environmentally sustainable developmental goals and specific, long-term benefit-producing forms of investment projects would be for such a global system of redistribution—well, that is of course entirely unclear from this exercise. Equally unclear is what the appropriate organizational form for such a global redistributive authority would be.

On the basis of purely fiscal calculations, such a project does not appear to be completely unfeasible. Redistribution rates of up to 40-some per cent are not un-imaginable: government expenditures do hover in the 20 to 50 per cent range in most wealthy states. Of course the sudden addition of such sums to the current government expenditures is unrealistic, but so would have seemed the current government expenditure rates to most observers a mere hundred years ago. Since under the current system, a significant proportion of government expenditures is military spending—2.6 per cent of the overall world GDP, to be more precise (SIPRI 2002)—and the "high-income countries ... have the highest per capita military spending" (SIPRI 2002), there are plenty of areas in which tremendous reductions are possible. Since, if implemented, part of the sums to be transferred from the wealthy to the poor states would be spent on infrastructural investment goods and items of collective consumption made in the wealthier states, the more affluent economies would also enjoy some of the immediate demand-increasing benefits of the plan. In all likelihood, if it were to succeed, global-redistributive fiscal reform would have to be a long-term objective, phased in gradually and implemented flexibly, through constant adjustments.

Some basic tenets of global economic liberalism, and the organizations devoted to enforcing it, urge all of us to think about the economic process in rather purely monetary terms. Perhaps these key elements of global economic liberalism could be turned around to argue that the economic resources of the world do not mandate the current, obscenely exaggerated system of unequal distribution. What if they could support a more reasonable and acceptable form of social organization, one that would provide for a global distribution of income that is significantly less unequal than today? That would afford the vast majority of humankind a quality of life and dignity that is, today, the privilege of those born and living in states on the higher levels of the global income pyramid. It appears that much could be achieved even without resorting to any, wildly utopian imagery of complete and full income equality. Humankind does have the resources to make available much more adequate basic social and economic infrastructure, nutrition, shelter, health care, education, and general social security to the citizens of the poorest states than it provides now. Much improvement could be achieved by organizing a system of global redistribution that would put an end to the current, absurd levels of global inequality and alleviate the truly inhuman misery of the extreme poor.

While it appears at least potentially feasible on a purely speculative, fiscal basis, successful implementation of a project of this kind—as always is the case, Karl Polányi has taught us, with economic institutions—would require the construction of social institutions leading to political action on part of the sane and responsible majority of humankind. The fact that the purely economic means do exist but no project of global redistribution has emerged as yet suggests that currently existing social and political institutions may not be suitable for conceiving and implementing such a project. They were certainly not designed for this purpose.

Given the unfathomable magnitude of global state-to-state inequalities today, humankind is left with two basic alternatives: creating an organizational

framework that is suitable for global redistribution or the ultimate immoral act
of doing nothing. While it appears much less costly in the immediate short run,
the latter amounts to an explicit admission that the moral unity of humankind is
a fiction, and that the community of humans is willing to accept, and live with,
a historically very recent phenomenon, a global structure of inequality that
systematically splits humankind into disjunct, geographically separate groups
with a perniciously uneven distribution of opportunities for life between the
two groups. To put it plainly, the latter choice opens an abyss of unforeseeable
consequences concerning the survival of humankind.

Pursuing the morally more acceptable and geopolitically wiser alternative—
organizing collective social and political action for the establishment of a global
system of economic redistribution—appears, hence, to be one of the most pressing
challenges for political and social organizations, movements, states, and supra-
state forms of public authority alike, more or less irrespective of their specific
location in the current system of global inequality. Whether such a project is
feasible through peaceful means cannot be decided at the moment—simply
because nobody has ever attempted such an exercise. The United Nations' "Decade
for the Eradication of Poverty," with its recommendations, calls for action and
encouragements addressed to states and supranational organizations, serves as a
useful baseline: At least it helps in considering just how far we must still go.

References:

Arrighi, G. (1991), 'World Income Inequalities and the Future of Socialism', *New Left Review* 189, 39–65.
Bata, M. and Bergesen, A. (2002), 'Global Inequality: An Introduction', *Journal of World-System Research* 8(1), 2–7.
Bergesen, A. and Bata, M. (eds.) (2002), *Special Issue on Global Inequality. Journal of World-System Research*, 8(1–2).
Firebaugh, G. (1999), 'Empirics of World Income Inequality', *American Journal of Sociology* 104, 1597–630.
IBRD (2002), *World Development Indicators*. CD-ROM dataset. Washington, DC: The World Bank.
Korzeniewicz, R. P. and Moran, T. P. (1997), 'World-Economic Trends in the Distribution of Income, 1965–1992', *American Journal of Sociology* 102, 1000–39.
Korzeniewicz, R.P., Stach, A., Patil, V. and Moran, T.P. (2004), 'Measuring National Income: A Critical Assessment', *Comparative Studies in Society and History* 46(3), 535–86.
Maddison, A. (2001), *The World Economy: A Millennial Perspective*. Paris: OECD.
Maddison, A. (2003), The World *Economy: Historical Statistics*. Paris: OECD.
Polanyi, K. (1957), 'The Economy as Instituted Process', in Polanyi, K., Arensberg, C.M. and Pearson, H.W. (eds) *Trade and Market in the Early Empires. Economies in History and Theory*. Glencoe, IL: The Free Press.
Silver, B.J. and Arrighi, G. (2001), 'Workers North and South', *La rivista del manifesto*, 19 (July–August).
SIPRI (2002), "Highlights from the SIPRI YEARBOOK 2002." http://editors.sipri.se/pubs/yb02/highlights.html.

UN (1995), 'Observance of the International Year for the Eradication of Poverty and Proclamation of the first United Nations Decade for the Eradication of Poverty', *UN document A/RES/50/107*. New York: United Nations.

UNDP (2003) *Human Development Report 2003*. New York: United Nations.

Index

Ethics in an Era of Globalization

representation 6, 18, 21–2, 31–4, 36–8, 45,
    71, 91, 100, 103–4, 135–6, 164, 178–9,
    202
  democratic representation *see*
    democracy
representative *see* representation
resistance 30–31, 60–61, 103, 106, 126,
    136, 143, 156, 158, 161, 165
  resource 5, 7, 10, 15, 37, 45–6, 65–8, 82,
    100, 104, 106–7, 109, 119, 137, 144,
    153, 159, 161, 165, 178–80, 182,
    187(fn), 201(fn), 218–19, 235
  natural resource 37, 153, 179, 187(fn)
respect 2, 9, 14, 16, 18–19, 25, 34, 44, 46,
    51, 58, 60–61, 70–71, 80, 86, 97, 104,
    107, 115–16, 120–21, 126, 138, 142–3,
    145, 165, 172, 176(fn), 183, 189,
    197(fn), 200, 207–8, 220
rhetoric 59(fn), 98, 138, 151, 161, 167
Ricoeur, P. 4, 27, 34–5, 38
Robertson, R. 141–2, 145
Robinson, F. 122, 131, 199, 200
Robinson, W.I. 153, 157, 167
Rorty, R. 19, 24
Rousseau, J.-J. 136

Sachs, G. 62
Sachs, J. 56, 64, 72
Sachs, W. 114, 131
sanction 76, 122, 140
Sandel, M. 122, 131
Seckinelgin, H. 211, 214
secular 41
security 20, 80, 82, 116, 121, 135, 143,
    151–2, 158, 161, 192, 207, 209, 235
self 2, 4, 20, 23, 33–5, 52, 62, 65(fn), 69,
    80, 99, 102, 105, 108, 110, 119, 144,
    154, 158, 163, 165, 199–200, 202–3,
    205, 210
  self-determination 23, 79, 80, 191
  self-interest 27, 31, 34, 38, 62–3, 84, 105,
    116, 151, 173, 183, 200, 210
  self-transformation 4, 19
seller 63, 145, 179
semantic *see* sense-making
Sen, A. 83, 93–4, 160–61, 170
sense-making 3, 10, 17, 44, 47, 50, 56,
    65–6, 140, 183
sensibility 35, 76, 92, 140

sentiment 62, 138–9, 141
shelter 116, 119, 235
Shinoda, H. 190, 195, 211, 213, 214
Singer, M. 2, 198
Singer, P. 8, 160, 171–4, 176–9, 181–6
Smith, A. 29, 32, 34, 138
social
  social being 19, 27, 34, 101
  social cohesion 31
  social ethics 14
  social network *see* network
  social ontology 19, 102
  social policy 17
  social relation 14, 33, 105–6, 157
  social services 60, 67, 151–2
socialism 64, 66–7
socio-economic 45, 79, 151, 156, 158,
    164–6, 190(fn)
solidarity 4, 5, 13, 18, 22–5, 27–8, 31, 37,
    42, 61, 69–70, 81–2, 119, 128, 138,
    190, 199, 203
space 2, 9, 29, 36–7, 46–7, 51, 57, 76,
    77(fn), 88, 100, 110, 158, 167, 183–4,
    200, 203–8, 210
Spinoza, B. 85(fn), 91, 93
spirit 2, 30, 77(fn), 83, 97
St Clair, A.L. 7–8, 51, 149, 154–5, 158–9,
    161, 165, 169, 170
stakeholder 15, 17, 21, 90
Stiglitz, E. 168
Stoics 52, 91, 191
structural 42, 52, 78–9, 151, 156–8, 162–3,
    179, 198
subjectivism 6, 9–10, 34, 203–7
subjugation 136, 165
subordination 5, 175, 193
subsidiarity 82
subsistence 22, 103, 121
suffering 7, 8, 23–5, 45, 62–3, 84, 88, 101,
    136, 138, 144, 152, 156–7, 171, 176–7,
    180, 185
supplement 20, 24–5, 101, 105
sustainability 1, 25, 46, 60, 63–4, 68, 70,
    79, 81, 116, 119, 151, 153, 155, 166,
    195, 208, 234
sympathy 103, 138, 175, 182, 185

Tamir, Y. 196, 214
Taylor, C. 109, 111, 122, 131